Taking on the Pledge of Allegiance

Taking on the Pledge of Allegiance

The News Media and Michael Newdow's Constitutional Challenge

Ronald Bishop

State University of New York Press

Published by
State University of New York Press, Albany

Printed in the United States of America

For information, contact State University of New York Press, Albany, NY
www.sunypress.edu

Production by Ryan Morris
Marketing by Michael Campochiaro

Library of Congress Cataloging-in-Publication Data

Bishop, Ronald, 1961–
Taking on the Pledge of Allegiance : the news media and Michael Newdow's Constitutional challenge / Ronald Bishop; foreword by Nadine Strossen
p. cm.
Includes bibliographical references and index.
ISBN 978-0-7914-7181-4 (hardcover : alk. paper)
ISBN 978-0-7914-7182-1 (pbk. : alk. paper)
1. Newdow, Michael—Trials, litigation, etc. 2. Bellamy, Francis. Pledge of Allegiance to the Flag. 3. Flags—Law and legislation—United States. 4. Religion in the public schools—Law and legislation—United States. I. Title.

KF228.N524B57 2007
342.7308'52—dc22

2006100311

10 9 8 7 6 5 4 3 2 1

Contents

Foreword

Ron Bishop's valuable book documents in detail the media's inaccurate and unfair coverage of Michael Newdow's important constitutional litigation concerning two fundamental sets of rights that the Supreme Court long has protected: first, parents' rights to make basic decisions about the education and upbringing of their own children—in particular, their children's moral and religious education—free from government coercion;[1] and second, the right of all individuals, including public school students, to be free from government pressure—even subtle and indirect pressure—to affirm religious beliefs.[2]

Specifically, Newdow asserted a quite limited, although undeniably important, claim. He challenged the "pledge policy" at his daughter's public school, which required that teachers daily lead the students in "pledg[ing] allegiance to . . . one nation *under God*." Newdow maintained that this policy violated his parental right to influence his young daughter's religious beliefs, and also violated the individual freedom of religion and conscience that the First Amendment's Establishment Clause protects from government pressure.[3]

Contrary to pervasive media exaggerations about the scope of Newdow's litigation, which Bishop chronicles, Newdow did *not* challenge the requirement that students recite the Pledge in its original form, before the 1954 federal law added the words "under God" expressly to counter "Godless Communism" during the Cold War. Nor did Newdow challenge the recitation of these added words in any context other than public school classrooms, and he certainly did not seek to strip all religious references from public life, notwithstanding the widespread, overblown media accounts that mischaracterized his claims in these ways, which Bishop discusses.

The media's manifold distortions of Newdow's significant case included the failure to acknowledge that what he was seeking, above all, was to protect his cherished parental relationship with his beloved daughter. In the face of the limitations that the family law system had imposed on his relationship with his daughter, as a result of his custody battles with her mother, Newdow was fighting to maintain that relationship as fully as possible, including the core element of that relationship that the Supreme Court had repeatedly recognized: parents' rights to instill their own moral or religious values in their own children, rather than permitting government schools to proscribe or prescribe particular religious beliefs for all children.

Far from lauding Newdow's devotion to his daughter, and his determination to maintain a meaningful relationship with her, to the contrary, the media tended to demonize him as an egocentric individualist who was taking advantage of his biological relationship with his daughter to advance his own ideological agenda. It is especially ironic that Newdow was most harshly assailed by spokespeople for the religious and political right—who, as Bishop shows, were disproportionately represented in the media coverage—given Newdow's paramount commitment to aims that they also espouse: reducing government power to intervene in family relationships, and, in particular, reducing the power of government schools to impose on children majoritarian values concerning religious beliefs that conflict with their parents' beliefs.

Even judges, including Supreme Court justices, who rejected Newdow's religious liberty claim, did agree with his central contention that "he has a right to expose his daughter to [his] views [about religion] without the State's placing its *imprimatur* on a particular religion."[4] These judges rejected his religious freedom claim essentially on factual—rather than legal or principled—grounds, since they viewed the pledge as "a patriotic exercise, not a religious one."[5] In short, had these judges viewed the Pledge as a religious exercise, they apparently would have upheld Newdow's claim. Moreover, many legal, historical, and religious experts did fully endorse Newdow's claim that public schools may not require students to recite the words "under God" in the Pledge.

This substantial support for Newdow's legal claims, including from ideologically diverse judges and other experts, was another essential aspect of his case that the media coverage badly distorted. As Bishop documents, the media generally disparaged and trivialized Newdow's legal claims, implying that they had garnered the support of only a few judges on an allegedly—but not actually—extremist liberal court, the U.S. Court of Appeals for the Ninth Circuit.

Consider just a few of the many facts that the media coverage obscured, but which underscore the serious merits of Newdow's religious liberty claims, and their broad support among ideologically and religiously diverse experts:

- The Ninth Circuit judge who authored the much maligned opinion upholding Newdow's claim, Alfred Goodwin, *is* a Republican, who had been appointed to the court by a conservative Republican president, Richard Nixon.
- The many "friend of the court" briefs that were filed in the Supreme Court supporting Newdow's contentions included briefs submitted by leading historians, legal scholars, religious scholars, theologians, religious organizations, and individual religious leaders.
- Of the three Supreme Court justices who addressed the merits of Newdow's claims,[6] one "conclude[d] that, *as a matter of our precedent, the Pledge policy is unconstitutional.*"[7] Notably, that justice can hardly be dismissed—as so many members of the media attempted to dismiss the Ninth Circuit judges who had ruled in Newdow's favor—as an extreme liberal; it was none other than Clarence Thomas, the conservative Republican who had been appointed by Republican president George H. W. Bush!

Despite Justice Thomas's expressed disagreement with the Court's pertinent Establishment Clause precedents, to his great credit, he carefully examined these precedents and candidly concluded that their reasoning rendered the challenged Pledge policy even more clearly unconstitutional than other practices the Court had previously struck down, including school-sponsored prayer at graduation ceremonies. As Justice Thomas explained, in part:

> A prayer at graduation is a one-time event, the graduating students are almost (if not already) adults, and their parents are usually present. By contrast, very young students, removed from the protection of their parents, are exposed to the Pledge each and every day.
>
> Moreover, . . . although students may feel "peer pressure" to attend their graduations, the pressure here is far less subtle: Students are actually compelled (that is, by law . . .) to attend school. . . .[8]

In further support of Newdow's religious liberty claim, Justice Thomas also cited Supreme Court precedents that "squarely held that the government cannot require a person to declare his belief in God," as well as others that held "that the Establishment Clause prohibits government from appearing to take a position on questions of religious belief."[9] In noting his disagreement with these governing precedents, Justice Thomas underscores that Newdow's claim could be rejected only if the Supreme Court undertook a wholesale, radical revision of its long-standing Establishment Clause jurisprudence, overturning all of the precedents he cited, as well as many others.[10] As Justice Thomas recognizes, short of gutting its modern Establishment Clause jurisprudence, and holding instead that the Establishment Clause "does not protect any individual right,"[11] the Court would have to affirm the Ninth Circuit's ruling striking down the Pledge policy.

As Bishop demonstrates, the media accounts of Newdow's litigation were replete with quotes from politicians (Democrats and Republicans alike) scathingly denouncing and deriding the Ninth Circuit's conclusion that Supreme Court precedent compelled a ruling in Newdow's favor.[12] But these media accounts did not note that this very same conclusion was also reached by such a prominent conservative jurist as Clarence Thomas. Nor did they note that only two Supreme Court justices rejected Newdow's religious freedom claim under the Establishment Clause, or that one of those two stressed that "it is a close question."[13]

In sum, the media coverage of Newdow's case wrongly impugned the virtues of both his legal claims and his motives in pursuing them. Bishop's exposé of the media's caricature of this particular individual pursuing a particular Establishment Clause claim is an important contribution to an essential general effort: to redress the same kinds of distortion and demonization that mar most media coverage of any religious liberty claims under the Establishment Clause. For example, by dwelling on Newdow's avowed atheism, the media coverage of his case purveyed a misimpression that has pervaded coverage of Establishment Clause issues more generally: the dangerously wrongheaded notion that strong enforcement of the Establishment Clause benefits only, or primarily, those who are irreligious or antireligious. Former Supreme Court justice Harry Blackmun, himself an observant Christian, strongly repudiated this very charge when it was leveled by a dissenting opinion, objecting to the Court's ruling that a government-sponsored religious display violated the Establishment Clause's guarantee of government-free religion. As Justice Blackmun wrote:

> [The dissent] apparently has misperceived a respect for religious pluralism, a respect commanded by the Constitution,

as hostility or indifference to religion. No misperception could be more antithetical to the values embodied in the Establishment Clause.

Michael Newdow valiantly fought to curb government's coercive power over parent–child relationships and over individual beliefs regarding religion, two cherished sets of fundamental rights that have understandably been precious to generations of Americans, regardless of their particular beliefs concerning family matters, religion, politics, or anything else. It is therefore not surprising that Newdow's extraordinary efforts to uphold these fundamental general rights earned the support of many legal experts, as well as many religious leaders, who hold very divergent specific beliefs.

In light of the pervasive media stigmatizing of those who champion the Establishment Clause's ban on government-sponsored religion, it is not surprising, although it is disheartening, that the media largely chose to ignore this wide-ranging support for Newdow's efforts. Bishop's trenchant critique should inspire members of the media, when covering similar issues in the future, to exercise the rights that the First Amendment's Free Press Clause guarantees to them with more respect for the rights that the First Amendment's Establishment Clause guarantees to all of us.

Notes

For research assistance with this foreword, Professor Strossen thanks her chief aide, Steven Cunningham (New York Law School '99).

1. See, for example, *Pierce v. Society of Sisters*, 268 U.S. 510 (1925) and *Meyer v. Nebraska*, 262 U.S. 390 (1923).

2. See, for example, *Lee v. Weisman*, 505 U.S. 577 (1992).

3. This clause, the very first in the Bill of Rights, provides: "Congress shall make no law respecting an establishment of religion. . . ." The Supreme Court long has held that it, along with most other Bill of Rights provisions, applies to all government bodies and officials, including those at the state and local levels. See *Everson v. Board of Education*, 330 U.S. 1 (1947).

4. *Elk Grove Unified School District v. Newdow*, 542 U.S. 1, 23 (2004) (Rehnquist, C. J., concurring in the judgment) (with whom Justices O'Connor and Thomas joined) (rejecting the majority's conclusion that Newdow lacked sufficient rights concerning his daughter's education to have "standing" to pursue his claims). *Accord, Newdow v. U.S. Congress*, 328 F. 3d 466, 490 (9th Cir. 2003) (Fernandez, J., concurring and dissenting)

(concurring in the portion of the majority's opinion upholding Newdow's standing to challenge the Pledge policy because it "interferes with his right to direct the religious education of his daughter," idem at 485).

5. *Elk Grove Unified School District v. Newdow*, 542 U.S. at 31 (Rehnquist, C. J., concurring in the judgment). *Accord*, *Newdow v. U.S. Congress*, 328 F. 3d 466, 473 (9th Cir. 2003) (O'Scannlain, dissenting from the denial of rehearing en banc) (joined by five other judges) (rejecting the holding of the majority of the Ninth Circuit panel that the Pledge is "a religious act").

6. Five justices concluded that he lacked "standing" and hence did not address the merits of his claims, and a sixth, Justice Scalia, had recused himself from the case.

7. Idem at 49 (Thomas, J., concurring in the judgment) (emphasis added).

8. Idem at 46–47.

9. Idem at 48.

10. See idem at 45 ("I would take this opportunity to begin the process of rethinking the Establishment Clause."); idem at 50 ("[T]he Establishment Clause is best understood as a federalism provision—it protects state establishments from federal interference but does not protect any individual right.").

11. Idem at 50.

12. *Newdow v. U.S. Congress, et al.*, 328 F. 3d 466, 488 (9th Cir. 2003) (denying petitions for rehearing and rehearing en banc and issuing amended, superseding opinion) (Goodwin, J.) ("[T]here can be little doubt that under the controlling Supreme Court cases the school district's policy fails. . . .") (citing cases also cited by Justice Thomas to support the same conclusion).

13. *Elk Grove Unified School District v. Newdow*, 542 U.S. 1, 37 (O'Connor, J, concurring in the judgment). The only other justice to rule against Newdow on the merits of his Establishment Clause claim was then chief justice Rehnquist. See idem at 18 (Rehnquist, C. J., concurring in the judgment)

Nadine Strossen
Professor of Law, New York Law School
President, American Civil Liberties Union

Acknowledgments

Before we embark on our journey, a few heartfelt words of thanks to the reporters, legal scholars, attorneys, and judges who took valuable time from their busy schedules to discuss with me, by phone and e-mail, coverage of the Newdow case. Thanks also to my former and current students, whose ideas, and challenges to my ideas, keep me intellectually honest. My time with them in the classroom has been the most rewarding professional experience of my life.

Extra special thanks and love to my wife, Sheila, and my son, Neil, who put up with me as I conducted research, compiled information, hastily clipped newspaper articles, and then, finally, wrote the book. They are my two true loves, and I dedicate this book to them.

Introduction

> Individuality is fine, as long as we all do it together.
>
> —Major Frank Burns from the TV series *M*A*S*H*

In my sophomore year of high school, my homeroom teacher was a man named Ernie Steinman. Tall and bespectacled, he was not one for a lot of rules. Homeroom in late 1970s northern New Jersey was an unruly ritual. Most mornings, we (or at least my closest friends at the time and I) straggled in and, after staring out the window and waking up a bit (we had not been raised on the ritual of morning coffee that so many kids observe today), talked and would eventually make enough noise to drown out the few announcements about school events that Ernie would try to make. Our lack of structure, not to mention our lack of decorum, would probably make the standardized testing industry and the teachers and parents they have frightened for the last quarter century or so wince out of frustration.

There was one ritual in particular that Ernie did not make us observe: saying the Pledge of Allegiance, as children in most schools across the country did each morning. At the beginning of the school year, he announced—mentioned in passing is a more accurate characterization—that we would not say the Pledge. Before you more conservative folks begin mounting an effort to track Ernie down so that he can defend himself on *The O'Reilly Factor*, I should say that it is unclear to me now, 25 years later, if his choice was one of conviction or of convenience. Like us, Ernie saw homeroom as a 10-minute obstacle, something to be endured. Either way, though, Ernie's action planted a tiny seed of rebellion (if not critical thinking ability) in my adolescent head.

Since I was not an avid fan of hard rock music (at the time, anyway), and didn't smoke or drink, not saying the Pledge was as rebellious as I got, and I loved it. It wasn't an antinuclear power protest march (which my parents probably wouldn't have let me go to) or burning my draft card (which I was too young to have), but it was a stand. I was cool—in my own mind, anyway. Our friends couldn't believe that we got away with not saying the Pledge. Ernie could have sold tickets to our homeroom.

I thought of Ernie as a lawsuit filed in 2000 by "avowed atheist" Michael Newdow made its way through the courts. Newdow claimed that the inclusion of the words "under God" in the Pledge of Allegiance amounted to an unconstitutional endorsement of religion. Newdow believes that requiring his daughter to sit in her classroom at Florence Markofer Elementary School and listen while her classmates recited the Pledge amounted to coercion. She was free not to recite the Pledge, but Newdow contends (and many educational psychologists might agree) that a classroom full of fourth graders is not a spot conducive to practicing nonconformity.

In June 2002, the Ninth Circuit U.S. Court of Appeals surprised the country, and shocked conservatives, when it found first that the Pledge itself was unconstitutional, and then, in an amended opinion, that the mention of God in the Pledge was an unconstitutional breach of the wall that separates church and state. President Dwight D. Eisenhower, responding in 1954 to members of Congress and to pressure from the Knights of Columbus (the nation's largest Catholic organization) and a slew of editorials and stories published by the Hearst newspaper chain, approved the addition of "under God" to the Pledge as a politically expedient reaction to the alleged insinuation of "atheistic Communism" into our lives. Elisabeth Sifton (2004) points out that President Eisenhower "saw no harm in affirming that America, battling against godless Communism was doing so 'under God'" (p. 13). The Ninth Circuit's original decision brought a firestorm of criticism from citizens, scholars, and public officials, coming as it did in the still long shadow of the September 11, 2001, attacks.

In an almost surreal coincidence, on Flag Day 2004 the Supreme Court overturned the Ninth Circuit's ruling. The high court did not address whether the words "under God" were unconstitutional. Instead, the justices held that because Newdow did not have legal custody of his daughter at the time she was hearing the Pledge (Newdow and the little girl's mother never married, and later ended their relationship), he lacked standing to sue in the first place. For those who supported Newdow's effort to remove "under God" from the Pledge, the Court's side trip was good news. Someone else, they claimed, will come along, mount a similar challenge, and perhaps nudge the Court to finally issue a ruling on the constitutionality of "under God." Many folks, including a number of print and broadcast journalists, believed the Court simply ducked the issue. They had the chance to end this discussion—or at least come to the rescue of the Establishment Clause—and blew it.

But let's backtrack a bit: On the day in June 2002 that the Ninth Circuit handed down its controversial decision, broadcast and print journalists almost immediately began to marginalize Newdow. More important for our journey, reporters assured the American people that the U.S. Supreme Court would almost certainly overturn the Ninth Circuit's crazy decision. Cooler heads—make that ideologically correct heads—would eventually prevail.

Instead of treating Newdow and the Ninth Circuit's decision in a balanced fashion, the news media framed both as aberrations—it was a crazy publicity stunt by a radical atheist, and a radical act by a hopelessly liberal, often overturned federal circuit court. In the days after the decision, the news media acted as what one group of scholars (Donahue, Tichenor, & Olien, 1995) have called a "guard dog" for the government, and, in a broader sense, as protectors of the ideas supposedly at the ideological heart of America. Newdow was a threat to these ideas. Broadcast journalists almost panicked when the Ninth Circuit ruled, and news outlets provided a stage for equally panicked politicians to make orchestrated grandstand appeals to the nation's patriotism.

But as the case made its way to the Supreme Court, the frames seemed to change. In interviews conducted during 2004 and 2005, several journalists who at one time thought Newdow would fall flat on his face, especially before the Supreme Court, were amazed at the depth of his preparation and the eloquence he showed in arguing before the justices.

At this point, you may be thinking: of course Newdow was marginalized—he's an atheist, clearly operating outside the mainstream of American life. Just 10 percent of us are atheists. Consider this: the news media, for better or worse, construct or reflect a picture of what's going on the world. But it's a limited picture, one painted by only a few folks who, in essence, don't want to alienate us—cause us to change the channel, flip radio stations, visit another Website, or stop plunking down our money for a copy of the newspaper. This picture can't be too controversial—unless Michael Moore happens to have made it. Financial success goes a long way toward finding you a place on the news media's agenda. But it's what happens to someone like Moore—or Newdow—once they have that place on the agenda that is at issue here. As much as we talk about how our nation values diversity, and journalists talk and write about dealing with as many sides of every story as possible, we have our limits, limits that are narrowed in times of national crisis, real or otherwise.

But even if Ernie Steinman was just trying to clear more time for himself during homeroom, what's so wrong about not saying the Pledge? Why do we choose to look past the purely political reasons behind the addition of "under God" to the Pledge in 1954? Somewhere in my at times misspent public education, I learned that one person who believed strongly in an idea, or who believed that "the system" was flawed to the point it was hurting people, could actually change it. Journalists have helped make it no fun to be "the little guy" anymore—maybe because the social, political, and economic decks are stacked against the idea. Maybe they believe that few of us have the energy for dissent anymore. For every Colleen Rowley (the FBI agent who testified before Congress in 2002 about the bureau's failings) and Dr. Jeffrey Wigand (the tobacco industry scientist who revealed to journalists that tobacco companies artificially manipulated nicotine levels in cigarettes, only to have journalists try to kill the story for purely financial reasons), there are probably scores of other folks who want to act but don't. Still, it's heartening to know that more folks are blowing the whistle on their employers. The U.S. Department of Justice reports that the number of whistleblower suits involving government contracts jumped from 82 in 1990 to more than 300 per year (Caruso, 2004, p. F-1).

While it's probably true that money does enter the minds of some whistle-blowers, it would be nice (not to mention fair) if journalists considered the "because it's the right thing to do" theme in writing their stories. Journalists are "on your side" (a popular name for regular investigative reporting segments) when your liposuction goes awry and your phone service is subpar, but when it comes to folks challenging our dominant institutions, rituals, and norms, they backpedal, and instead rely on tested tropes that make the challenge seem less threatening. And anyway, the public reward isn't that great. Rowley had her moment before Congress, but the news media often suggested that, right or wrong, she was an angry former employee. Wigand had his movie, *The Insider*, and before that a celebrated (and initially censored) interview with *60 Minutes*, but he also endured death threats and spies hired by his former employer following his every move.

And maybe folks don't jump at the chance to blow the whistle because of the endless raft of vitriolic single-mindedness they will catch from those who believe that the government and large corporations are almost always on their side. Such was the fate of former CIA operative Mary McCarthy, who in April 2006 was dismissed amid claims by the

Bush administration that she leaked sensitive information about the president's controversial domestic surveillance program. Journalists permitted administration officials to lay bare and dissect the process of leaking, a process essential to the craft of reporting, and rarely contextualized the McCarthy leak by mentioning that administration officials have quite a long track record of leaks.

Which brings us back to Michael Newdow, and the purpose of our journey: how the news media covered his suit challenging the Pledge. What symbolic hurdles do the mass media put up in the path of someone like Newdow? Recent events—newspapers acting more like *USA Today*, with its digestible news stories, color, and factoids, than the *New York Times*; broadcast news outlets begrudgingly emulating the right-wing looniness that emanates from the Fox News Channel; the changes in broadcast regulation that have enabled ideologues like Rupert Murdoch (who owns the Fox News Channel) and monoliths like Clear Channel to turn our airwaves into a perpetual cross between *Girls Gone Wild* and *Ripley's Believe It or Not*; an endless supply of enthusiastic Australian men selling us everything from car wax to commodity futures—does not allow for an individual with a simple point to make to make it. That is, unless that person follows a culturally approved, not too challenging or controversial, script. It's easy to blow your shot, too; we have not seen too much in recent months of Jessica Lynch, the brave young soldier whose story was co-opted and altered by the military to make her seem more heroic.

Then there's what America's master cutter-and-paster, columnist George Will (who does a great job of hiding his conservative bearings and connections from the American public), has accurately called a "confessional culture." We will say almost anything, confess to almost anything, loudly and publicly. The more "in plain view" we are when we confess, the better. It helps if our self-flagellation earns us a shot in the limelight—usually on a talk show or on reality television. The popularity of both genres has a lot to do with the demise of broadcast regulation mentioned earlier. So there's just too much competition—mindless, self-absorbed competition—for someone with a real idea.

And then there's the most obvious fly in the Newdow ointment: his challenge to the Pledge was viewed as a direct attack on God. You just don't do that in a nation allegedly founded on religious tolerance. Zealotry, and kowtowing to the zealots, is right behind baseball and collecting Beanie Babies on our list of favorite pastimes. More important (and more ominously), the zealots, in the form of the religious right, exert a disproportionate amount of influence on our culture, our lawmakers, and our president.

We'll spend part of our time together exploring the historical parallels that surround the decisions to add "under God" to the Pledge, and the Supreme Court's June 2004 ruling. For now, let's start with one: in 1954, the United States government claimed that the words were necessary to help the nation fend off a pernicious enemy (Communism) that was largely concocted by overzealous, ultraideological politicians. Politicians and journalists made similar arguments concerning Newdow's challenge to the Pledge. To battle Communism, the government, in the form of Representative Joseph McCarthy, stripped many of their civil liberties, caused others to turn on acquaintances, ended the careers of innocent people, and told us it was for the good of the nation and the sanctity of our institutions. Senator McCarthy's spirit seems to permeate the Patriot Act, a law deemed necessary by the government to fight another vague enemy: terrorism.

But if we actually believe journalists when they talk about the importance of fairness and balance, the press should explore all sides of the issue, not just join the politician's call to suck it up, come together, and be patriotic. And no matter what the country's evangelical Christians and Mel Gibson (and the hundreds of millions of dollars he earned from the grossly inaccurate film *Passion of the Christ*) say, God—or at least the evangelical view of a haughty, vengeful God—is enjoying a cultural resurgence, an enormous cultural comeback, thanks at least in part to the efforts of conservative politicians to make patriotism and religious faith mean roughly the same thing, as author Susan Jacoby (2004) argues.

"The apostles of religious correctness," Jacoby notes, "attempt to infuse every public issue, from the quality of education to capital punishment, with their theological values" (2004, p. 1). Journalists should not let this happen, at least not without an occasional challenge. They should do more than blindly laud President Bush for his repeated acknowledgments that his faith is an integral part of how he governs. They should do more than paste Tim LaHaye and Jerry Jenkins, authors of an apocalyptic series of novels, on the cover of *Newsweek* magazine (May 24, 2004) and congratulate them for selling 62 million books whose themes are built on unsupported ideas about the end of the world to which very few of us adhere. Journalists should resist the temptation to relegate individuals like Newdow "to a kooks' corner of American history," as Jacoby notes.

So far, they haven't had a lot of success at resisting: when journalists do cover atheists and atheism, it is positioned as a misguided (most of the time) or aberrant (some of the time) view, one directly opposed to what most "sane" Americans believe. Madelyn Murray O'Hair, perhaps the world's most famous atheist, is also a focal point for journalists, mainly because of her erratic behavior and still mysterious death. All journalistic roads—in the portrayal of atheists, at least—lead back to O'Hair.

While Michael Newdow is not as colorful as O'Hair, bits and pieces of past coverage of O'Hair have found their way into coverage of Newdow. As his suit progressed, we learned just as much about Newdow's singing talents and his quirky CD of songs in which he professes his opposition to religious indoctrination as we did about his lawsuit. Tame stuff when compared to O'Hair, whose death continues to be shrouded in mystery, but it still conveys the impression that Newdow is outside the mainstream of American life—journalists should simply tell us that LaHaye and Jenkins are too.

Before we embark (and in the interest of full disclosure), I must reveal a few important facts to the reader: First, I am a liberal. I believe that attacking Iraq was a bad, politically motivated idea hatched largely to rid the world of what many conservative Christians in this country believe is a backward religion (remember when President Bush called the war a "crusade," then took it back?) and to benefit the companies (like Vice President Dick Cheney's former employer, Halliburton) who obtained the contracts to supply the struggling people of Iraq with goods and services and to reward individuals like newly anointed Iraqi Prime Minister Iyad Allawi, who used many of the same tactics and weapons (supplied by us) to try to rid the world of Saddam Hussein more than a decade ago.

Second, I am an atheist. Let me qualify that a bit: I don't believe in God, but even more important, I'm not a big fan of labels. My strongest belief is in thinking for oneself. I believe wholeheartedly in the separation of church and state, and am troubled by the insinuation of religion into so many aspects of our lives. The news media, chastened by a relatively small number of ultrazealous conservative Christians, has allowed this to happen. I also happen to agree with Newdow that the words "under God" should be removed from the Pledge of Allegiance. To me, they sound like an endorsement of Christianity. If we truly believe in diversity, then we should mention Allah and Vishnu in the same breath as God. Try telling that to the Christian right or to the Catholic Church. The fact that Newdow is an atheist was one very large strike against him going in to this controversy. As Elisabeth Sifton (2004) noted in *The Nation*, Newdow was "a perfect opponent" in the eyes of the Bush administration. In addition to being an atheist, he was not married to his daughter's mother, Sandra Banning. Banning is an evangelical Christian who told reporters on many occasions that her daughter did not mind reciting the Pledge.

When the Pledge was revised to include "under God" in 1954, the country had turned equating a lack of religious belief with communism into a national pastime. As Joan DelFattore (2003) explains, atheism has always been "considered close to treason," where publicly expressing the depths of one's religious beliefs is generally seen as "an affirmation of patriotism and love of freedom" (p. 68)—this is particularly true in times of national crisis, even manufactured ones.

And anyway, the Pledge, as originally written by Francis Bellamy, a socialist and former Baptist minister, was meant to be a "straightforward statement of the American public school system's commitment to the assimilation of all immigrants," as Susan Jacoby notes (2004, p. 287). In short, he wanted the Pledge to symbolize bringing people, or in this case, schoolchildren, together. Bellamy, who adamantly believed in the separation of church and state, would have been appalled, Jacoby writes, by the addition of "under God" to the Pledge.

Ironically, he had written the Pledge at least in part as a slam at the Catholic school system, which was operating independently, and busily racking up tax subsidies from local governments throughout the early and middle 20th century. Eventually, however, the Catholic Church tired of trying (and failing) to convince its own followers not to attend the public schools, Jacoby suggests (2004, p. 308). Into the breach stepped the Knights of Columbus, the world's best known Catholic laypersons' organization, to lead the lobbying effort to have "under God" added to the Pledge.

Third, I was also at one time a journalist. My distaste for some of the practices that crept into the field during my stint as a reporter and editor (discussed in the next chapter) is one of the primary reasons—that and my love of teaching, of course—that I find myself today in the classroom, loving every minute of my time with my students. We have returned to a time when many journalists are expected to express themselves through their reporting—to provide perspective along with the facts. Just as damaging to the national discourse on important issues is the growing tendency of journalists now to talk about themselves and the news-gathering process as stories unfold. As the 20th century began, journalists, mostly in an effort to make money for their bosses, agreed that objectivity and balance would win and keep the trust of readers. Today, it seems (sadly) that bias and pointed political rhetoric—"dueling talking points" as Jon Stewart, host of *The Daily Show*, has called them—are the tools that help many reporters accomplish the same goal.

I can only hope that the reader won't hold these things against me. I believe strongly in approaching any intellectual act—writing, speaking, teaching—without an ideological agenda. But making this exercise even harder is the fact that nobody, it seems—even journalists—approaches an act of communication these days without one. Some journalists have even written about abandoning objectivity altogether. This is probably not that much of a reach, since some have already abandoned careful evaluation of information provided by individuals and groups in the name of rushing to provide what appears to be "balance" in their stories so that they don't anger the far reaches of the political and religious right.

As a result, the boundary, however fragile or imagined, between reporting and commentary is gone. Pundits, who swallow up a shocking amount of news airtime, shout at each other, parry in a cowardly fashion from the precipices of their dogmatism, never really intending to listen to one another, or to their guests. We shouldn't be shocked, then, that Newdow received less than complimentary treatment from journalists. But, as perhaps a reporter would say, there's more to the story than that.

Chapter 1

Master Myths, Frames, Narratives, and Guard Dogs

Journalists at first paid little attention to Michael Newdow's suit. Several of the journalists with whom I spoke about Newdow argued there was a good reason for the absence of coverage: the suit, originally filed in Florida, was dismissed by a federal judge in the Eastern District of California a little more than six months after it was filed. In addition, Newdow, who earned a law degree from the University of Michigan, chose to represent himself. I instruct my journalism students to jump at such an obvious "David v. Goliath" story. But he was mounting his challenge in Sacramento, California—not Los Angeles, New York, or Washington, where much of a reporter's attention is typically focused—without a lawyer, and he had lost on the district court level.

So much for David and Goliath.

One journalist, who covered the case for the *New York Times*, said he would not have dreamed of pitching the story—at this stage, anyway—to his editor. "Nobody would have thought this suit would succeed," he said (A. Liptak, personal interview, July 2004). "Here's this little guy who can't even get a lawyer." On top of that, the reporter said, the district court gave Newdow, in essence, "the back of its hand" when it dismissed the suit. "There was no news there," Liptak said. A reporter for the *San Francisco Chronicle* who covers the Ninth Circuit acknowledged that he had never even heard of Newdow until the Ninth Circuit issued its controversial ruling in June 2002 (B. Egelko, personal interview, July 1, 2004).

I conducted a series of computer searches using the Lexis-Nexis database in 2003, 2004, and 2005. I searched for news articles, editorials, and broadcast transcripts that appeared in the nation's major daily newspapers and television networks from the day Newdow filed his suit in March of 2000 to May 15, 2005. I also conducted lengthy e-mail and telephone interviews in 2004, 2005, and 2006 with several of the journalists who covered the case, several of the attorneys involved in the case, and a number of interested observers.

As I read and reread the newspaper articles and news transcripts, I looked for key themes and narrative strands, keeping in mind Jack Lule's idea that news "comes to us as a story" (2001, p. 3). News is composed of what Lule believes are "enduring, abiding stories." In covering what goes on in the world, journalists tap "a deep but nonetheless limited body of story forms and types." This reliance on certain story forms is no surprise, writes Lule, given our love for stories. "We understand our lives and our world through story," he argues (p. 3).

Perhaps more important, Lule contends that familiar myths—"the great stories of humankind" (p. 15)—regularly come to life in news reporting. Lule defines myth as "a sacred, social story that draws from archetypal figures to offer exemplary models for human life" (p. 17). Myths empower society to express its "prevailing ideals, ideologies, values, and beliefs." They are, Lule writes, "models *of* social life and models *for* social life" (p. 15). Myths are not evident in every news story, as Lule cautions, but in many instances journalists draw upon "the rich treasure trove of archetypal stories" to revisit those shared stories that help us make sense of the world in which we live.

Lule's analysis of news produced seven of what he calls "master myths": the *victim*, whose life is abruptly altered by "the randomness of human existence"; the *scapegoat*, deployed in stories to remind us of "what happens to those who challenge or ignore social beliefs"; the *hero*, there to remind us that we have the potential for greatness; the *good mother*, who offers us "a model of goodness in times when goodness may seem in short supply" (p. 24); the *trickster*, a crafty figure who usually ends up bringing "on himself and others all manner of suffering," thanks to his crude, boorish behavior; the *other world*, which enables us to feel good about our way of life by contrasting it, sometimes starkly, with ways of life elsewhere (as when reporters wrote of life in the former Soviet Union during the Cold War); and the *flood*, in which we see the "destruction of a group of people by powerful forces," often because they have "strayed from the right path" (p. 25).

Lule's assessment meshes with Richard Campbell's claim that while we talk a good game when it comes to individualism, we really embrace it only when it is situated in what John Fiske calls our "communal allegiances" (quoted in Campbell, 1991, p. 142). Our path in life should not be so unique that we forget how to conform, or that journalists are unable to make it seem like we conform. Put even more simply, you can take individualism only so far.

And while journalists routinely criticize powerful institutions, they do so by "personalizing" issues, or casting them as battles between individuals. This shift comes with a cost. "The social origins of events are lost," Lule writes. I tell my journalism students "news" is "anything that breaks the routine." Such an approach may ensure that they produce good stories, but it also robs journalism of its ability to place events in historical context, as John Fiske contends.

In his excellent book on the mythic structure of the CBS newsmagazine *60 Minutes*, Campbell (1991) argues that the show portrayed former president Ronald Reagan as embodying Middle American values despite the fact that they he and his wife, Nancy, were wealthy, powerful people. Similarly, in a story on Joyce Brown, a homeless person from New York, the program symbolically moved her from the "periphery" to "a central location more in line with a consensual middle ground" (p. 151). Those from the periphery fare better with journalists, Campbell argues, if they are able to make their arguments in a "common sense" fashion.

The late celebrated columnist Molly Ivins, a staunch liberal from Texas, was a frequent guest on television news and discussion programs, despite her ideological leanings and her ongoing criticism (maybe "lampooning" is a better word) of President Bush. The reason? She's smart—and funny. Bill Moyers, a brilliant, skilled journalist who recently retired as host of the PBS program *NOW*, was a television fixture, despite some very harsh criticism of the Bush administration during his stint as *NOW* host and editor. Why? Again, he's smart, eloquent, and speaks "liberal" in a way that even centrists—not to mention conservatives—can stomach, even appreciate.

Reporters tend to draw nonconformists like Ivins and Moyers "back into the consensus," as Stuart Hall argues (quoted in Campbell, 1991, p. 151). By doing so, these individuals manage to reaffirm the communal allegiances noted by Fiske. Individuals who resist, or who espouse, excessively radical viewpoints are "not allowed to speak directly, but are reported, that is, mediated if their point of view is represented at all," argues Fiske (ibid., p. 153).

Consider the case of 2004 presidential candidate Howard Dean, the former governor of Vermont. Journalists credited him with breathing fresh air into the political fund-raising and outreach process by using the Internet to, for example, set up "meet-ups" across the country. Soon, other candidates were copying Dean. He was the front-runner; that is, until mainstream journalists started talking about how truly liberal he was, and how he might scare off Democrats looking for a more centrist alternative—which we eventually got in Senator John Kerry. But the moment that crystallized this unease for reporters was the "I Have a Scream" speech following Dean's disheartening third-place finish in the Iowa caucuses. I'm sure you remember the scene: Dean, sleeves rolled up, trying to calm the fears, and stoke the passions, of more than 3,000 crestfallen Iowa volunteers, exhorting them, pumping his fist, and then finally letting out a raspy scream.

At that moment, Dean crossed the line separating "breath of fresh air" and fire-breathing nonconformist. He was soon seen as a liability to the party. He had to defend his enthusiasm; journalists asked him to explain why he colored outside the lines, why he for the moment burst out of the typical political package. "Was it over the top? Sure, it was over the top," he told Diane Sawyer of ABC's *PrimeTime Live*. Dean, with his wife, Judy, now by his side, felt no regrets. "I'm not apologetic because I was giving everything to people who gave everything to me," he said ("Dean: I Have," 2004).

Reporters probably felt all along, perhaps with good reason, that Dean never had a legitimate shot at the nomination. To be sure, his speech damaged his standing. But reporters soon committed what I believe is a key error: they started *writing and intoning about* how Dean's standing had been damaged—and little else about his ideas. We read about his temper and Judy Dean's desire to continue practicing medicine if her husband won—to my amazement, women seeking self-fulfillment by pursuing a career is still an alien concept to many people.

So when a public figure is too controversial, reporters move that person to what Daniel Hallin (1986) has called the "sphere of deviance." Occupying this space are "those political actors and views which journalists and the political mainstream of society reject as unworthy of being heard" (pp. 116–117). Journalists resolutely guard the boundary between this zone and the "sphere of legitimate controversy," where public officials are allowed to determine how and when we discuss important issues. Those in the "sphere of deviance" rarely get near the innermost sphere in Hallin's model, the "sphere of consensus," where hallowed ideas and values—Hallin calls it the "region of motherhood and apple pie" (p. 116)—are kept and protected, in part by journalists whose actions suggest that debate on these ideas and values would be pointless. When consensus on an issue wanes, reporters intensify their focus on objectivity, Hallin suggests. But with that focus comes reliance on official versions of events. Those figures that challenge the consensus are sent packing—symbolically, anyway—to the "sphere of deviance." Some are simply treated like unruly children; others are exposed and criticized for their nonconformity.

But these assessments of how journalists treat dissenters beg the question: How *did* Newdow manage to earn so much coverage, especially in light of the fact that the symbolic deck was stacked against him? I fully expected to find that reporters invoked the "scapegoat" myth—that they simply acted as a conduit for the government's position on (and for public outcry about) Newdow's suit, and subsequently held Newdow up as an example of what happens when someone has the audacity to challenge one of our most beloved ritualistic expressions of patriotism, audacity amplified in the minds of many in our collective reaction to the 9/11 attacks. My analysis reveals, however, a more complex deployment of the master myths discussed by Lule.

Frame Analysis: Journalists *Make* the News

An explanation of framing begins with this idea: journalists *make* the news. Not "make" in the sense that they are the subjects of their own coverage, but "make" in the sense that they piece together the stories we see and read each day from the information available when the story unfolds. In doing so, they highlight some parts of a story, making them seem more significant than other parts. Frames direct our attention to certain aspects of a story. Some scholars argue that frames even suggest to us how we should view a story—the "preferred reading" of the facts.

Like journalists, we develop and deploy frames to help us make sense of the world around us. Let's try a simple example: think about setting up a photograph—during a recent family get-together, perhaps, or a memorable vacation. You don't try to include everything in the shot; you *select* what will go in the photo—nice scenery, local citizens, maybe your hotel room—and what you'll leave out, based on what you think your friends and family will want to see. The photo may some day come to represent the totality of your trip (you'll look at it and say, "Boy, I really loved our trip to Williamsburg), but it's really just a slice of that trip built with pieces you choose and arrange.

It's the same with news. A reporter makes a series of careful choices about the information, quotes, visuals, and descriptions that go into a story. A reporter covering a protest march, for example, is faced with a great deal of information—the marchers, information about their positions on issues, reactions of residents and merchants—so organizing it in some fashion is vital, especially when a story is, in the words of John Fiske, "unruly."

Frames help the reporter understand a story, and, eventually, help the reader or viewer understand the story. The key difference is that journalists, unlike our intrepid tourist-photographer, are supposed to observe a code of ethics that requires they cover a story in a fair, balanced, and objective fashion. Thus, even though a journalist might not have the time or the space to create an exhaustive report about an event, he or she is obligated to piece together what famed journalist Bob Woodward calls "the best available version of the truth"—a version that is accurate, and that does not favor a particular worldview or ideology.

Framing is a popular tool in academic research; there have been literally hundreds of articles written in which scholars use frame analysis to evaluate the depth and balance of news coverage. Noted sociologist Erving Goffman (1974) began the dialogue on framing. He wrote that a frame is a "principle of organization which governs events—at least social ones—and our subjective involvement in them" (p. 11). Frames enable us to "locate, perceive, identify, and label a seemingly infinite number of concrete occurrences" (p. 21). We use frames to make sense of the world around us. Journalists create news frames to help them "simplify, prioritize, and structure the narrative flow of events (Norris, 1995, p. 357). As Oscar Gandy (2001) explains, frames "are used purposively to direct attention and then to guide the processing of information so that the preferred reading of the facts come to dominate public understanding" (p. 365).

Kathleen Jamieson and Paul Waldman (2003) contend that frames are "the structures underlying the depictions that the public reads, hears, and watches" (p. xii). Framing takes place when journalists "select some aspects of a perceived reality and make them more salient in a communicating text" (Entman, 1993, p. 52). By attempting to organize experiences for readers, journalists "highlight some bits of information about an item that is the subject of communication, thereby elevating them in salience" (p. 53).

At the heart of my work is the use by reporters of "keywords, stock phrases, stereotyped images, sources of information, and sentences that provide reinforcing clusters of facts or judgments" about Newdow, his motives in challenging the Pledge of Allegiance, and the reactions of public officials (Entman, 1993, p. 52) and their actions. Through their reporting, Paul D'Angelo (2002) argues, journalists provide "interpretive packages" of the positions of parties who have a political investment in an issue. In so doing, journalists "both reflect and add" to what William A. Gamson and Andre Mogdiliani (1987) call the "issue culture" of a topic. Of particular relevance for our journey are the contentions, summarized by D'Angelo, that frames limit our political awareness, limit activism, and "set parameters for policy debates not necessarily in agreement with democratic norms" (p. 877). Journalists select sources because they are credible, and believe that even a long-standing frame has value because it contains "a range of viewpoints that is potentially useful" to our understanding of an issue (p. 877).

But what happens when some views are excluded? Todd Gitlin, a world-renowned sociologist, explored how the news media, specifically the *New York Times* and CBS News, covered the activities of a group of activists known as Students for a Democratic Society (SDS). SDS was at the forefront of the opposition to America's involvement in the Vietnam War. Between 1960 and 1965, the news media ignored SDS, in part because the group did not try to attract the media's attention. By 1965, antiwar protests had begun to capture the attention of more people. Therefore, they had become more newsworthy. As a result, reporters began to cover SDS.

Gitlin (1980) argued that frames are "persistent patterns of cognition, organization, and presentation, of selection, emphasis, and exclusion, by which symbol-handlers routinely organize discourse, whether verbal or visual" (p. 7). Frames give shape to what parts of a story are told, what parts are given prominence, which sources are used, what groups are marginalized through their portrayal as deviant or illegitimate, and what words are used to describe the parties to a story.

In covering antiwar protests, reporters made fun of how Vietnam War protestors dressed, how they spoke, and of their goals. They likened SDS to violent neo-Nazi groups, and paid an unfair amount of attention to right-wing groups. Reporters focused on disagreements among SDS members, and showed them to be deviant by suggesting that the group included communists. They underestimated the number of SDS members, and suggested that the group was not getting its point across. Reporters relied on statements from government officials and did not gather additional information that might have helped them paint a clearer picture of the group's activism.

In short, reporters marginalized SDS. They undermined the group's efforts to "present a general, coherent political opposition." Reporters suggested that activists spent all of their time and effort on "single grievances" which the significant institutions in society can fix without "altering fundamental social relations"—in other words, without real change. Reporters from the *Times* went from portraying SDS as a bona fide movement to a "menace" in seven months. Editors at the *Times* were concerned that conservatives would charge that the paper was sympathetic to Communism, claims Gitlin. Reporters also suggested that SDS was bent on persuading young people to avoid the draft. Reporters spotlighted tactics, not goals or ideas. But as Gitlin argues, reporters were only being true to their job routines; they covered "the event, not the condition; the conflict, not the consensus; the fact that 'advances the story,' not the one that explains it" (p. 122). Reporters paid a great deal of attention to spokespeople who "most closely matched prefabricated images of what an opposition leader should look and sound like: theatrical, bombastic, and knowing and inventive in the ways of packaging messages" (p. 154) for maximum media exposure. The group's goals and ideas were less important because they made for less compelling stories.

My own research reveals that journalists have marginalized 21st-century antiwar protestors by using several new frames. First, the movement is large and encompasses a diverse range of people, but its diversity is just as much a weakness as it is a strength. Antiwar activism is too broad, lacks focus, and is on a never-ending quest to define itself. The movement was partially driven by an eclectic mix of aggressive young people and Vietnam War protest veterans whose zeal and computer-savvy on the one hand, and a tendency to go through the motions for old times' sake on the other, hampered the movement's progress. Those from the "middle ground" who protested came to the movement suddenly, and at times did so only when protest fit their schedule.

Second, journalists went from undercounting protestors to focusing almost solely on the number of protestors at each rally, and on the diverse range of their activities. By the time the United States attacked Iraq, reporters were doing little more than telling readers how many protestors were protesting, where they were protesting, and how many were arrested. Missing was intelligent discussion of the issues raised by the protestors. Their arguments were reduced to chants, signs, and the phrase "no blood for oil."

The "veterans" interviewed by reporters are stuck in the 1960s. They are still devoted to the cause, but are irrelevant. Reporters permitted them to stand at the stylistic barricades erected by colleagues whose writing was analyzed by Gitlin. The use by journalists of Gitlin as a source is a somewhat disconcerting nod to the fact that 1960s style protest is not relevant. Despite covering efforts by protestors to attract "Middle America," stories tended to focus on preachers (veteran protestors) and students (their contemporary counterparts). Reporters also created the impression that these sentiments sprung up out of the blue, and lacked continuity with earlier antiwar activism. There was little discussion of demonstrations against the Persian Gulf War, and none about antiwar sentiment directed toward Grenada, Somalia, Bosnia, or Kosovo.

Third, coverage suggests that the ambivalence felt by protestors about challenging their government lends at least some support to the idea that this round of protests was unpatriotic. Reporters give ample space and time to angry, profane individuals who question the patriotism and love of country shown by protestors.

Fourth, if protestors aren't old and irrelevant, they are faceless and violent. We can't identify with them because they are too busy running through the streets, joining themselves together with PVC pipe, chaining themselves to things and too each other, and blocking traffic. Further, today's protestors are well versed in how to use the media to get their message across and to mobilize support. Protestors can generate attendance, journalists suggest, but have no real impact on policy. It is as if protestors are either going through the motions, are worried about fitting activism into their busy lives, or are protesting only because it is fashionable. Whatever their motivation, their efforts are fruitless, journalists suggest.

Then as now, reporters pushed protestors to the edges of the frame. Journalists judged them to be not as newsworthy as the other aspects of the war, even though there was a great deal of antiwar sentiment in the nation at the time. When protest *was* covered, it was treated as being outside the mainstream, even though the right to disagree with our government and show our disagreement in the form of protest is a right that we cherish. Such treatment is not limited to antiwar protestors. Journalists—particularly broadcast journalists—have framed opponents of the World Trade Organization as strident and destructive. Further, journalists have long treated the views of many environmental activists as outside the mainstream. Some groups, like Greenpeace, do cross the ethical line with some of their more destructive actions. But in the early 1960s, journalists permitted government officials and corporate leaders to dismiss Rachel Carson, author of *Silent Spring*, arguably the most significant treatise on the destruction of the environment, as an unqualified troublemaking spinster.

In the chapters that follow, we will explore how journalists used several distinct frames to position Newdow as an erratic outsider who had the audacity to challenge one of this nation's most revered rituals in a time of national crisis.

Narrative Analysis

A third valuable tool for exploring news coverage of the Pledge is narrative analysis. Walter Fisher (1987) defines narrative as "symbolic actions—words or deeds—that have meaning for those who live, create, or interpret them" (p. 58). In short, we are all storytellers. In fact, "enacted dramatic narrative is the basic and essential genre for the characterization of human actions" (p. 58). Fisher firmly rejects the claim that narrative is not grounded in rationality. "[N]o form of discourse is privileged over others because its form is predominantly argumentative," Fisher argues. "No matter how strictly a case is argued—scientifically, philosophically, or legally—it will always be a story, an interpretation of some aspect of the world that is historically and culturally grounded and shaped by human personality" (p. 49).

While the focus of narrative analysis is the individual story, it is possible to explore a number of stories that cohere as a larger story—a "metastory" (Berdayes & Berdayes, 1998) that functions "to generate a more inclusive perspective, and to expand the possibilities and range of debate" (p. 113). A metastory can provide the researcher with a clearer understanding of the culture that produces the narrative. Sonja Foss (1996) argues that narrative "functions as an argument to view and understand the world in a particular way" (p. 400). It enables the researcher to explore and define "a coherent world in which social action occurs" (Berdayes & Berdayes, 1998, p. 109).

Narrative analysis also enables the researcher to explore assumptions at work in the narrative. Researchers can isolate and examine closely the "linguistic and cultural resources" drawn on by the creators of a narrative. This enables the researcher to assess how these resources persuade the reader to accept the narrative as a realistic portrayal of events and people. Keep in mind, too, that some narratives resonate longer, and have more cultural authority, than others. One narrative can, over time, come to dominate our understanding of a person or an issue.

Try this: ask a Republican about former president Ronald Reagan. You'll get something like, "Oh, he encouraged America to love itself again" and be told what a great communicator he was—and you'll probably get a sizable dose of his enduring adoration for his wife, Nancy. What you won't hear are his ignorance of the growing AIDS crisis in the world, and his involvement in the Iran-Contra scandal. You get "the shining city on the hill" narrative. It's incomplete, inaccurate—but it hangs together and it sounds good.

Thus, we use narrative, Foss (1996) argues, to "help us impose order on the flow of experience so that we can make sense of events and actions in our lives" (p. 399). For the purposes of this analysis, narrative's most salient quality is that it "provides clues to the subjectivity of individuals and to the values and meanings that characterize a culture" (p. 401). Narratives typically include logical reasons for the actions of the participants. They also reflect the values that drive these actions. These values, claims Fisher, "determine the persuasive force of reasons." They enable individuals who hear the narrative to decide whether they will act on it. But the question that always tantalizes me is: what happens if the narrative isn't made up of accurate information—that truth has been sacrificed for the sake of a good story? The stories that your parents tell about you, for example, resonate like crazy. They become powerful because, in part, they hold together and are told with conviction.

Thus, special attention will be paid during our journey to what journalists invited their readers and viewers to think—and not to think—about Newdow and his lawsuit. Jamieson and Waldman (2003) argue that nothing is more important to journalists than a compelling narrative, one that will attract and keep readers. Journalists, they argue, work to "deliver the world to citizens in a comprehensible form" (p. 1). Elements and ideas that might damage a narrative's coherence—how well the story hangs together—will be avoided or discarded by the reporter.

As an example, consider how popular women's magazines like *Vogue* and *Redbook* cover eating disorders like anorexia nervosa and bulimia. The narrative that emerges from articles in these publications offers a distorted picture of what life is like for someone suffering from an eating disorder. Victims typically suffer alone, trapped by their selfishness and perfectionism, while stunned family members and peers stand by, watching as the disease suddenly takes hold.

In the latter stages of the narrative, writers blame the media both for the victim's illness and for the overall increase in the number of cases of eating disorders. This narrative provides a distorted picture of what goes on outside the discourse of dieting—outside the symbiotic relationship between food companies and diet product makers carried out in the pages of women's magazines. Editors of women's magazines probably would not want to despoil an editorial approach built around the "health and beauty consciousness" discussed by Robin Andersen (1995, pp. 15–17). These articles disrupt the diet-friendly editorial environment sold by women's magazines to their readers and to their advertisers.

But this level of sensationalism does little to advance understanding of eating disorders. As David Morris (1998) explains, "[P]ostmodern ideals of beauty do not circulate in an innocent realm of fantasy but support and promote a consumer economy" sustained by creating "strangely immaterial needs" (p. 154), chief among them the need for a perfect body. But the information that fuels this narrative is not placed in context. We see only the "privatized landscape" of the anorexic's experience. Women's magazines deploy this metastory not for genuine change, or to encourage debate about the need to diet; instead, it allows women's magazines to continue normalizing diet while paying narrative lip service to the experience of those who suffer from eating disorders.

The "Guard Dog" Function of Reporting

Our final theoretical stop is the "guard dog" function of journalism advanced by George Donahue, Philip Tichenor, and Clarice Olien (1995). Journalists (and journalism professors) talk a great deal about how journalists are supposed to act as "watchdogs." They monitor the conduct of public officials and large corporations, and expose corrupt behavior for the public's benefit. Starting with the Watergate scandal, the list of corporate and governmental acts of misconduct revealed by journalists is impressive.

But Donahue and his colleagues (1995) see the journalist's role differently. They argue that journalists often play the role of guard dog. Think of an alarm system—I use the popular Slomin Shield in my classes to illustrate these ideas. But journalists don't sound "the alarm" to protect their readers; they do so to protect large cultural institutions, institutions that, frankly, don't need their help. They act when "external forces present a threat to local leadership" (p. 116). Journalists tend to go after individuals, but often fail to explore the institutional flaws that cause the threats. It would be like reporting a string of murders without exploring how the alleged perpetrators were so easily able to obtain weapons.

Journalists are trained to act as "sentry" for dominant institutions, patrolling the perimeter, searching for threats, and sounding the alarm when one is identified. The dominant institution may have no idea why the alarm is being sounded. When a threat causes conflict, journalists address it in "a constrained way and only on certain issues and under certain structural conditions" (p. 116). They seek to reinforce, not challenge, these institutions, and lead the community back toward cohesion.

We can see the "guard dog" in action by briefly exploring coverage by print journalists of the internment of Japanese-Americans. On February 19, 1942, President Franklin D. Roosevelt signed Executive Order 9066, which empowered the secretary of war to "exclude any and all persons, citizens, and aliens, from designated areas in order to provide security against sabotage, espionage, and fifth column activity" (Daniels, 1993, p. 129). Immigrants born in Japan ("issei") and second generation Japanese-Americans ("nisei") were not allowed to work or travel anywhere on the West Coast. They were eventually rounded up and sent first to "assembly centers," and then to one of ten relocation centers run by the civilian-staffed War Relocation Authority.

We now know that the threat of "fifth column activity" never existed. A key FDR adviser, General John DeWitt, lied in a report to the president about alleged acts of spying by Japanese-Americans. Among the most ardent advocates for relocation were then California Attorney General Earl Warren, later a revered champion of civil rights, and Secretary of War Henry Stimson, who encouraged the president to pursue evacuation as a viable means of ending the alleged Japanese-American threat to national security.

Journalists fell right in line, although not right away. Two strands of news coverage emerged immediately following the attack on Pearl Harbor. The first focused on efforts by Japanese-Americans to show their patriotism, their support for the war effort, and their loyalty to the United States. One headline in the *Los Angeles Times*, for example, read "Japanese-Americans Pledge Loyalty to the United States" ("Japanese-Americans Pledge," 1941). The Japanese-Americans Citizens League guaranteed its "fullest cooperation and its facilities to the United States Government." The Japanese consul in Los Angeles even apologized to the United States for Japan's actions.

Slowly, however, the tone of the coverage shifted, once the government developed its ill-conceived policy for dealing with the alleged threat. On December 8, 1941, the *Los Angeles Times* referred to California as a "zone of danger" (Daniels, 1993, p. 28). Of the thousands of Japanese-Americans living in the area, "some, perhaps many are good Americans. What the rest may be we do not know, nor can we take a chance in light of yesterday's demonstration that treachery and double-dealing are not major Japanese weapons" (p. 28). The paper called on "alert keen-eyed citizens" to look out for what were surely "spies, saboteurs, and fifth columnists in their midst" (Daniels, 1981).

As Donahue and his colleagues (1995) argue, reporters pay a great deal of attention to "nation and society—their persistence, cohesion, and the conflicts and divisions threatening that cohesion" (p. 116). Jamieson and Waldman (2003) agree, arguing that journalists "report from a sense, perhaps visceral, perhaps cerebral, that their reporting should instill public faith in the proposition that, despite its flaws, the democratic system does work" (p. 130). To do that, they must tell us what is and what is not a "threat" to that system. Journalists write to show us not only that democracy survives threats (like those mounted by Newdow), it also corrects underlying problems with the system. Journalists may be wary of powerful individuals, but they express a staggering amount of reverence for the institutions through which their power is exercised (p. 136). Thus, much of their reporting seeks an answer to the question, "did the system work?"

Chapter 2

A Case of First Impression

In his suit, originally filed in March 2000 in Sacramento federal court, Michael Newdow argued that both the California law that requires schools to conduct "appropriate patriotic exercises" (section 52720 of the state's Education Code) and the Elk Grove and Sacramento School Districts policies requiring elementary school students to say the Pledge to start each school day violated the Establishment Clause of the U.S. Constitution. These policies were clear attempts by district officials to indoctrinate Newdow's then five-year-old daughter with "religious dogma."

Newdow argued that he, not the government, had the right to instruct his daughter about religion. Every day, his daughter had been "compelled to watch and listen as her state-employed teacher in her state-run school leads her and her classmates in a ritual proclaiming that there is a God, and that ours is "one Nation under God." Even though the Pledge had been challenged on three previous occasions, Newdow believed that his was a "case of first impression" or "a novel, new or undecided interpretation of law that comes before a court" (www.legalexplanations.com, 2005). Newdow was the first person to name the president and Congress in a Pledge case.

Elk Grove School District superintendent David Gordon contended that Newdow's daughter had not been coerced into saying the Pledge; district policy allowed her to "opt out," or sit quietly while the Pledge was recited. Newdow would argue that he did not have to prove that his daughter was coerced. In 1992, the Supreme Court ruled in *Lee v. Weisman*, 505 U.S. 577 (1992), that students who had to listen to a benediction given at their high school's graduation ceremonies had been coerced into hearing religious dogma. In his daughter's classroom, the coercion was even more "forcefully present," since her teacher led a daily recitation of the Pledge. Newdow discussed the "opt out" provision with his daughter's teacher and principal, but concluded it would be impossible for her to "opt out" without feeling like an outsider. Newdow did not, as many journalists would later suggest, question the government's motivations for or its right to encourage patriotism. He objected to the government's inclusion of "religious dogma" to achieve that goal.

A Call for Change

In his complaint, Newdow summarized for the court the Pledge's history. A brief, more objective summary will suffice for our purposes. Written as part of preparation for marking the 400th anniversary of Christopher Columbus's now debated discovery of America, the Pledge first appeared in the popular Boston-based children's magazine *The Youth's Companion*. Francis Bellamy, a socialist and former Baptist minister, in 1892 wrote the Pledge, which originally read: "I Pledge allegiance to my Flag and to the Republic for which it stands: one Nation indivisible, with Liberty and Justice for all."

Author Susan Jacoby (2004) notes that Bellamy was removed from his minister's post in Boston for "preaching against the evils of capitalism" (p. 287), a message that today's journalists, many of whom work for large corporations with a vested interest in sustaining capitalism, might ignore or marginalize. Bellamy also was a firm believer in the separation of church and state. Jacoby speculates that he would have been "horrified" at the government's decision to add "under God" to the Pledge. In fact, the Pledge was originally intended to reflect the commitment of our public schools to assimilate the growing number of immigrants, Jacoby writes.

Journalists who covered Newdow's suit in 2002 would repeatedly note that Bellamy was a socialist, and that he was fired for expressing his socialist beliefs, but they failed to explore his belief in separation of church and state (other than brief discussions of the Pledge as a "completely secular document" [Dobbs, 2003]—discussions precipitated by supporters of Newdow) and, perhaps more important, the original purpose of the Pledge. "His Pledge was a call for change in a nation dominated by robber barons and big business," said CBS News reporter John Blackstone (2002).

Blackstone's characterization was a bit off the mark: Bellamy wanted to make children of immigrants feel welcome in their new schools. Blackstone interviewed Peter Dreier, a professor of politics at Occidental College, who added that Bellamy sought to "promote a national sense of fairness, equality, an egalitarianism and opportunity." This is closer to, but still not fully reflective of, Bellamy's original intent. For journalists, it was enough that Bellamy was a socialist who had, to the extent that he espoused values we all supposedly cherish, seen the light.

Ironically, children in Catholic schools joined children in the public schools in reciting the Pledge after World War I. "Catholic educators, originally suspicious of the Pledge's secular intent, decided that the words, even without a nod to the deity, could do no harm and would help demonstrate the Americanism of American Catholics" (Jacoby, 2004, p. 287). It was the Knights of Columbus, an organization founded by a Catholic priest and whose mission is to "render financial aid to members and their families," that spearheaded the effort in 1954 to change the Pledge.

Changes to the Pledge came in 1923, when the words "my Flag" were replaced by "the Flag of the United States," and in 1924, when the phrase became "the Flag of the United States of America." In 1942, President Roosevelt signed into law rules that governed display of the flag. The law replaced the one-armed salute to the flag suggested by Francis Bellamy with the "hand over heart" ritual we all know. Officials felt that Bellamy's original salute would remind the nation too much of the Nazi "Heil Hitler" salute (Jacoby, 2004, p. 287). The law also included this version of the Pledge: "I Pledge allegiance to the flag of the United States of America and to the Republic for which it stands, one Nation indivisible, with liberty and justice for all." Nothing in the Pledge to that point, claimed Newdow, smacked of religion.

The trouble began when Congress, in an overzealous attempt to stop the spread of "godless Communism," a phrase repeated religiously (if you will) by a number of reporters writing after the Ninth Circuit's decision in Newdow's favor, moved to add "under God" to the Pledge. A *Washington Post* columnist, writing in 2002, added a bit of misanthropic rhetorical flourish to Congress' original purpose: "to strengthen the rhetorical contrast between our God-fearing nation and the godless commies" (Fisher, 2002, p. B-1).

The *New York Times* took a more temperate view. Amendment of the Pledge "was a petty attempt to link patriotism with religious piety," a *Times* editorial stated, "to distinguish us from the godless Soviets." But borrowing a page from those who argue that the religious content of the Pledge is little more than "ceremonial deism," the *Times* contended that sheer repetition of the Pledge had made its reference to God innocuous. "A generic two-word reference to God tucked inside a rote civic exercise is not a prayer," the editorial said. While Congress and the president may have erred in adding the phrase, getting rid of it now "would cause more harm than leaving them in."

But by adding "under God," Newdow argued, Congress invalidated the law passed in 1942 that codified the Pledge. Citing a 1993 Supreme Court ruling (*Church of Lukumi Babalu Aye v. City of Hialeah*, 508 U.S. 520, 533), he contended that a law "lacks facial neutrality if it refers to a religious practice without a secular meaning discernible from the language or context." The Court's ruling in *Lukumi* was the culmination of a controversy surrounding live animal sacrifices performed by adherents of the Santeria religion. When a number of members announced plans to build a church in Hialeah, Florida, the city council passed a resolution reflecting the "concern" of residents about "religious practices inconsistent with public morals, peace, or safety." In the resolution, the city affirmed its commitment to barring these practices. At the same time, officials passed an ordinance that prohibited ritual animal sacrifice.

Members of the Santeria church filed a civil rights suit, claiming that the Hialeah law violated their constitutional right to practice religion. A federal district court judge in Miami dismissed the suit, ruling that the government's interest in preventing "health risks and cruelty to animals" was sufficiently compelling, even though, the judge acknowledged, the law was not "religiously neutral." Regulating religious practices does not violate the First Amendment when those practices threaten the public's health, the judge said. A federal appeals court panel in Atlanta affirmed the judge's ruling.

Striking down the ordinances as unconstitutional, the Supreme Court restated a principle at the heart of its previous Establishment Clause rulings: the First Amendment "forbids an official purpose to disapprove of a particular religion or of religion in general," just as it forbids the endorsement of a particular religion. "[I]f the object of a law is to infringe upon or restrict practices because of their religious motivation, the law is not neutral," wrote Justice Anthony Kennedy for the Court. "Official action that targets religious conduct for distinctive treatment cannot be shielded by mere compliance with the requirement of facial neutrality," Justice Kennedy wrote. Hialeah officials had unfairly targeted the Santeria ritual when it passed the law, the Court said.

What of the Honest Atheist?

The tendency of journalists to marginalize Newdow has precedent in the fawning treatment by reporters in the 1950s of efforts by lawmakers to amend the Pledge. In 1953, Louis Rabaut, a liberal democrat from Michigan, introduced House Joint Resolution 243, which proposed the addition of "under God" to the Pledge. Rabaut hoped that the amended

Pledge would provide to young people "a deeper understanding of the real meaning of patriotism" (Christian Family Coalition, 2005). Patriotism, Rabaut noted, "is a devotion to an institution that finds its origin and development in the moral law and commands our respect and allegiance so long as it provides that liberty and justice for all in which freemen can work out their own immortal destinies."

Rabaut's resolution languished for almost a year. It wasn't until President Eisenhower heard a February 7, 1954, sermon by Reverend George Docherty of the New York Avenue Presbyterian Church in Washington, DC, that the movement to add "under God" began in earnest. Jack Lule, whose work we touched on in chapter 1, would argue that Docherty was the first true hero in the story of the push to amend the Pledge. He reminded us that we could take the fight to communism if we only paused to reexamine and embrace the ideas that made the country great.

Eisenhower listened intently in the front pew (where Abraham Lincoln had once sat) that Sunday as Docherty argued that to leave "under God" out of the Pledge "is to omit the definitive character of the American way of life." Recognition of God's hand in our affairs was "the one fundamental concept that completely and ultimately separates Communist Russia from the democratic institutions of this Country," Docherty said. Two world wars and what Docherty (1954) called "the tragedy of nineteenth century democratic liberalism" had "shattered the illusion that you can build a nation on human ideas without a fundamental belief in God's Providence" (p. 6). Further, the First Amendment called only for the separation of church and state, not "the separation of church and life" (pp. 7–8). To be totally inclusive, "under God" means everybody—there should be no religious test for those who immigrate to the United States.

Journalists for the *Washington Post* treated Docherty's sermon like the act of a true hero. In an article that ran the day after the service, reporter Kenneth Dale (1954) told readers that "the minister of Lincoln's church" had forcefully suggested "that the words Lincoln inserted in the Gettysburg Address—'under God'—be inserted" into the Pledge (p. 12). "Belief in God is the distinguishing factor" between the United States and the Soviets, wrote Dale.

"What then of the honest atheist?" Docherty (1954) asked. It turns out that the reverend didn't quite mean "everybody," after all. He called atheists "spiritual parasites" (p. 9) that live off of the "accumulated spiritual capital of Judaio (sic)-Christian civilization" and "deny the God who revealed the divine principles upon which the ethics of this Country grow" (p. 9). An atheist "cannot deny the Christian revelation and logically live by the Christian ethic. And if he denies the Christian ethic, he falls short of the American ideal of life" (p. 9). The reverend suggested that atheists were only interested in hedonistic pursuits. "The American way," wrote Dale, is more than "going to the ballgame, and eating popcorn and drinking Cola-cola (sic)" (1954, p. 12).

Being an American "is a freedom that respects minorities but is defined by a fundamental belief in God," Docherty said at the end of Dale's article. Our way of life, claimed Docherty, was put at risk by "modern, secularized godless humanity." Dale then added, "or communism." The last few paragraphs of Dale's article suggest that the atheist is partially to blame for the country's problems and for the alleged threat to its security. We also see evidence of two master myths, as described by Lule: the *scapegoat* (used by storytellers to remind us what happens to those who go against the consensus) and the *trickster*, who is done in by his or her own boorish behavior. The atheist is essentially a spiritual and ideological freeloader without any real moral compass.

The sermon was well received by more than 500 clergy visiting Washington, DC, in May 1952. They belonged to a group called the Washington Pilgrimage, described by the *Post* as "a religious-patriotic group" (Dole, 1955, p. 10). Once they heard Docherty's sermon, members "took up the idea and sounded out leading ministers across the country," most of whom liked Docherty's concept. But not only did the group's lobbying violate the separation of church and state, it was also against the law. Sounds an awful lot like the Catholic Church's attempt to sway voters in 2004 when it suggested that Catholic politicians who support a woman's right to choose should not be given communion.

And nearly a year after the president signed the Pledge bill, the *Post* was still burnishing Docherty's credentials as a hero. Consider this lead from a March 1955 story: "Thirteen years ago a young Scotch minister stood on a jetty at Scapa Flow and watched an American warship, the Washington, glide to anchorage" (Dole, 1955, p. 10). The *Post* reporter continued: "Overhead an ack-ack barrage, the most tremendous in the British naval base's history, gave out a welcome. Through the ear-splitting cacophony fluttered the Stars and Stripes at the vessel's stern." How could Docherty know then "that one day words of his would change the salute to the flag?" (p. 10).

In 1951 the Knights of Columbus had decided to begin all organization meetings and functions with the "improved" version of the Pledge. The group would later become a key player in the campaign to revise the Pledge. But nothing really happened, claimed journalists, until the president heard Docherty speak. His intolerant rumination would resurface as a small, but significant part of the coverage of Newdow. Journalists recounted Docherty's story about how a conversation with his son about what he had done in school one day made Docherty realize that the

Pledge lacked a reference to God. His struggle for a sermon topic was over. "I had found my sermon," he told the *Washington Post* in 2002 (Broadway, 2002).

Having sung "God Save Our King" as a boy, Docherty had "an advantage over American parents" who struggled with describing our nation's connection to God, wrote the *Post*'s Larry Broadway. The "erudite Scotsman" realized that the Pledge must include the recognition by "the Founding Fathers that the country exists because of God and through God." Without the mention of God, the Pledge was just average—it "could be a Pledge of any republic," Docherty said. "I could hear little Muscovites repeat a similar Pledge to their hammer-and-sickle flag in Moscow with equal solemnity."

So taken was Eisenhower with Docherty's message that he purportedly told the pastor "I think you've got something" after the February 7 service (Gibb, 2002a). A day later, Congressman Charles Oakman of Michigan reportedly introduced a bill calling for the insertion of "under God." His colleague from Michigan, Senator Homer Ferguson, two days later introduced a companion measure, citing Docherty's sermon as his inspiration.

Not one of the reporters who wrote about Docherty took issue with his blatantly bigoted language, perhaps because many people use similar language to refer to the Soviet Union and its citizens during the almost completely manufactured "Red Scare." What's troubling is how often we hear this kind of language today—often from right-wing radio talk show hosts like Rush Limbaugh and celebrated authors like Ann Coulter. Here's Limbaugh (2005) on the importance of tolerance in religion: "the religious left in this country hates and despises the God of Christianity and Catholicism and whatever else. They despise it because they fear it, because it's a threat, because that God has moral absolutes."

But God is also tolerant and forgiving, even when some mount an unfounded campaign claiming that liberals are trying to destroy Christmas, as Bill O'Reilly did in the winter of 2005. And consider Coulter's (2005) take on the ideal approach to interacting with predominantly Muslim countries: "We should invade their countries, kill their leaders and convert them to Christianity. We weren't punctilious about locating and punishing only Hitler and his top officers. We carpet-bombed German cities; we killed civilians. That's war. And this is war." That kind of "tolerance" just warms the heart, doesn't it?

Still the staunch guardian of the Pledge, Reverend Docherty "was not fazed" in 2002 by the Ninth Circuit decision that "rattled Congress and raised ire cross-country"—ire that Docherty had a hand in fueling nearly 50 years earlier. Neither age nor declining health had "robbed" Docherty's "gentle but Scotch-stubborn optimism," wrote a *Pittsburgh*

Post-Gazette reporter. He was certain that the Ninth Circuit's ruling would eventually be reversed. "It may take some time . . . but there's no problem. And that was only San Francisco," he said, a subtle denigration of the city's perceived liberal attitudes on social issues. Docherty's 2002 Pledge sermon left him "a little tired," but unbowed (Gibb, 2002b).

A Contradiction in Terms

Docherty's bigotry, and Congress' desire to denigrate communism, were key elements in Newdow's complaint. He excerpted a congressional report on the issue: "The inclusion of God in our Pledge . . . would further acknowledge the dependence of our people and our Government upon the moral directions of the Creator." The change would also "deny the atheistic and materialistic concepts of communism" (H.R. 1693, p. 154). Echoing Docherty, Senator Homer Ferguson remarked, "an atheistic American . . . is a contradiction in terms," an opinion that Newdow found "detestable" and "abhorrent." Another sponsor of a Pledge bill, Oliver Bolton of Ohio, called the White House and suggested that the bill be signed by President Eisenhower on Flag Day, and that a ceremony "and even a few minutes on T.V." would be appropriate to mark such an occasion. "He recommends that a Protestant, a Catholic, and a Jew be in the group," wrote Homer Gruenther, the president's congressional liaison.

At least one media outlet, CBS News, shared in the celebration, but only briefly mentioned its religious flavor. On June 14, 1954, the network covered a "New Glory for Old Glory" celebration that revolved around the official raising of the flag over the U.S. Capitol. Revered journalist Walter Cronkite, who hosted the broadcast, could hardly contain his enthusiasm: "Way back when—remember when American flags fluttered from every home on special holidays? It was a wonderful sight—and we hope the tradition will be begun again."

The only mention of the Pledge revision came from CBS News reporter Ron Cochran, who observed that Homer Ferguson and Louis Rabaut were uttering the "new Pledge of allegiance [*sic*] to the Flag authorized by a new law signed only a few minutes ago by the President." Concluded Cronkite: "'New glory [*sic*] for Old Glory'—a wonderful idea and maybe if we all remember to display our flags today and every special day—we will remember more clearly the traditions of freedom on which our country is founded." As the flag ascended, a bugler played "Onward, Christian Soldiers"—more proof, claimed Newdow, that the intent of the bill was the "injection of the majority's favored religious doctrine into the nation's Pledge." Perhaps because reporters assumed the country was so caught up in the anti-Communist fervor, they did not look for any opposition to the Pledge amendment.

The *Washington Post*'s story on the signing of the bill reads like a high school civics presentation. In the story's lead, the reporter quoted the president as saying that the change to the Pledge will add to our arsenal of "spiritual weapons which forever will be our country's most powerful resource" (Harrington, 1954, p. 45). Speaking to the nation about the resolution, Eisenhower stressed that "from this day forward, the millions of our school children [*sic*] will daily proclaim in every city and town, every village and rural schoolhouse, the dedication of our Nation and our people to the Almighty." The change to the Pledge brought new hope to those plagued by violence and "deadened in mind and soul by a materialistic philosophy."

Post writer Catherine Harrington also described for readers how Rabaut and Ferguson led a group of dignitaries in saying the revised Pledge for the first time as members of the American Legion raised the flag. We would see this image again nearly 40 years later when journalists aimed their cameras and primed their notebooks as members of Congress showed their patriotism after the Ninth Circuit's ruling by reciting the Pledge on the Capitol steps.

The power of the Pledge even squelched a bit of rivalry between Rabaut and Ferguson that had bubbled up over authorship of the bill. Rabaut, who first formally suggested the change, blocked House approval of Ferguson's measure. In the spirit of national unity and thinly veiled discrimination, Ferguson "bowed to Rabaut's pride of authorship and passed the House bill so the President could sign it on Flag Day," wrote Harrington (1954, p. 45).

Instead of offering readers a dissenting view, Harrington spent the rest of the article talking about how the Daughters of the American Revolution—hardly a radical group—marked the flag's 177th birthday. Readers learned that the president general of the Daughters presented a flag to the national president of the Girl Scouts of America for use at a scouts camp in Maryland. A month before President Eisenhower signed the bill, the *Post* reported a tremendous amount of public support for the revision. On May 18, 1954, reporter James Haswell noted that members of Congress were being inundated with mail supporting the change. The government had taken three steps to "remind Americans of their religious heritage," Haswell wrote: a bill introduced by Rabaut requiring the U.S. Post Office to cancel mail with a new "pray for peace" stamp, Senator Ferguson's resolution on revising the Pledge, and a new eight-cent stamp featuring the words "in God we trust," introduced by the postmaster general (p. 10).

Haswell revisited the sentiments expressed by Docherty, our newly minted hero, in his February 7 sermon. Without God in the Pledge, Haswell wrote, "Russian children with perfect sincerity could adopt it to salute the Communist flag." Readers were reminded that Communism "rejects the very existence of God" (p. 10).

At least Haswell didn't use the word "Muscovites."

For its part, the *New York Times* offered a brief, but thorough description of the event, then ran three full paragraphs of President Eisenhower's statement, without amplification or clarification ("President Hails Revised Pledge," 1954, p. 31). Both the *Times* and the *Post* ran headlines that said the president "hailed" the revised Pledge. The *Times* also reported that Rabaut and Ferguson had put behind them their dispute over who authored the revision. If Ferguson (or any of the congressmen who sponsored Pledge legislation) had acted opportunistically in introducing his own version of the bill, journalists didn't report on it. Jack Lule might argue that the president was treated like a hero for signing the revision into law, but the heroic efforts of Rabaut and Ferguson were not lost on reporters.

Up until June 14, the *Times* had sporadically covered the revision controversy, offering readers short news stories in April 1953, when Rabaut first introduced his resolution ("Pledge Revision Asked," p. 38) and then in May 1954 ("Revised Pledge Gains," p. 33) when, as the movement to revise the Pledge was picking up steam, the House Judiciary Committee reported favorably on Rabaut's resolution.

The Greatest Peril

The favorable coverage of the Pledge revision by the *Times* and the *Post* pales when compared to the nationwide campaign in support of the change mounted by Hearst Newspapers. It began on April 28, 1954, with an editorial in the *New York Journal-American* (owned by Hearst) headlined simply, "Under God." The editorial warned readers that "unless we can get some action," Senator Ferguson's resolution, like Rabaut's, would die in committee. Like all of the other players in this drama, the *Journal-American*'s editorial board stirred our fears of Communism:

> It seems to us that in times like these when godless Communism is the greatest peril this nation faces, it becomes more necessary than ever to avow our faith in God and to affirm the recognition that the core of our strength comes from him. ("Under God," 1954a)

The founder of Hearst Newspapers, William Randolph Hearst, knew more than a little about whipping up national angst with largely inaccurate information. In 1896, Hearst sent reporter Richard Harding Davis and renowned artist Frederic Remington to Cuba to cover the burgeoning conflict between forces loyal to Spain and Cuban insurgents. Once Davis and Remington got there, they found little to satisfy Hearst's appetite for the kind of scandal that would drive circulation. When Davis wired Hearst that nothing of note was happening, Hearst allegedly replied, "Please remain. You furnish the pictures and I'll furnish the war" (Schudson, 1978, p. 62). Sounds almost like the Bush adminstration strategy of hiring and paying journalists to promote its programs.

Hearst ran a story from Davis (with pictures from Remington, who had returned to New York) on February 10, 1897, about three Cuban women who were allegedly stripped and searched by Spanish officers as the ship they were on headed for Key West, Florida. Remember that Remington was still in New York. Somehow, though, he managed to produce a troubling picture of the scene for publication in Hearst's newspapers. In actuality, female matrons, not savage Spanish soldiers, searched the women. At least that's what the women told reporters for the *New York World*, run by Hearst's archrival, Joseph Pulitzer. The woman depicted by Remington denied that she had been searched by the Spanish officers.

Davis had not indicated in his article that matrons had searched the women. Still, he was incensed, and took the unusual step of writing to the *World* to explain what had happened. He blamed Remington, and said "had I seen the picture before the article appeared, I should have never allowed it to accompany the article" (Schudson, 1978, p. 63). Davis claimed to be objective, but in his story he had unmistakably expressed horror at how the Spanish soldiers had acted. Thus, as journalism historian Michael Schudson explains, Davis and so many of his colleagues, then and now, were simply "actors in the drama of the newspaper world" (p. 64).

From April until June 1954, the Hearst newspapers relentlessly promoted the revision to the Pledge. The same day the editorial ran, the *Journal-American* ran a story that detailed the company's "drive to have Congress change the oath of allegiance to the American flag to have it conform to the nation's faith in God" (Flythe, 1954a, p. 14). The *Journal-American*'s William Flythe described the "pressure" that was "being exerted on the Senate and House Judiciary Committees for quick action."

In the story's third paragraph, Flythe (1954a) almost seemed to be issuing a direct order to the nation and to members of Congress: "The words 'Under God' are to be included in the familiar oath spoken by millions of Americans wherever the flag is shown" (p. 14). Flythe then offered readers nine uninterrupted paragraphs of Ferguson's explanation of why the revision was so important. The only objection to the change cited by the senator stemmed from the possibility that it "would require the destruction of existing Pledge and reprinting of new ones" (p. 14). That's it—printing costs? With the exception of a few dissenting letters to the editor, Hearst's reporters did not include a single source in their stories who was opposed to the Pledge amendment.

Readers learned two days later that the Catholic War Veterans were behind the Pledge revision effort. They sought the president's support "in the growing campaign" to add the words "under God" ("Ask Ike," 1954). Soon, New York City mayor Robert Wagner was on board, urging "swift Congressional adoption" of the revision ("Mayor Backs," 1954). In the first few paragraphs of each article to run in the *Journal-American*, the support and endorsement of the drive by Hearst Newspapers was made plain. For his part, Mayor Wagner said the proposed revision deserved "the full support of all," and would go a long way toward reminding everyone "that our traditional heritages can and will be maintained only under Divine Guidance" ("Mayor Backs," 1954).

Action on the revision moved quickly. On May 5, both the House and the Senate subcommittees approved Rabaut's resolution, primarily because it was the first one submitted, and was the only one to include the new Pledge in its entirety. Ferguson reportedly interrupted a Senate subcommittee meeting to push for his version of the legislation. Ferguson's resolution would have put "under God" after "indivisible," where Rabaut's resolution placed the words after "nation."

The *Journal-American* noted Ferguson's willingness to concede the point, as long as the measure was passed quickly. "As the Pledge now reads, any communist could make it," he told the subcommittee, "but when we make the Pledge under God we outlaw the godless nations" (Flythe, 1954b, p. 10). There was tremendous public support for this push to "outlaw the godless nations," at least according to the *New York Journal-American*. The American Legion, the American Legion Auxiliary, the Veterans of Foreign Wars, and the New York League of Business and Professional Women were only a few of the organizations that rallied in support of the revision. Three years earlier, the American Legion had embarked on its own "Back to God" campaign, through which it encouraged "regular public worship, daily family prayer, and the religious instruction of our youth" ("Legion Head," 1954, p. 10). Without this broad range of support, the *Journal-American* noted in a May 13 editorial, "this campaign would never have developed the force that it has" ("Under God," 1954b).

And national support for the campaign was "something to take heart from in these times of anxiety and crisis." The support cancelled out whatever "temporal divisions separate them" and gave conclusive evidence that "they are united under God, so that this nation is in absolute truth, as the Pledge would read, one nation under God." Concluded Hearst's editorial writers, "That is good to think of these days." ("Under God," 1954b). So, when President Eisenhower signed the revision into law on Flag Day, "the solemn vow will have a deeper meaning" (Flythe, 1954c, p. 4), the *Journal-American* noted in a story on June 9, thanks to the addition of "under God," and the lobbying efforts of Hearst Newspapers, efforts that clearly violated the journalistic ideals of fairness and objectivity.

Governmental Hostility

Newdow contended that atheists in the United States became the target of the kind of "governmental hostility" suggested by Justice Kennedy the moment Congress moved to amend the Pledge. President Eisenhower's statement after signing the revision into law "demonstrate[d] that the Act was not only promulgated for a religious purpose, but that it was intended to have a religious effect" (Appendix H, p. 5). He cited Justice William Brennan's dissenting opinion in *Marsh v. Chambers*, 463 U.S. 783, a 1983 case in which the Supreme Court upheld the practice of starting each day of the Nebraska state legislative session with a prayer.

Writing for the majority in *Marsh*, Chief Justice Warren Burger said, "[T]he practice of opening legislative sessions with prayer has become part of the fabric of our society." The creators of the Constitution did not believe that such a practice amounted to "a proselytizing activity" or the government's "seal of approval of one religious view." As evidence, Burger noted that the new Congress approved the language of the Bill of Rights three days after it approved the appointment of paid chaplains. The framers would not have endorsed a practice that violated the new Constitution.

Brennan, a staunch liberal, disagreed. He took the majority to task for failing to subject the Nebraska practice to any of the tests used to determine if a law violates the Establishment Clause. Perhaps the most well known of these tests emerged from the Court's 1971 decision in *Lemon v. Kurtzman*, 463 U.S. 783, 797, in which the justices struck down tax subsidies for parochial schools. To withstand an Establishment Clause challenge, it must be shown that a state law has "a secular purpose," that the law's effect "neither advances nor hinders religion," and that the law does not "foster an excessive entanglement with religion."

Calling on God for guidance in the performance of legislative duties "is nothing but a religious act," wrote Justice Brennan, who was joined in his dissent by Justice Thurgood Marshall. As for the majority's argument that prayer at the start of legislative sessions was part of the "fabric of our society," Brennan noted that history is not always a good teacher. James Madison, who voted to authorize appointment of chaplains, came to believe that the practice was unconstitutional.

Brennan also argued it was incorrect to focus solely on the intent of Congress in enacting the Bill of Rights. The Bill of Rights did not come to be simply because Congress "came up with a bright idea one morning," Justice Brennan wrote. The enactment "was forced upon Congress by a number of the States as a condition for their ratification of the original Constitution." It was thus incorrect to treat any policy authorized by the framers as "presumptively consistent with the Bill of Rights."

Brennan paid homage to the "inherent adaptability" of the Constitution. Much has been written about the schism between "strict constructionists" and those who believe the Constitution is a living document, one "meant to last for the ages," as Brennan explained. Brennan was a champion of the latter camp. "We have recognized in a wide variety of constitutional contexts that the practices that were in place at the time any particular guarantee was enacted into the Constitution do not necessarily fix forever the meaning of that guarantee," he wrote.

In light of our more diverse cultural makeup, practices that at one time seemed appropriate "may today be highly offensive to many persons, the deeply devout and the nonbelievers alike," Justice Brennan argued. Prayer is "serious theological business," a business that Congress is not equipped to enter. "It is simply beyond the competence of government, and inconsistent with our conceptions of liberty, for the State to take upon itself the role of ecclesiastical arbiter," Brennan concluded.

The dangerous flip side of the government's endorsement of religion is the continuing denial of freedom to those who do not believe in God, a denial made easier by the recent flood of religious ideas and symbolism caused, at least in part, by the news media's unwillingness to offer readers and viewers any critical analysis of them. "Atheism is a religious belief system protected as strongly as theism," Newdow said in his complaint. Addition of "under God" to the Pledge has caused those who believe in God "to perceive the Pledge as an endorsement of their theism, and for atheistic Americans . . . to perceive the Pledge as a disapproval of their atheism."

In 1985, the Supreme Court concluded that the "individual freedom of conscience protected by the First Amendment embraces the right to select any religious faith or none at all" (*Wallace v. Jaffree*, 472 U.S. 38). Put simply, the Constitution enables us to enjoy freedom of religion *and* freedom from religion. Having just sat through yet another discussion (during an April 2005 edition of NBC's *Meet the Press*, whose host is a practicing Catholic) of whether newly consecrated Pope Benedict XVI will soften his hard-line stance on homosexuality, on women in the priesthood, and on abortion, I continue to believe that it is becoming more difficult to find an unreligious moment in offerings from the mass media. Religious content on television in ostensibly less zealous packages is not new. I watched the television show *Davy and Goliath* (produced by the Lutheran Church) as a kid, and know full well that Mister Rogers, one of my favorite television personalities, was an ordained Presbyterian minister. But I prefer tolerance and critical thinking to a full-blown assault on my senses, as happened when NBC broadcast the miniseries *Locusts* in 2006.

An Endorsement of Discrimination

To Newdow, the presence of "under God" is a governmental endorsement of discrimination against atheists, who make up about 10 percent of the U.S. population. Atheists already have it bad, Newdow claimed. "The voting public," he argued, "shuns atheists." The publicity from his suit, Newdow anticipated, would make it impossible for him to win elected office, something he would be unable to do in six states, where the law states that candidates must claim a belief in God in order to run. To date, not a single atheist has been elected to public office, according to the organization American Atheists.

Journalists chose not to explore this part of Newdow's argument. Instead, they worked to shore up American ideals and institutions that were purportedly threatened by Newdow, whose actions were tied by reporters (if loosely) to the 9/11 attacks. In the first stories about the Ninth Circuit's ruling, Newdow was referred to as a "self-proclaimed atheist" as if atheism was somehow illegitimate because Newdow was not officially endowed with his beliefs by a higher power and by a church structure that believed only it was the proper keeper of that higher power's inspiration. Journalists eventually settled on the term "avowed atheist." While the government pays lip service to religious tolerance, it continues this "ludicrous and unconstitutional affront" to atheists and agnostics, Newdow argued. His flair for turning a colorful phrase (he said the Pledge's wording represents an "impermissible interlarding" of church and state) eventually became a key theme in news coverage of his suit. Reporters chided Newdow's relentlessness, which manifested itself in his tendency to ramble.

But it was ceremonial deism, not the perceived mistreatment of atheists, that would cause federal judge Peter Nowinski to dismiss Newdow's suit. The Elk Grove School District asked the judge to rule only on the constitutionality of the Pledge. Only one court at that point, the Seventh Circuit Court of Appeals, had addressed the issues raised by Newdow. In *Sherman v. Community Consolidated School District* (980 F. 2d 437), the court in 1992 ruled that the Pledge was not an endorsement of religion. At issue in *Sherman* was an Illinois law that required public school students to begin their days with a recitation of the Pledge. Richard Sherman, then a student in Wheeling, Illinois, brought the suit along with his father, Robert. A year earlier, a federal judge in Chicago found that the Illinois law satisfied the three-prong *Lemon* test. Richard was not compelled to say the Pledge, and was not penalized for choosing not to. Further, said the three-judge panel, "[a]ny peer pressure to conform that Richard may have experienced, the court believed, does not justify silencing pupils who are willing to recite the Pledge." While the decision was not the rule of law in the Eastern District of California, it was persuasive enough to cause Judge Nowinski to recommend that Newdow's case be dismissed.

The Tenor of the Times

An exchange between Newdow and Judge Nowinski suggests one possible reason for the reluctance of judges to invalidate the Pledge: the conservative tenor of the times. During a hearing in May 2000, Newdow told Nowinski that he was well aware that "no judge wants to be responsible for taking God out" of the Pledge. According to a transcript cited in Newdow's memorandum, the judge replied: "What you last said couldn't be more accurate. In this day and age no one wants to take that step. I don't think anybody's going to." Certainly not in 2007, when uncritical treatment of evangelical Christians seems to pour from many mainstream media outlets; when, for example, journalists fawn over Tim Lahaye and Jerry Jenkins as if they were conducting interviews for Oprah's Book Club. And consider the comment made by MSNBC reporter Martin Savidge, hours after the death of Terri Schiavo, who had become a conservative cause célèbre; Savidge reported that Michael Schiavo's "movements are unknown at this time," as if Michael Schiavo was a criminal on the run from police.

Judge Nowinski held the Elk Grove policy and the Pledge only to the endorsement of religion test, a test that Newdow argued the policy does not pass. Judge Nowinski also ignored a laundry list of Supreme Court rulings, including *Lee v. Weisman*. Newdow claimed that the judge "sorted" through dicta (observations made by judges that often are not part of the reasoning behind a decision) to find "a few equivocal statements to reach the conclusion he obviously desires." A court can reject dicta if it finds they do not affect an argument, they are not based on the facts in the case, or they are unnecessary.

While Judge Nowinski was not the first federal judge to "have wounded America's atheistic religious minority due to contorted legal doctrine, his reliance on the prejudices of others does not save him here." Most of us, Newdow argued, are unaware of the injustice felt by atheists and agnostics when they experience the religious idea expressed in the Pledge, an idea used by the government to promote patriotism. "They don't recognize how detestable it is to send one's child to the public schools and have them inculcated with a religious belief that is the antithesis of that which they wish to instill," Newdow wrote. A federal judge must evaluate wrongs committed against dissenters "from the point of view of both the Constitution and the minorities they are sworn to protect."

Perhaps the most compelling part of Newdow's memorandum is his claim that the exchange with Judge Nowinski was clear evidence that he would use "whatever means" to keep the words in the Pledge. The ongoing discrimination of atheists (and the failure of judges to treat their claims as worthy of the court's time) was an abuse of power, Newdow suggested. He cited Justice Felix Frankfurter's concurring opinion in *Youngstown Sheet & Tube Co. v. Sawyer*, (343 U.S. 579, 594 (1952). There, the justice noted, "accretion of dangerous power does not come in a day. It does come, however slowly, from the generative force of unchecked disregard of the restrictions that fence in even the most disinterested assertion of authority." Judges are appointed to protect the rights of everyone, even those who espouse unpopular views.

Newdow also blamed the judicial system for what he called the "disarray" in Establishment Clause rulings. The judiciary has chosen to "assault logic, invent sophistry, twist prior case law and completely disregard a denial of fundamental religious liberties" because, as Judge Nowinski noted, "no one wants to take that step." The Supreme Court's landmark 1954 ruling in *Brown v. Board of Education of Topeka*, 347 U.S. 483 (1954), in which the Court struck down the doctrine of "separate but equal," was a victory for the nascent civil rights movement, but it was also a stark reminder that the Court had "relegated a segment of Americans to second-class citizenship for more than half a century" with its 1896 ruling in *Plessy v. Ferguson*, 163 U.S. 537 (1896), Newdow noted. "How many individuals did they injure as a result? And how many lower courts contributed to this abrogation of civil rights by adhering to a doctrine which, by its very essence, existed solely due to prejudice and injustice?"

Justice Harry Blackmun's comment in *Allegheny County v. Greater Pittsburgh ACLU*, 492 U.S. 573 (1989), seems to support the idea that the Pledge is not an Establishment Clause violation: "Our previous opinions have considered in dicta the motto and the Pledge, characterizing them as consistent with the proposition that government may not communicate an endorsement of religious belief." However, in 13 dicta written by Justice Blackmun in *Allegheny County*, he stressed that the government and religion must remain separate. In one instance, for example, he wrote that "the bedrock Establishment Clause principle [is] that, regardless of history, government may not demonstrate a preference for a particular faith." Judge Nowinski selected the one dictum that seems to suggest otherwise, but Newdow claimed this was simply an "observation" about the ideas expressed by his fellow justices.

In one of the memorandum's stranger passages, Newdow argued that the dictum cited by Judge Nowinski was not only a dictum, it was "a dictum about dicta," and thus could be of only limited support to his point. Justice Blackmun was responding to a dissenting opinion by Justice Kennedy, who acknowledged that federal law "contains religious references that would be suspect under the endorsement test." Newdow speculated that Blackmun knew his colleagues held differing views about the Pledge, and was simply "choosing his battles." Perhaps he was planting the seeds for a challenge to Justice Kennedy's dictum. Judge Nowinski chose Justice Blackmun's dictum despite the fact they were both of equal legal value, Newdow argued.

On July 21, 2000, U.S. district judge Milton Schwartz, sitting in Sacramento, approved Judge Nowinski's recommendation, dicta and all, and dismissed Newdow's suit. Newdow filed a notice of appeal with the Ninth Circuit U.S. Court of Appeals five days later.

Chapter 3

An Impermissible Message of Endorsement

In their response to Newdow filed with the Ninth Circuit, the school districts argued that while the Supreme Court had not yet directly addressed the question of whether the Pledge was constitutional, it has—in dicta found in several cases, including *Lynch v. Donnelly*, 465 U.S. 668 (1984), and *Allegheny County v. Greater Pittsburgh ACLU*, 492 U.S. 573 (1989)—held that "the inclusion of 'under God' in the Pledge passes constitutional muster" (School District's brief, p. 6). The high court in *Lynch* ruled that the Constitution does not, in fact, require that church and state be kept completely separate; "it affirmatively mandates accommodation, not merely tolerance, of all religions, and forbids hostility toward any," the district argued, citing the high court's decision.

While California law does require school districts to "conduct appropriate patriotic exercises" (School District's brief, p. 5), the Pledge is just one way that districts can comply. In a 1968 case (*Smith v. Denny*, 280 F. Supp. 651), a Sacramento federal judge ruled that reciting the Pledge was not an Establishment Clause violation, and that the only penalty that might be suffered by students who choose not to recite the Pledge was the "alleged ostracism as a result of exercising his or her alleged constitutional rights."

All branches of government, the districts argued in their brief, have acknowledged "the role of religion in American life from at least 1789." There is constitutional support for the government's refusal to adopt an "absolutist" view of the Establishment Clause, the kind of view Newdow urged the Ninth Circuit to take. The Supreme Court in *Lynch* likewise refused to take the path of "mechanically invalidating all governmental conduct or statutes that confer benefits or give special recognition to religion in general or to one faith" (p. 9). The key question for the justices has always been: does a law establish or endorse religion?

The district offered a short list of governmental acts that support their contention: designation of Thanksgiving and Christmas as national holidays, employment by Congress of chaplains, using taxpayer money to pay military chaplains, and support museums that "display religious paintings depicting such events as the birth of Christ, the crucifixion, and the resurrection," (p. 7), and national days of prayer proclaimed by the president.

These actions serve only "legitimate secular purposes," a term used by Justice Sandra Day O'Connor in her concurring opinion in *Lynch*. The Pledge and our national motto—"In God We Trust"—are "constitutionally acceptable forms" of what the Court in *Allegheny County* called "ceremonial deism" (p. 8). The Pledge is simply "an affirmation of the heritage of this country." The conclusion that this affirmation violates the Establishment Clause requires "an extreme and rigorous twisting of the language of the many courts of the United States." Attorneys for the districts did not address Newdow's contention that the policy and the Pledge contribute to the treatment of atheists as second-class citizens—and that the government uses Newdow's taxes to fund this treatment.

In his Ninth Circuit brief, Newdow expanded his personal narrative and his defense of atheism. He asked the Ninth Circuit to "immediately and permanently cast aside any negative view of atheists," whose ranks purportedly include composer Irving Berlin, Thomas Edison, and Mark Twain. Society has not come around, Newdow argued, citing a 2000 Pew Research Center poll that revealed that 52 percent of Americans view atheists either unfavorably or very unfavorably (p. 11).

And while our nation's institutions "reflect a firm conviction that we are a religious people, those institutions by solemn constitutional injunction may not officially involve religion in such a way as to prefer, discriminate against, or oppress, a particular sect or religion," Newdow argued, citing Justice William Brennan's concurring opinion in *Abington School District v. Schempp*, 374 U.S. 203, 231 (1963).

Yet this is exactly what happened when Congressman Louis Rabaut, author of a congressional resolution in 1953 to amend the Pledge, asserted, "an atheistic American is a contradiction in terms." The government's desire to show that we were different than the Soviets is not, Newdow contended, a valid reason for advocating a particular religion. In the end, the goal of our government was to "proclaim the moral superiority of a particular religious ideal" (p. 14). He accepted as valid the districts' desire to encourage patriotism in their students. But the change made in 1954 was purely religious in nature, and was based on the invalid idea that "belief in God is morally superior to atheism" (p. 20).

Newdow had harsh words for Judge Nowinski's recommendations—harsher, perhaps, than those he used in objecting to them after they were issued. The judge invoked the *Lemon* test, but did not explain his analysis. With no evidence that the act had anything but a religious purpose, the Pledge failed the first prong of the *Lemon* test, and, thus, the test as a whole. Later in his brief, Newdow suggested that Judge Nowinski had cooked up a "wily scheme" to bypass *Lemon*: citing the only Supreme Court dictum that hints the Pledge is constitutional, claiming that the dictum "alludes" to the endorsement test, using *Lemon* "alongside the endorsement test in a sentence," and hoping "that the proximity of these two 'tests' will suffice to turn the First Amendment on its head" (pp. 52–53). The judge did not exercise "particular care," as required by the Supreme Court (*Grand Rapids School District v. Ball*, 473 U.S. 373, 390 (1985)) in evaluating the claim that the Pledge constitutes an impermissible endorsement of religion. He labeled "ridiculous" the judge's statement that the Pledge would not be "perceived by [theists] as an endorsement, and by [atheists] as a disapproval, of their individual religious choices."

The judge also seemed to ignore the Supreme Court's description in *Minersville School District v. Gobitis*, 310 U.S. 586 (1940), and *West Virginia State Board of Education v. Barnette*, 319 U.S. 624 (1943), of the Pledge as having significant power to "inculcate sentiments of loyalty and patriotism," Newdow argued. If the Pledge's original purpose was to "inculcate" patriotism, then the amended Pledge's purpose was to "inculcate," and advance religion, a practice barred under the Constitution. It is "simply absurd," said Newdow (p. 35), to conclude that Congress and the president had anything else on their minds other than the endorsement of monotheism when they amended the Pledge.

Newdow seemed to recall his exchange with Judge Nowinski (detailed in the previous chapter) during which the judge said that none of his colleagues on the bench would want to remove God from the Pledge. "However anxious it might have been to avoid its politically unpopular constitutional duty, the District Court was required to consider this contradiction," Newdow claimed. Judge Nowinski erred when he disregarded Newdow's contention that he had been made to feel like an "outsider" by the presence of "under God" in the Pledge. He also failed to acknowledge relevant Supreme Court rulings, including the Court's landmark 1962 ruling in *Engel v. Vitale*, 370 U.S. 421, in which the justices held that a daily recitation by New York schoolchildren ("Almighty God, we acknowledge our dependence upon Thee, and we beg Thy blessings upon us, our parents, our teachers and our Country") clearly violated the Establishment Clause.

If a student-led prayer at a high school football game "unquestionably" violated the Clause, as the Supreme Court found in *Santa Fe Independent School District v. Doe*, 530 U.S. 290 (2000), then "religious dogma initiated by Congress, executed by the government's teachers, and instilled daily in the public school classrooms cannot possibly be permissible" (pp. 40–41)," Newdow argued. Judge Nowinski ignored "mountains of unequivocal dicta" from the Supreme Court that use of the words "under God" violated the Constitution, and then chose to rely on "one or two very questionable statements" in crafting his recommendations (p. 42). On the day of Newdow's hearing before Judge Nowinski, the Supreme Court rejected this approach (*U.S. v. Morrison*, 120 S. Ct. 1270). Relying on a single dictum "is simply not the way reasoned constitutional adjudication proceeds," Chief Justice William Rehnquist wrote for the Court.

The Ninth Circuit's Ruling

In its June 26 decision, the Ninth Circuit panel (Judges Ferdinand Fernandez, Alfred Goodwin, and Stephen Reinhardt) offered a brief clinic in constitutional law before turning to Newdow's Establishment Clause claim. Recall that Newdow demanded in his original complaint that the president (then Bill Clinton) "alter, modify, or repeal" the Pledge by taking out "under God." In an opinion written by Judge Goodwin, the panel noted that it is beyond a court's authority to tell the president what to do. Moreover, the Speech and Debate Clause of the Constitution bars the courts from instructing Congress "to enact or amend legislation" (p. 9112). One wonders if former Congressman Tom DeLay and those who attack purported "judicial activism" have actually read the clause.

Article 1, Section 6 of the Constitution stipulates that federal legislators are "privileged from Arrest during their Attendance at the Session of their respective Houses, and in going to and returning from the same; and for any Speech or Debate in either House, they shall not be questioned in any other Place." The clause not only protects lawmakers from the consequences of debate; if they act in the "sphere of legitimate legislative activity," they cannot be, for example, prosecuted if something bad happens as a result of legislation (www.uslegalforms.com/lawdigest/legal-definitions.php).

Newdow also mistakenly argued that since the amended Pledge violates the Establishment Clause, Congress is not covered by the Speech and Debate Clause. Judge Goodwin reiterated that as long as an action by Congress "falls within the legitimate legislative sphere," its members may not be "questioned in any other Place," as the Constitution describes. The clause's protection would be meaningless if it could be taken away by a "mere allegation that a valid legislative act was undertaken for an unworthy purpose," Judge Goodwin wrote.

But the Ninth Circuit panel also ruled that Newdow had standing to bring his suit, since his daughter was still enrolled in school in the Elk Grove Unified School District. To establish standing, a person must show that they suffered an "injury in fact" that is caused by the actions of another party. It must also be shown that a favorable decision by the court will remedy the injury. Here, Newdow challenged a policy that he believed interfered with his right to provide religious education to his daughter, a right affirmed by the Ninth Circuit in 1985 (*Grove v. Mead School District No. 354*, 753 F.2d 1528, 1532) and again in 1999 (*Doe v. Madison School District No. 321*, 177 F. 3d 789, 795).

Perhaps more significant was the panel's discussion of whether Newdow himself suffered an "injury in fact" from the changes made to the Pledge in 1954. In its 1982 ruling in *Valley Forge Christian College v. Americans United for Separation of Church and State, Inc.*, 454 U.S. 464, the Supreme Court found that just suggesting a "psychological consequence" purportedly caused by creation of a governmental policy was not enough to sustain an Establishment Clause claim. Since then, however, the high court has expanded standing to the point that the mere enactment of a law may be a violation of the Establishment Clause.

Alabama legislators passed a law in 1981 that authorized schools to provide a moment of silence for "meditation." A year later, the law was changed so that the period of silence could be used for meditation or prayer. Students were free to meditate, to pray, or to do nothing at all, Judge Goodwin noted. But when the law was amended, it was clear that lawmakers had only a religious intent in passing the law: they wanted to encourage students to pray during the moment of silence. The law lacked "any clearly secular purpose," the Court ruled. And it is safe to assume, the judge added, that the high court explored standing before turning to the merits of the suit challenging the statute (*Wallace v. Jaffree*, 472 U.S. 38 (1985)).

Fifteen years later, the high court struck down a New Mexico school district policy that allowed student-led prayer at high school football games. Just passing this law, the Court said, violated the Establishment Clause, since it had "the purpose and perception of government establishment of religion," Judge Goodwin wrote, quoting the Court's opinion in *Santa Fe Independent School District v. Doe*. Like Alabama lawmakers, Santa Fe school district officials had only a religious purpose in mind when they created the student-led prayer policy." Thus, the mere enactment of the policy was enough to sustain an Establishment Clause claim. Any "objective observer" would conclude that the school district was encouraging students to pray, Judge Goodwin noted.

With this standard in mind, the appeals panel turned to the 1954 change in the Pledge. Insertion of "under God," Judge Goodwin wrote, "was not meant to sit passively in the federal code unbeknownst to the public." Sponsors of the legislation built their case on existing state Pledge laws. Further, their goal was to have schoolchildren across the country reciting the words "under God" as part of the Pledge. "The children of our land," said Representative Louis Rabaut, a cosponsor of the bill, "will be daily impressed with a true understanding of our way of life and its origins." This is as serious an injury as those suffered by students who were required to obey the Alabama law and Santa Fe school prayer policy. The 1954 act was in fact a "religious recitation policy" that violated Newdow's right to shape his daughter's religious education.

Turning to the merits of the act, the judges found that it failed all three of the tests developed by the Supreme Court to evaluate Establishment Clause claims: the three-pronged *Lemon* test, the so-called coercion test first seen in *Lee v. Weisman* (in which the Court ruled that the government cannot "coerce anyone to support or participate in religion or its exercise"), and the "endorsement" test first described by Justice Sandra Day O'Connor in her concurring opinion in *Lynch v. Donnelly*, 465 U.S. 668, 694 (1984). In *Lynch*, the Court allowed city officials in Pawtucket, Rhode Island, to include a nativity scene in its Christmas display, as it had for more than 40 years. The city owned and maintained the nativity scene, had no contact with church officials about it, and used it to celebrate Christmas and its history—a "legitimate secular purpose" in the eyes of the Court.

Still, the Court's decision provided Justice O'Connor an opportunity, wrote Judge Goodwin, to clarify the law. The Establishment Clause bars government officials from making religion "relevant in any way to a person's standing in the political community," Justice O'Connor wrote. A revision of the *Lemon* test, the endorsement test is not met when government becomes entangled with religious institutions, or when government officials endorse—or show their disapproval for—a particular religion. Endorsement makes those who do not believe feel "that they are outsiders, not full members of the political community," Justice O'Connor wrote. Those who adhere to the endorsed religion quickly learn that they are "insiders, favored members of the political community."

The Ninth Circuit panel flatly rejected Judge Nowinski's finding that the reference to God in the Pledge was ceremonial—an argument heard again in the recent controversies surrounding the display of the Ten Commandments in courthouses in Alabama and in Pennsylvania. Inserting "under God" made the Pledge more than an acknowledgment that many people believe in God, the panel held. Moreover, the revised Pledge went beyond simply recognizing the importance of faith to the Founding Fathers—a faith that did not, many historians agree, take a denominational shape. "To recite the Pledge is not to describe the United States; instead, it is to swear allegiance to the values for which the flag stands: unity, indivisibility, liberty, justice, and—since 1954—monotheism," Judge Goodwin wrote for the panel.

"Under God" is not a neutral phrase. It would be like saying we were a nation "'under Jesus,' or a nation 'under Vishnu,' a nation 'under Zeus,' or a nation 'under no God,'" wrote Judge Goodwin. These are not neutral statements. The government endorsed the ideals found in the Pledge, and was trying to instill in students respect for these ideals when it changed the Pledge in 1954. The fact that students were not required to say the Pledge was irrelevant; the government was clearly endorsing one religious view, and was forcing students "to declare a belief," as the Court ruled in *Barnette*, in concepts that are more "idealistic" than "descriptive," given the actual state of the country. As Justice O'Connor had suggested, the Pledge makes those who do not believe in God feel like outsiders with little, if any, impact, on the "insider" political structure.

Turning to the coercion test, the court noted that the Pledge has put students, even those students who may wholeheartedly endorse the Pledge, in a truly difficult position: they can either say the Pledge, complete with religious content, or "opt out," and risk incurring the scorn and ridicule of their peers. Peer pressure, in the words of the justices who ruled in *Lee v. Weisman*, is "as real as any overt compulsion." Even having to listen to the Pledge, when one does not believe in God, or is critical of the government, "has a coercive effect." Even President Eisenhower wanted to ensure "the dedication of our Nation and our people to the Almighty," as was discussed in the previous chapter.

The Elk Grove School Board fared only slightly better when the court moved on to the *Lemon* test. The board mistakenly looked at the entire Pledge in arguing that it has only a secular purpose: "solemnizing public occasions, expressing confidence in the future, and encouraging the recognition of what is worthy of appreciation in society." The goal in amending the Pledge was to differentiate us from the Soviets, who were part of a system "whose philosophy is at direct odds with our own," wrote Judge Goodwin, citing the House report on the act. Putting God in the Pledge was a clear acknowledgment of our dependence "upon the moral directions of the Creator." In the bargain, we could "deny the atheistic and materialistic concepts of communism with its attendant subservience of the individual."

Judge Goodwin reminded the parties that in *Wallace*, the Supreme Court stressed that the First Amendment "embraces the right to select any religion or none at all." We should be free to choose what we believe in. This freedom is not limited to those who believe in God; the First Amendment extends tolerance "to the disbeliever and uncertain," the *Wallace* court said. Advocates of the 1954 act tried to block future challenges to the Pledge by stressing that officials at the time were only recognizing "the guidance of God in our national affairs." This, too, is an endorsement of religion, the judges ruled.

In a footnote, the panel took issue with how the Seventh Circuit U.S. Court of Appeals reached its ruling in *Sherman*. The Seventh Circuit judges ruled that if recitation of the Pledge *and* prayer in the classroom are unconstitutional, then the Pledge "becomes unconstitutional under all circumstances." The court then rejected its own reasoning, saying that the First Amendment "does not establish general rules about speech or schools" and "calls for religion to be treated differently."

Judge Goodwin said the panel had "some difficulty understanding this statement; we do not believe that the Constitution prohibits compulsory participation, as in *Barnette*, but permits compulsory religion as in this case. If government-endorsed religion is to be treated differently from government-endorsed patriotism, the treatment must be less favorable, not more" (p. 9130).

Finally, the Seventh Circuit failed to apply any of the tests discussed in this chapter before ruling in *Sherman*. Lower courts cannot simply ignore Supreme Court precedent. The high court requires that alleged Establishment Clause violations be "held to the scrutiny of the established tests," the panel noted (p. 9131).

The depth of the Ninth Circuit's decision was lost on many journalists, especially in the days immediately after the panel ruled. They hastily concluded that the Pledge had met its demise and framed the court's decision as precipitating a national crisis. In fact, the Ninth Circuit panel found only that the Elk Grove policy and the inclusion of "under God" in the Pledge violated the Establishment Clause.

Currency Beware!

Those who wanted the Pledge kept intact—the majority of Americans—found a champion in Ninth Circuit judge Ferdinand Fernandez. In a sharply worded, sometimes colorful dissenting opinion, Judge Fernandez contended the majority based its ruling on an erroneous reading of the Establishment Clause, which exists, he said, not "to drive religious expression out of public thought" but to "avoid discrimination" against a religion. Thus, the tests cited by the majority are only of limited value. Of utmost importance is "neutrality," the judge said. The Establishment Clause is designed to offer equal protection to members of all faiths.

The most cited excerpt of Judge Fernandez's dissent was his argument that the danger that "under God" will produce a theocracy "is so miniscule [*sic*] as to be *de minimis*" (p. 9132)—a contention supported, the judge argued, by findings in a long series of cases, including *County of Allegheny v. Greater Pittsburgh ACLU*, *Lynch v. Donnelly*, and *Wallace v. Jaffree*. Call it "de minimis" or "ceremonial deism," the bottom line for Judge Fernandez was that the words "under God" do not endorse religion, or damage an atheist's right not to practice religion, "except in the fevered eye of persons who would like to drive all tincture of religion out of the public life of our polity" (p. 9134). There have been "no signs of incipient theocracy springing up since the Pledge was amended in 1954."

If the high court were to agree with Newdow, the judge said, performance of patriotic songs would eventually be banned. "And currency beware!" the judge said. The majority should not have limited itself to "elements and tests" while ignoring "the good sense and principles that animated those tests in the first place." The cost, according to Judge Fernandez? "[R]emoving a vestige of the awe we must feel at the immenseness of the universe and our own small place in it, as well as the wonder we must feel at the good fortune of the country" (p. 9136).

Liberal—Oh Really?

So exactly how liberal is the Ninth Circuit U.S. Court of Appeals? A brief discussion of this question will give us a solid foundation on which to build an analysis of news coverage of the decision in *Newdow v. The Congress of the United States of America et al.* Duke University law professor Edwin Chemerinsky (2004), who advised Newdow as he prepared to argue before the Supreme Court, argues that the news media was "simply wrong" when reporters claimed that the circuit was the most liberal appeals court in the country, and was reversed more often than any of the other 12 circuit courts. Even the *New York Times*, self-appointed leader of the nation's "elite" media, said that the *Newdow* opinion came from "the nation's most liberal appeals court" (Nieves, 2002a, p. A1).

But according to Chemerinsky, reporters, perhaps caught up in the desire to prove that they and their employers are not liberal, mischaracterized the Ninth Circuit's makeup and rulings. Take the claim about the frequency of Supreme Court reversals: during the high court's 2002 term, it reversed decisions from the nation's federal appeals court about three-fourths (74 percent) of the time. The justices reversed the Ninth Circuit *exactly* three-fourths of the time. But you wouldn't know that by reading coverage of the *Newdow* ruling—reporters were too busy casting the appeals panel, like Newdow, as a threat to our values. Judge Goodwin and Judge Reinhardt were portrayed as Newdow's accomplices in his push to bring down God, mom, large gas-guzzling cars, celebrity worship, baseball, and apple pie.

In the words of one reporter, "The Ninth Circuit is famous for its loopy, ultraliberal rulings that run against the grain of other federal courts and are often overturned by the Supreme Court" (Allen, 2003, p. M3). The truth is that the Ninth Circuit is not reversed any more often than other federal appeals courts, as Chemerinsky pointed out. Reporters also created the false impression that the Supreme Court would inevitably "fix" the outrageous ruling by the Ninth Circuit panel. That's not what courts do, claims Chemerinsky. "It is wrong to equate a reversal with a mistake by the lower court," he said (2004, p. 2). We all must abide the high court's rulings, "but that does not mean that its rulings are 'right' and reversed lower courts are 'wrong,'" Chemerinsky argued. The issues dealt with by the courts are complex; judges sometimes disagree—neither circumstance is good news for the journalist, who has typically been encouraged by journalism professors and their editors to find the "black and white" in every story.

And with a mix of political leanings represented on the Ninth Circuit, the makeup of the panel that rules in a case is significant—as it is in every federal appeals court. "The identity of the judges always has mattered and especially so in these ideologically divided times," wrote Chemerinsky. "There is no way to construct a human system in which value choices must be made that will not depend on who occupies the positions" (p. 3). The real danger comes when judges, following the misguided lead of journalists, start trying to show that they are not liberal "by being more conservative in their rulings, especially in high-profile cases" like Newdow's (p. 4).

A "Bumper Strip Headline"

I will undoubtedly earn a spot on the U.S. Olympic understatement team by noting that reaction to the Ninth Circuit's June ruling, explored more thoroughly in the next chapter, was furious and largely negative—at least that's how reporters characterized it. One member of the U.S. Senate, a body supposedly less raucous and more refined than the House of Representatives, called Judge Goodwin, author of the opinion, "stupid." Goodwin fired back: "I never had much confidence in the attention span of elected officials for any kind of deep thinking about important issues," he told a reporter (Hoppin, 2002). "When they pop off after what I call a bumper strip headline, they almost always give a superficial response."

And as was discussed in the previous chapter, it is the country's more conservative national complexion that may be at the root of the tongue-lashing received by the court. Goodwin believes that the harsh reaction was at least in part caused by "this wrap-yourself in the flag frenzy." What else explains members of Congress practically sprinting out of their chambers to sing "God Bless America" on the steps of the U.S. Capitol, or the poorly considered, politically expedient responses by our elected officials to the Ninth Circuit's ruling?

As if to suggest that even liberals thought Judge Goodwin was too liberal, the *New York Times*' first story on the ruling recalled how Supreme Court justices Thurgood Marshall, Harry Blackmun, John Paul Stevens, and William Brennan—liberals all—ruled that mentions of God on money ("In God We Trust") "were protected from the Establishment Clause because their religious significance had been lost through rote repetition" (Nieves, 2002a, p. A20). Even these "liberal lions" could find a place in their hearts for ceremonial deism.

One part of this story is particularly troubling: the *Times* reporter suggests (fair is fair: it may be an error) that we have to be protected *from* the Establishment Clause. We can't let it do its work too well, lest all religious thought and impulse be driven from our heads and hearts. And here I thought the Clause existed so that tax dollars wouldn't be used to pay for church-based organizations, and so that township council meetings won't be held at the local Catholic church.

The *Times* reporter also described support for the Ninth Circuit's ruling as "muted." Sporadic maybe, but tell me if this statement from Barry Lynn, executive director of Americans United for Separation of Church and State (AU), a religious liberty watchdog organization (full disclosure: I subscribe to AU's e-mail advisory service) strikes you as muted: "This decision shows respect for freedom of conscience. You can be a patriotic American regardless of your religious belief or lack of religion. Our government should never coerce school children [*sic*]—or anyone else—to make a profession of religious belief." Sounds pretty firm and resolute. But let's go further: "America is an incredibly diverse country with some 2,000 different religions and denominations, as well as millions of Americans who profess no religion at all. Government actions should respect that diversity" ("Public Schools Can't," 2002).

I thought that journalists, especially those on the broadcast side, *liked* individuals who expressed their thoughts loudly, but succinctly. Let's compare Lynn's comments to comments made by Jay Sekulow, chief counsel for the American Center for Law and Justice (an organization that opposed the Ninth Circuit's ruling): "I think the opinion is absurd" (Nieves, 2002a, p. A20). Later, Sekulow would say that the court had "created a constitutional crisis for no reason."

So now I'm confused. Maybe Lynn and those who supported Newdow simply looked "muted" when compared to Newdow—of course, the basis of that comparison is a portrayal of Newdow by reporters as hell-bent on stripping God from our lives. Or maybe journalists have made the ability to muster sound-bite righteous indignation into their chief criterion for using quotes.

Chapter 4

A Reputation for Unorthodox Opinions

Coverage of the Ninth Circuit's June 26 decision by journalists suggests that they were taken by surprise. But as journalists for network and cable news outlets began to deal with what quickly became a very "unruly" story, again using John Fiske's term (quoted in Campbell, 1991), they started to lay the foundation for several frames that suggested the Ninth Circuit's ruling was an aberration, and would almost certainly be reversed by the Supreme Court.

Recall that Donahue, Tichenor, and Olien (1995) argue that journalists act as "sentry" for dominant institutions, keeping an eye out for threats, and sounding the alarm when one is identified. They do not sound the alarm to protect their readers; they do so to protect large cultural institutions that probably would not otherwise need their help, and that may not know why the alarm is being sounded in the first place. Journalists tend to go after individuals, and rarely question the underlying power structure.

Journalists tend to deal with a threat, write Donahue and his colleagues, in "a constrained way and only on certain issues and under certain structural conditions" (1995, p. 116). They seek to reinforce, not challenge, these institutions, and lead the community back toward cohesion. Journalists initially thought that Newdow had little chance of succeeding. When he lost at the district court level, their speculation proved correct for the moment. So, to borrow a military phrase, journalists were able to "stand down"—the threat, however insignificant, had been neutralized.

Once the Ninth Circuit issued its ruling, many journalists assumed the role of sentry with renewed, almost excessive, vigor, as if to compensate for their earlier failure to take Newdow's suit seriously. Reporters had already bent over backward to support the nation. They expressed—sometimes very publicly—their patriotism, in a clear abandonment of journalistic principles. Some wore lapel pins and flag ribbons on the air. Many journalists criticized the actions of their colleagues. A spokesperson for ABC News noted, "Especially in a time of crisis, the most patriotic thing journalists can do is to remain as objective as possible." Stacey Woeffel, news director at a television station in Columbia, Missouri, instructed his reporters to "leave the ribbons at home" so as to assure viewers that they were not "influenced by the government in informing the public" (Malkin, 2001).

One conservative commentator, Michelle Malkin (2001), denounced Woeffel's stance. "The media snobs are at it again. Wrinkling their noses at flag pins and patriotic ribbons," she wrote. They act as if they are "lethally allergic to red, white, and blue. Do they plan on boycotting the Fourth of July, too?" Malkin claimed that those journalists who declined to express their patriotism were "simply embarrassed to identify with the average citizen," who doesn't view "flag-waving as a maudlin exercise." Some reporters, including a few for television stations in my area of the country, still wear the pins.

Reporters wear "an invisible uniform," explained Roy Peter Clark (2001), a senior scholar at the Poynter Institute. "They carry their patriotism in their hearts, not on their sleeves." Journalists should only carry the "instruments of their craft—notebooks, digital cameras, laptop computers, and now videophones" as they endeavor to "perform an unpopular job crucial to democratic life, providing the oxygen of information so that citizens can breathe and choose."

But as with so many of these attempts to defend journalism, the defense came with an unabashed assertion of patriotism. Clark pointed out later that he "flies two flags at home." His dog, a Jack Russell terrier named Rex, "each night rips the guts out of a stuffed bunny we've named Osama Bin Laden." Clark also expresses his patriotism through music: at a professional conference, he accompanied 50 journalists on piano as they sang "America the Beautiful."

Isn't it enough to just do your job?

There were other shows of solidarity. MSNBC, the cable news network owned by NBC (a subsidiary of General Electric) and Microsoft, anointed itself "America's News Channel" in the months following the 9/11 attacks. A billowing flag became a very obvious part of the Fox News Channel's on-air graphics package. Journalists would tell you that they sacrificed their professional standards in order to reassure the country that we would get through this time together.

But perhaps more troubling is that reporters saved government officials the trouble of having to create and deploy frames around which to build a narrative that would see us through the crisis caused by Newdow. We clearly knew what broadcast journalists thought of the Ninth Circuit's ruling almost before Congress and President Bush reacted. To reassure Americans that the spirit of the Pledge was intact, they devalued the Ninth Circuit's opinion by repeating several assertions: the Ninth Circuit was extremely liberal, the U.S. Supreme Court almost routinely reverses the Ninth Circuit's decisions, and the impact of the controversial decision was limited to the states within the circuit. The radical ruling would harm no one else until the high court resolved the issue. Further, journalists repeatedly suggested that Newdow was determined to eradicate all mentions of God from public life. Taken together, these thematic elements reinforced the idea that Newdow was far outside the mainstream, particularly when it came to the Pledge.

The Scapegoat

In this chapter the focus will be the work of broadcast journalists and cable talk show hosts who covered the Ninth Circuit decision in the days after the June 26 ruling. I analyzed transcripts of 85 news and talk show broadcast segments from June 26 to July 4, 2002, during which Newdow's suit was discussed. Newdow appeared in or was interviewed by journalists in many of these segments.

Both broadcast and print journalists cast Newdow as an erratic outsider, or a "scapegoat," to use Jack Lule's (2001) term. Lule notes that society tends to tolerate only a moderate amount of dissent. Those who dissent "usually are not permitted to question basic values, let alone the very structure of society," Lule writes (p. 63). The *scapegoat* myth enables reporters to "make an example" of anyone who dares to take on our dominant institutions. Lule also points out that journalists typically portray the scapegoat as "embodying the sins of society." Atheism is not a sin, but in the minds of many Americans, particularly fundamentalist Christians, it rises to that level. At the very least, not believing in God is clearly outside the mainstream. "Myths degrade and demean the Scapegoat in stories then define sin and dramatize its punishment," Lule contends (p. 63). The news media effectively plays their role as "agents of social control" by offering distorted, negative coverage of anyone who threatens the status quo, particularly when the government encourages the view that the fabric of our nation is imperiled.

Lule's exploration of news coverage of the late Black Panther Huey Newton reveals that reporters "demeaned and devalued" Newton in their stories by diminishing the importance of his activism, suggesting his work was in vain, focusing on his violent death, and by repeatedly mentioning his criminal record (pp. 71–77). "Because he strained against societal preconceptions and journalistic conventions of political protest, he was strategically and emphatically vilified," Lule concluded. Thus, journalists accept only a limited range of behaviors from those who challenge the status quo before they begin to diminish their message.

Lule's description of how journalists covered Newton meshes nicely with Donahue and his colleagues' claim that a "guard dog" reporter waits for a cue from the government before assuming its "sentry" role. President Bush and members of Congress clearly and emphatically denounced the Ninth's Circuit ruling. Congress showed its disgust for the decision by convening on the steps of the U.S. Capitol to recite the Pledge (emphasizing the words "under God") and to sing "God Bless America." But instead of taking members of Congress to task for what was clearly an act of political pandering, journalists gently chided them, and conveyed to viewers how reassuring their actions were in light of Newdow's threat to the Pledge.

Holy War

It would take only a few hours after the Ninth Circuit's decision for journalists to push Newdow into the role of scapegoat, a role he would play almost for the duration of what CNN's Greta Van Susteren (2002) referred to as a "holy war." Her choice of words is ironic, in light of the criticism President Bush received for his ill-timed (and later retracted) reference to the war in Iraq as a "crusade."

Step one in the construction of the first postdecision frame was for journalists to gauge and convey public reaction. I'm always a bit wary when a reporter finds instant widespread support (or rejection) of an idea or cause. How often do we hear politicians claim that "the American People" applaud or reject a particular policy? This could be too harsh of me: of course it's impossible to elicit the opinion of every person in the country—that's why we have polling organizations. Still, it is at least plausible to argue that journalists sometimes jump the gun when it comes to definitive statements about public opinion. Just think for a moment about how much stock journalists place in polls. They are trusted and easy-to-grasp indicators of public opinion on a subject.

But as a professor of mine once said, "Polls show what polls show." Journalists do little to clarify or expand on a poll's results, and even less to expose their limitations. They recount poll results instead of explaining the underlying issues. A clear-cut reaction fits a narrative of "America Under Siege" than a range of opinions held with differing degrees of conviction and built on different pieces of information. Perhaps journalists simply believed that overwhelmingly negative reaction to the Pledge decision was inevitable.

With that in mind, it did not surprise me to hear *CBS Evening News* reporter John Blackstone (2002) report on June 26 that reaction to the Ninth Circuit ruling was "swift and emotional." NBC's Tom Brokaw (2002a) exaggerated the impact of the decision in the opening to the June 26 *NBC Nightly News*: "Suddenly, the world seems to have been turned upside down again." The Pledge, "that staple of American classrooms, and Boy and Girl Scout meetings," had been declared unconstitutional. CNN International's Jonathan Mann (2002) asked simply, "Is nothing sacred?" It is not up to journalists, at least those operating under the definition of objectivity discussed in my newswriting classes, to speculate about what is and is not "sacred." But again, journalists were trying to cast this stunning opinion in familiar terms. Discussion of what is and isn't "sacred" means more to the typical news viewer than a discussion of Establishment Clause cases.

NBC reporter Pete Williams included in his June 26 story a clear, emphatic quote from Barry Lynn, president of the AU: "When you interject the controversy about religion into it, you turn a proclamation of patriotism into a religious creed, and that's something Congress should not do" (Brokaw, 2002a). To provide balance for Lynn's opinion, Williams used a far more inflammatory quote from the dissenting opinion in the Newdow case written by Ninth Circuit judge Ferdinand Fernandez.

The Pledge does not promote religion, Williams said, "except in what he called the fevered eye of people who would like to drive all trace of religion out of public life" (Brokaw, 2002a). Williams offered his viewers no middle ground. He cast those who supported Newdow as zealots. There is normal—reciting a fully intact Pledge every day in America's schools—and there is abnormal—embodying those who fail to acknowledge the significance of this ritual.

Thus, within the *holy war* frame viewers saw a key theme: Newdow would not stop in his single-minded quest to alter the Pledge—this was *his* holy war, so to speak. "Some people, though, wonder, where does it end?" the *Today Show*'s Katie Couric (2002) said in an interview with Newdow. Reporters conveyed the impression that Newdow was zealous, even reckless, in trying to purge God from public life. Choosing not to say the Pledge, as endorsed by the Supreme Court in *Barnette*, was an unsatisfactory option. "Why isn't that enough for you . . . to say to your daughter, 'You don't have to participate in reciting the Pledge of Allegiance'?" Couric asked Newdow.

"This is not your first lawsuit," intoned Robin Roberts of ABC's *Good Morning America* (2002) in an interview with Newdow the day after the Ninth Circuit's ruling. "You even sued the President because at his inauguration there was a Christian prayer." Newdow acknowledged filing that suit, and a suit to have God removed from our currency. "People hearing that might—might feel that's—that's a bit extreme," Roberts said.

Newdow explained that he was "upholding the Constitution," in a way he considered "very patriotic." But Roberts reminded Newdow (and her viewers) of the anger aroused by the Ninth Circuit's ruling: "You have offended quite a few people, and there's been such an—an outrage." Newdow noted that Americans were angry at the Supreme Court when it issued its landmark 1954 ruling in *Brown v. Board of Education of Topeka*, but Roberts missed the parallel he was trying to draw. "There are so many children who want to say the Pledge of Allegiance," she said.

And anyway, some reporters suggested, this battle was fought and won when President Eisenhower amended the Pledge in 1954. We reached consensus on the Pledge a long time ago, Mr. Newdow, and now you come along and threaten it with your lawsuit. Journalists almost seemed to sense that they would not be able to bring Newdow back into the conformist fold, as Lule might suggest. He simply wasn't making sense.

"Many people, I believe, thought that this matter had long ago been decided the other way," said a constitutional expert interviewed by CBS reporter John Blackstone (Roberts, 2002b). "And now the issue has been revived again." Inclusion of this quote again suggests that dissent and discussion, of these ideas at least, are not to be encouraged. Here, we see reporters begin to accept the mantle of "sentry" suggested by Donahue and his colleagues.

But in these early hours after the ruling, the government had only made brief (but emphatic) comments about the decision. Some reporters chose to hit the ground running, rather than wait for government officials to castigate Newdow. It would have been a shock to most of the planet if President Bush congratulated Newdow for his bravery and said "why not?—two fewer words will make the Pledge easier to say," but reporters clearly had begun their patrol for threats as the government was crafting a response.

This theme would continue as the case moved to the Supreme Court. "Let us pray—oops, strike that—let us hope that motherhood and apple pie are not on a court docket somewhere," mused CNN's Candy Crowley on the June 26 edition of *CNN Newsnight* as viewers again saw members of Congress recite the Pledge of Allegiance on the steps of the Capitol. "It's a perfect issue to be on Capitol Hill around the Fourth of July. Don't you think?" she asked her colleague, Anderson Cooper. Cooper (2002) took a swipe at the ultrapatrioitic Fox News Channel: "it's the kind of story Roger Ailes (the very conservative head of the Fox News Channel) dreams about." Newdow's atheistic spree would no doubt continue, at least according to reporters.

Crowley achieved two thematic flourishes in her on-the-spot analysis of Congress' show of patriotism: she diminished Newdow's claims by showing the level of support for the Pledge, but did so by gently poking fun at the politically opportunistic nature of that support. "Please stop and appreciate this moment," she asked Cooper (2002) between very animated quotes from members of Congress. "The decision is nuts," said Senate minority leader Tom Daschle.

Daschle's colleague, republican George Allen of Virginia, asked, "Will they imprison school choirs? Have the school directors imprisoned because the children are singing *God Bless America*?" Longtime senator Robert Byrd of West Virginia was quoted in Crowley's story as saying, "I hope the Senate will waste no time in throwing this back in the face of this stupid judge." Byrd's lack of respect for an esteemed judge notwithstanding, Crowley feigned amazement at the bipartisan distaste for the ruling, but in doing so reinforced the narrative emerging from early coverage: that Newdow was out of control; he would not stop until he had eradicated every mention of God from American culture.

We had our villain—our antagonist, if you want to get Shakespearean about it. The battle was between Newdow and (at this point) members of Congress and the president. Viewers saw a struggle among individuals. Careful consideration of ideas was rejected in favor of black hats and white hats. Rarely would journalists stray from this storyline in the weeks and months ahead.

Connie Chung's (2002) interview with Newdow, the first after the ruling, reinforced this narrative strand. Chung, doing her best impression of a "guard dog," had identified the threat to our dominant institutions, and did what she could to shred his argument. "Tell me, Mr. Newdow, is it your intention to go after *In God We Trust* and *God Bless America*?" Chung's badgering continued:

> CHUNG: You're saying that we change everything on all our bills that say "In God We Trust," as you well know, on the other side?

> NEWDOW: I'm suggesting that we adhere to the Constitution that says we shouldn't throw religious dogma in the middle of our government's actions . . .
> CHUNG: So you would support taking out "In God We Trust?" Is that what you're saying?

This was typically the extent of what Newdow was allowed to say. Reporters were quickly developing a "preferred reading" of Newdow's case, one that would not allow for full consideration of his reasons for filing suit in the first place. The saying, "keep your friends close and your enemies closer," applies here (believe it or not). Journalists would keep Newdow right where they could see him—by suggesting that he was the only one so possessed of the desire to expunge God from civic life. He was on a lonely quest, but reporters would keep us posted on his whereabouts. CBS reporter John Blackstone confirmed the image of Newdow on a lonely quest by reporting that he "is looking beyond the Pledge of Allegiance. From dollar bills to government buildings, he sees other references to God that have to go" (Roberts, 2002b). Like his colleagues, Blackstone suggests Newdow is an unthinking one-dimensional zealot.

Hands Over Hearts

On the June 26 broadcast of ABC's *World News Tonight*, the court's ruling was one of the broadcast's two lead stories, a strong indication of its importance. Anchor Peter Jennings (2002) told viewers that the story "certainly was a compelling one." The Ninth Circuit, he said, "has ruled today that reciting the Pledge of Allegiance in public schools is unconstitutional because it mentions God." The Ninth Circuit's ruling, he said, "unleashed a flurry of condemnation from politicians." Jennings then introduced a report by ABC reporter Jackie Judd.

Judd's story began with a shot of schoolchildren, hands over their hearts, reciting the words at the heart of the controversy: "One nation under God." In the weeks and months to come, viewers of television news would repeatedly see shots of people, often children, saying the Pledge. "American currency may declare that 'In God We Trust' and we may sing 'God Bless America' at the ballpark," said *CBS Evening News* anchor John Roberts (2002a), "but a federal appeals court in San Francisco ruled today that children in U.S. public schools should not recite the Pledge of Allegiance." The decision represented a slap in the face to American values and cherished rituals. Americans were the victims of Newdow's rampage. It was as if an assailant had opened fire on a crowd of people. "For generations," reported CBS' Blackstone during the broadcast, "it is the way the school day has begun, but a federal appeals court says two little words make it unconstitutional" (Roberts, 2002a).

Judd attempted to reinforce a sense of normalcy, reminding viewers that 26 states require schools to begin their days with a recitation of the Pledge. Then Judd introduced a second key thematic element in early coverage of the decision: "In the aftermath of 9/11, a handful of other states is considering doing the same," she said, bypassing for the moment the misguided bigotry that drove many of these decisions. Judd reminded viewers that students may decline to say the Pledge, although she did not mention the 1943 Supreme Court ruling that barred schools from compelling students to say the Pledge each day (Jennings, 2002).

Like many of his colleagues, CNBC reporter Steve Handelsman reminded viewers of a student's right to "opt out" of saying the Pledge (Hansen, 2002a). The *Today Show*'s Katie Couric (2002) turned this against Newdow; she prefaced her first question to Newdow in a June 27 interview by reminding viewers that "your second grade daughter doesn't actually participate when the Pledge of Allegiance is recited in her classroom, and yet you wanted to file this lawsuit." But the Ninth Circuit, according to Handelsman, "called that choice of participation or protest unacceptable" (Hansen, 2002a).

While Handelsman accurately characterized the Ninth Circuit's ruling in this excerpt (the panel found that Elk Grove's policy concerning the Pledge put "students in the untenable position of choosing between participating in an exercise with religious content or protesting") his reporting suggests that there is no middle ground for students—they either support or oppose the Pledge. They either say the Pledge or storm out of the classroom in protest. But it also suggests, as did much of the broadcast coverage, that those who stay and show their patriotism are to be commended. And those who do not—and those teachers who choose to leave the Pledge out of their morning routines—are somehow harming their students. CNN reporters even asked their own interns about the controversy. "They didn't even say the Pledge . . . because the teachers can't force you to say it," said CNN's Kelli Arena. "And so the classroom was so unruly with these kids sitting around and not saying it, that they just decided not to say it. So no one is jamming anything down anybody's throat here" (Snow, 2002).

Arena's colleague, Christine Romans, offered a somewhat incongruous conclusion to the discussion: "come on, this is just the Pledge of Allegiance." This segment suggests that unruly students should not enjoy the benefit of the ritual and its meaning. This privilege was reserved for the truly patriotic. The rest of us could just sit there and bask in our small victory, won, it seems, so that the truly patriotic didn't have to deal with us. Handelsman's report ended with a group of children reciting the end of the Pledge, followed by a cheer of "Yeah!" (Hansen, 2002a).

These reporters did their best to assure viewers that life would soon be back to normal. Aside from a sprinkling of pro-Newdow quotes, they did not give readers the chance to hear from officials—or from students—who felt the Pledge was indeed a violation of the Establishment Clause. It was their duty as "sentry" to restore order—and a sense of normalcy.

A day after the ruling, CNN reporter James Hattori visited a school in the Elk Grove School District. He suggested that school officials were successfully maintaining order in light of the Newdow ruling. "You can hear it, the Pledge of Allegiance recited as usual before classes got under way, including the words 'under God,' as usual" (Whitfield, 2002). School officials were not about to let this crazy atheist take away a cherished morning ritual, the tone of Hattori's report suggested. Throughout the early coverage, reporters used the word "usual" or "typical" to underscore the radical nature of the court's decision, and to assure viewers that life would go on.

The same day, CBS reporter John Blackstone said "pending further court action, this is still legal." Viewers then saw a shot of children "in Ms. Hobble's fourth grade class in Elk Grove, California" dutifully reciting the Pledge. The phrase "one nation under God," Blackstone noted, "was declared with particular exuberance this morning" (Roberts, 2002b). Blackstone spoke as if the schoolchildren were responding to a terrorist attack. His CBS colleague, Jane Clayson (2002), reported earlier in the day that the Pledge was "under fire."

Reporting on Judge Goodwin's June 27 decision to stay his earlier ruling pending completion of the district's appeal, CNN's Bill Hemmer (2002) echoed the hope of journalists that the Pledge would survive: "[i]t may be a long time, if ever, before kids have to stop saying the Pledge of Allegiance."

Broadcast journalists reporting in the hours after the Ninth Circuit ruling exhibited behavior that bordered on the frantic, as they tried to gauge what would happen in the wake of the ruling. Viewers soon learned that our elected leaders would act decisively, though not without some partisanship. Donahue and his colleagues (1995) would argue that reporters were simply waiting for a cue from the government—for a policy statement that they could use to shape their ongoing coverage of the controversy.

On CNN's *Inside Politics* on the afternoon of June 26, host Judy Woodruff (2002) noted that the Pledge controversy had quickly taken on a political flavor. Republicans would blame the Democrats, and their unwillingness to affirm President Bush's judicial nominees, for the mess. A memo from the National Republican Congressional Committee urged party members to contact their local school board to instruct them to "nullify" the Ninth Circuit's decision by saying the Pledge in their classrooms as usual. CNN's Bob Franken explained that Judge Goodwin was a Nixon appointee.

Democrats responded to the Republicans' assertions by attacking the Ninth Circuit's ruling with as much disbelief and vitriol as their Republican counterparts. Senator John Kerry, who a little more than two years later would become his party's nominee for president, would call the decision "half-assed justice."

But as politicians practically pushed each other out of the way to denounce the decision and reassert their patriotism, more information was added to the original version of the story. CNN political analyst William Schneider introduced Bellamy's authorship this way: "here's something you may not know . . . the Pledge of Allegiance was written by a socialist. Yes, a man named Francis Bellamy . . . who was pressured into leaving his church in Boston in 1891 because of his socialist sermons." Schneider's CNN colleague, anchor Anderson Cooper, would later note that the Pledge "was written by a Baptist minister, curiously enough a socialist" (Cooper, 2002). Ironically, in creating the Pledge, Bellamy wanted to foster "a national sense of fairness, equality, egalitarianism, and opportunity," said a scholar interviewed on *CBS Sunday Morning* (Osgood, 2002).

Woodruff ran a sound bite from former presidential press secretary Ari Fleischer, who explained that both the Supreme Court begins each session in October by saying "God save the United States and this honorable court" and Congress starts each day with a prayer. Fleischer also tried to limit the impact of the decision by noting that only the states within the Ninth Circuit were bound by its decision. And anyway, as reporter Pete Williams reported on the *NBC Nightly News* (Brokaw, 2002b), "school is mostly out" in these states. Williams's comment suggested that there was hope that students would not be impacted by the court's radical decision and that there was time to fix the damage done by the Ninth Circuit's ruling before school started again.

President Bush was in Arizona when the decision was handed down, comforting victims of a fire by telling them to "have faith in God almighty." While the president would never tell residents to disobey the law, Fleischer said, most Americans "have faith in God, and they're going to express it in the Pledge every day that they can." Congress would soon join them.

By 5:00 p.m. on June 26, the U.S. Senate unanimously passed a resolution directing its counsel to "intervene in the case to defend the constitutionality of the Pledge of Allegiance" (Blitzer, 2002). As CNN's Candy Crowley explained, "If there was a political Richter scale, this would have been an 8.5." The Ninth Circuit's decision "really rocked Capitol Hill and filled the hallowed halls with the sound of outrage" (Cooper, 2002).

Crowley's colleague, Anderson Cooper, said that President Bush's initial reaction to the ruling came while Bush was in Canada—"the place where you won't hear the Pledge, you'll only hear *O Canada*." Although it was a simple bridge between stories, Cooper's comment again signaled how far (physically and rhetorically) journalists would go to marginalize Newdow, and, in the bargain, nations that don't express their patriotism as forcefully as we do. CNN's Suzanne Kelly noted in a June 27 report that the Pledge was "a hallmark of American society, perhaps not fully understood by people outside the United States" (Mann, 2002). Kelly suggests that Americans are the only people in the world who understand freedom expressed in this fashion.

Then came the most defining moment in the early stages of this controversy: a few hours after the Ninth Circuit ruling, members of Congress assembled on the steps of the Capitol and recited the Pledge, followed by a rendition of "God Bless America." CNN anchor Miles O'Brien prodded viewers: "I assumed you noticed the emphasis for those two words out of the 31-word Pledge: under God." Reacting further to the show of solidarity by Congress, O'Brien said, "No one there quitting their day job, we hope. And we will Pledge to you right now that this will be a political issue for many days to come." As Candy Crowley explained in a later broadcast, "you get the feeling they'd have voted twice if they could" (Cooper, 2002). "Did I mention there was no daylight between them?" asked CNN's Kate Snow (2002) three days later, narrating a clip of the same scene. It was, in Snow's estimation, "a made-for-TV moment." Here, however, the packaging was acceptable to television reporters.

The tone in O'Brien's comments about Congress' actions suggests that Newdow's challenge to the Pledge was almost as much of a threat to America as Al-Qaeda. As Jamieson and Waldman (2003) would argue, O'Brien was simply holding out hope for his viewers that our political institutions would survive. But the firestorm caused by the decision gave journalists room to devalue the ruling by poking fun at politicians, and, by implication, at Newdow, while at the same time sustaining the idea that the ruling had in a few hours caused social chaos. "So you may be asking, 'what happens now?'" said CNN's Anderson Cooper. "Well, apologies to the Ninth Circuit Court, God only knows." Cooper's comment both diminished the appeals court panel, and played on our fears.

CNN anchors and reporters assured viewers that the government was on the case. CNN White House correspondent John King said the U.S. Department of Justice would quickly file a friend of the court brief in support of overturning the Ninth Circuit ruling. He quoted a senior White House official as saying the matter "will be resolved in the courts quickly. This decision, no doubt, will be returned" (Cooper, 2002).

King acknowledged that the White House was surprised by the decision, despite having followed the case as it made its way to the Ninth Circuit—but that wasn't the point: the government was ready to act. Bush administration officials "would love to have this debate come onto Washington in an election year," King said, "where the Supreme Court's conservative majority would throw out the decision quickly."

King's comment was not so much a statement of fact as it was a note of reassurance to his viewers. But it is certainly not reassuring to those of us who believe (the Court's decision in Bush v. Gore notwithstanding) that the justices' evaluation of a case is not tinged by ideology. The Court's purported conservative tilt is a topic of much discussion among journalists. Here, though, King makes it sound like a good thing, as if to say "don't worry, they'll take care of this."

Still Under Attack

America had withstood 9/11; it would certainly withstand an attack on the Pledge, at least according to broadcast journalists covering Newdow's suit. The timing of the Ninth Circuit's decision "couldn't have been worse coming after September 11," said one CNN news anchor (Mann, 2002). Journalists were now fully ensconced in the "guard dog" role. "This country feels threatened. It really is feeling very, very proud of what it stands for." Of course, "what it stands for" includes the encouragement and acceptance of dissent and the separation of church and state, but these concepts seemed alien to journalists covering Newdow's suit. Or perhaps the concepts were simply too complicated to be integrated successfully in the "black hat/white hat" narrative journalists were busily constructing. When the country is at war, nonconformists have to be rendered inert before they are recognized. Think of how many readers would be lost if journalists wandered outside this narrative and built the Newdow narrative on the idea that nonconformity—even atheism—might be a good thing.

All of this should not be surprising, given the tendency of journalists to accept the government's practice of making policy by looking at the world (and especially at Iraq) through a 9/11 prism. Only the most skilled (and progressive) reporters have taken issue with the government's use of the attacks on New York City and Washington, DC, as justification for a dubious military strategy that even some conservatives agree has severely damaged our standing in the world—not to mention an all-out assault on our civil liberties. I don't think it's an exaggeration to say that "life after 9/11" is the frame through which we experience much of our lives these days.

Nowhere in the early reporting of the decision could viewers find a reasoned discussion of Newdow's claims. CNN's Barbara Starr hinted that Judge Goodwin might have been correct "in the strictest sense of the Constitution" (Snow, 2002). But even the Constitution had to give way to the fearful public mood. "[T]here's no appetite for this in the American public," said Starr. In addition, journalists explored past challenges to the Pledge only to the extent that they supported the view, advanced by many conservatives, that God during the last two or three decades has been driven out of the public schools.

Judge Goodwin must be held responsible, reporters suggested. One reporter referred to him as the "so-called Pledge judge" (Hansen, 2002b). Newspaper columnist Bob Greene, appearing on a June 27 CNN news broadcast, said that "the judge's got to feel like a lonely guy, right now." Ironically, Greene added that one of the nation's great strengths is "not that we're so rigid and speak with a single voice. The best thing about this country is that we're more than 200 million voices, and everyone is just as strong as the other" (Mann, 2002). Perhaps, but even a cursory look at news coverage of Newdow reveals that those voices have value, and will be heard, only if they fall into line with what most of the other voices are saying.

Newdow was quoted by Judd (Jennings, 2002) on June 26 as saying that children "shouldn't have government telling them what a proper religious philosophy is." Judd balanced Newdow's sound bite with reaction from a disbelieving President Bush, who called the Ninth Circuit's decision "ridiculous." Broadcast journalists repeated Bush's one-word reaction in many subsequent stories. Republicans in Congress, said Judd, instructed local school boards to disregard the Ninth Circuit's decision. Viewers then saw Senator Robert Byrd of West Virginia challenge to Judge Goodwin: "I recited the Pledge and so has every other member of this body time and time again. Come, judge, put us in jail."

Building on Byrd's sentiment, Judd told viewers that the Ninth Circuit "has a reputation for unorthodox opinions" and that it is "reversed more often than any other circuit." CNN legal analyst Jeffrey Toobin went Judd one better, telling CNN anchor Kyra Phillips (2002) that the ruling was "certainly an extreme version of belief in the separation of church and state. Which is, of course, a bedrock principle in the Constitution." The inclusion of these facts, by Judd and by many other journalists, suggests that they were trying to reassure viewers that the Ninth Circuit's ruling was an aberration and could not possibly stand. Focusing on the Ninth Circuit's erratic, liberal tendencies also forced out any discussion of the value—or the Constitutional importance—of dissent in a free society.

The Supreme Court would certainly straighten out this mess, Judd suggested, especially since the justices had ruled in the past that the phrase "under God" is of only "minimal religious significance." The Ninth Circuit's ruling was a fluke. CNN's Toobin told Phillips: "this kind of generic religiosity has been really allowed by the courts for many years." The words "under God," he said, were "sufficiently generic, not an endorsement of any specific religion"—generic enough to cause some courts to allow them.

David Cole of Georgetown University Law School agreed: "It's been with us for so long," he told Judd, that the odds that the high court would uphold the Ninth Circuit were extremely slim. Nina Totenberg, National Public Radio's (NPR) Supreme Court reporter, echoed Judd's assessment: "[G]oing out on a limb . . . I would say the odds are pretty close to zilch" (Neary & Siegel, 2002).

Totenberg said it was inevitable that the U.S. Department of Justice would ask for a review of the decision by all 11 Ninth Circuit judges (an "en banc" review). "This was, after all, only a panel of the Court of Appeals," Totenberg told *All Things Considered* host Lynn Neary (Neary & Siegel, 2002). "And my guess is that the ruling . . . will die right there." But Judd ended her report by saying that a final decision might not come for some time. "Until then, the Pledge, 'under God' and all, will continue to be recited in many schools across the country" (Jennings, 2002). The next day, Judge Goodwin stayed his opinion. There was no need for the Department of Justice to push for an en banc review. "[A]lready on its own, the court appears headed in that direction," reported NBC's George Lewis, as if to say "they've come to their senses—it sure took them long enough" (Brokaw, 2002b).

But CNN's Kyra Phillips (2002) made it seem like the damage to the "bedrock principle" mentioned by Toobin had already been done. "And now the court is saying: students cannot hold religious invocations at graduations and can't be compelled to recite the Pledge," she said to Toobin. "It's just hard to understand when you have a President of the United States that always says, 'God Bless America,' or calls you to say the Pledge. Even asks Americans to come together in prayer on national television."

Toobin tried to calm Phillips by citing the Supreme Court's 1943 decision in *West Virginia State Board of Education v. Barnette*, in which the justices struck down a West Virginia law that required students to recite the Pledge. The Court's ruling came three years after it had upheld a decision by the Millersville, Pennsylvania, School Board to expel Lillian Gobitis, then 12, and her brother, William, then 10, for refusing to recite the Pledge because they were Jehovah's Witnesses. Susan Jacoby (2004) notes that the Court's ruling touched off "a wave of mob violence" against members of the church. More than 350 Witnesses were attacked in the two years following the decision (pp. 287–288).

Ceremonial Deism

Network journalists did allow Newdow to make his case, but only in short, repetitive bursts. Viewers saw and heard only variations on "the government should not be allowed to infuse God into public education." Rarely was Newdow given the chance to elaborate on this view. But the focus of experts called on by reporters to place Newdow's suit in context was not God or religion—it was history. Journalists endeavored to assure viewers that the presence of God in the Pledge was an example of the "ceremonial deism" discussed by the Supreme Court in a host of other cases. "We need common sense [*sic*] judges who understand that our rights were derived from God," said President Bush in an NBC story about the case (Couric, 2002).

David Gordon, then superintendent of the Elk Grove School District, noted in an interview on the *Today Show* that the Pledge "is kind of the centerpiece of how we teach our children about democracy, about civic values" (Couric, 2002). Earlier in the interview, Gordon noted that his town's "faith community" was aware of the "dividing line between coming into the schools and proselytizing and being a support for the schools in the community. And they do a great job for us." *Today* host Katie Couric did not challenge what to some might be a troubling, if limited, intrusion of the church into civic life.

Attorney Tom Goldstein, quoted by NBC's Pete Williams in his June 26 report on the Ninth Circuit's ruling, said that the inclusion of God in so many aspects of public life "isn't really signifying something religious. It's been part of our national culture for decades and sometimes more than a century" (Brokaw, 2002a). Before Goldstein's sound bite, viewers saw President Bush finish taking the oath of office in 2001 by saying "So help me, God," followed by a reminder from Williams that the Supreme Court—where this case clearly was headed—"begins its daily sessions with such a reference."

Buoyed by an interview with a historian who characterized the debate over separation of church and state as a "battle," reporter John Blackstone (Roberts, 2002b) on June 27 offered a measure of comfort to viewers of the *CBS Evening News*: "To many Americans, those symbolic references to God are more a matter of history and tradition than of religion. And in the end, that sense of tradition is likely to make the symbols difficult to dislodge." Reporting like Blackstone's ignores the fact that the Pledge itself is just over a century old, and was revised to include the words "under God" just a half century ago.

Outside the Mainstream

Newdow wasn't the only one who was cast as a nonconformist. The Ninth Circuit's ruling, said CNN's Jeffrey Toobin, was different. "[E]ven though this student could leave the room during the Pledge, which she clearly had a right to do, the mere saying of the Pledge by other students was found to be unconstitutional." It was this part of the Ninth Circuit's ruling that "was so unusual and sort of outside the mainstream," Toobin said (Phillips, 2002). And anyway, reported CNN's Suzanne Kelly, students who decide not to say the Pledge are "free to stand mute, looking on as their classmates recite the familiar lines." Use of the words "mute" and "looking on" does nothing to counter Newdow's claim that students would probably make a student who makes this decision less than comfortable. Any more than this would amount to special treatment, Kelly suggests (Costello, 2002a).

The court's interpretation of *Gobitis* and *Barnette* was "pretty extreme." For CNN International anchor Jonathan Mann (2002), being extreme was not limited to the court. In a June 27 report, he said, "To many people in the U.S., California is where the crazy things happen." Citizens may only having passing familiarity with the Constitution and with the court system, "but they know that their kids say the Pledge," Mann said.

What Toobin and Phillips did not recount for their viewers was the most significant section of Justice Robert Jackson's majority opinion in *Barnette*: "If there is any fixed star in our constellation, it is that no official, high or petty, can prescribe what shall be orthodox in politics, nationalism, religion, or other matters of opinion or force citizens to confess by word or act their faith therein" (quoted in Jacoby, 2004, p. 288). Perhaps unknowingly, journalists were allowing officials to do exactly that by so willingly disseminating the government's take on the Newdow decision.

CNN's Phillips (2002) seemed to need more reassurance that the Pledge would indeed survive the Ninth Circuit's ruling, so that school officials would be allowed to continue requiring the recitation of the Pledge. "So, Jeffrey, this still could be recited at schools, am I right?" she asked. The ruling, said Toobin, "does seem to say that the Pledge with the words 'under God' in it, cannot be recited."

"At all?" asked Phillips. Toobin said yes, but quickly added "that's what makes the opinion so extreme is that it—it seems to prohibit the saying of the words 'under God' in the classroom, as it is said in thousands of classrooms every day." Toobin concluded his analysis by reminding viewers that the Ninth Circuit was overturned more than any other appeals court, that the dissent by Judge Ferdinand Fernandez was strongly worded, and that an appeal was certain. "So this is far from the last word on the subject," he told Phillips.

Bob Franken, CNN's national correspondent, agreed, once again reminding viewers of the court's liberal tendencies. Trying to restake God's terrain, Franken noted the presence of the word God on coins. On "official buildings all over the United States, there are references to God," he said. Franken had earlier remarked that Newdow was "described in court briefings as an atheist," as if he had never seen an atheist before (Phillips, 2002). The scapegoating of Newdow had begun. Newdow would later be referred to as an "avowed atheist." A *CBS Evening News* reporter said Newdow was "an atheist from Sacramento, California." At least reporters were now using his name. One had referred to him as "a man who's a self-proclaimed atheist" (Neary & Siegel, 2002).

"This one has the possibility of Supreme Court written all over it," he remarked to Phillips in his June 26 report on the Ninth Circuit ruling. NBC reporter Pete Williams cited "legal experts" who argued that the decision "would likely be dead on arrival" when the Supreme Court convened in October 2002 (Barnicle, 2002). In a scene reminiscent of when journalists read from the steps of the Supreme Court from the justices' ruling on the contested 2000 election recount, Franken read from the Ninth Circuit's ruling. The judges, he said, ruled that use of the words "under God" was an endorsement of religion, not simply an acknowledgment that many of us believe in God.

Franken quickly jumped to the dissent written by Circuit judge Ferdinand Fernandez—the "one judge who was against this," as Franken put it. Franken's tone suggests that Judge Fernandez was the only judge willing to defend the Pledge, the only judge in touch with reality. In a later report (Woodruff, 2002), Franken would say that "of course, there was a dissent," as if it was inconceivable that there could be unanimity about Newdow's challenge to the Pledge.

Phillips agreed (again) that an appeal was inevitable. Franken stressed that going directly to the "court of public opinion" might bring a more expeditious end to the Ninth Circuit's madness. "[T]his is going to be one the talk shows are going to have a field day with," Franken said. Before concluding his report, he mentioned the court's liberal leanings one last time. "When the first bulletins came out about this, it was almost a sure thing that it would come out of the 9th Circuit," he told Phillips (2002).

And once journalists learned more about Michael Newdow, they quickly positioned him as an outsider, as they had done with the Ninth Circuit panel. Newdow appeared for the first time after the Ninth Circuit's ruling in an interview with former CNN anchor Connie Chung (2002), who continued the twin themes of outrage and disbelief in introducing Newdow. "To say that people all across the nation are outraged is an understatement," she began. She reminded viewers that the ruling only applied to the states that make up the Ninth Circuit, then reinforced the theme of opposition by adding that "opponents of the ruling span the country," an assessment that while probably true, was not backed up by any evidence.

Chung noted that the words "under God" were added to the Pledge when the United States was trying desperately to "combat atheistic communism." As if drawing a direct link between then and now, Chung said "about 1 million Americans are atheists." Newdow, "the most famous of them all," was, said Chung, "the man who started it all"—the lawsuit that caused all of this trouble. As if defending America's honor, Chung began the interview this way: "Mr. Newdow, I must ask you this very simple question: why?"

Newdow said that he did not like being made to feel like an "outsider" because of his religious views, something the Supreme Court has rejected. "But we're talking about school," countered Chung. "You're not in school anymore. It's your daughter who's in school, right?" Newdow said he sued on behalf of his daughter, but also as "a citizen who when I recite the Pledge of Allegiance, I'm required to countenance God, which I don't wish to do." Here, Chung suggests that Newdow is unnecessarily involving his daughter and it is she who may be most affected by a protracted lawsuit.

Later, Chung questioned Newdow's patriotism, a frequently used tactic by broadcast journalists covering this story. "Are you proud to be an American?" Chung asked Newdow. "Absolutely," said Newdow. Chung continued to explore the patriotism theme: many people, she said, "think that what you're doing is blatantly un-American." Chung then reminded viewers about Madelyn Murray O'Hair, the controversial atheist who successfully, in Chung's words, "got prayers out of public schools." By invoking O'Hair, Chung attempted to persuade viewers that atheism is an extreme view.

O'Hair came to be known as "the most hated woman in America," Chung noted. She asked Newdow if he was "prepared for that kind of identity, that tag." Chung's statement is a resounding invocation of the scapegoat myth discussed by Lule. Suggesting that Newdow might become "the most hated man in America" may be the ultimate marginalization. A June 27 report by CBS journalist John Blackstone included a quote by the Reverend Jerry Falwell that supported this reasoning: "It shows hostility towards people of faith, who constitute 96 percent of our population who believe in God" (Roberts, 2002b).

Blackstone did not question Falwell's extreme conservatism and intolerance of anyone who does not agree with his views on God. In a later report, also by Blackstone, Falwell ran truer to form; the decision by the Ninth Circuit, he said, "does not offend everyone except those who have a chip on their shoulder against people of faith and God everywhere" (Chen, 2002). Falwell was there to represent the fundamentalists, to ensure that reporters offered viewers a "balanced" story.

Chung was unwilling to let Newdow explain that patriotism does not mean unthinking devotion to the flag, or to America. Chung quickly ended this strand of dialogue, and moved on to Newdow's efforts to remove references to God from money and from "God Bless America."

Reporters would later suggest that Newdow brought the backlash to the ruling on himself. After all, he was, as one reporter suggested, fixated on "savoring" his victory (Mann, 2002). Several journalists suggested that Newdow filed the suit solely to attract attention to himself. "Across the country today, many blamed Newdow for imposing his views on everybody else," said *CBS Evening News* reporter John Blackstone (Roberts, 2002a). But soon, Newdow's work would be made easier by the trappings of celebrity. James Hattori of CNN began a June 28 report about Newdow this way: he "opens his own limo door when the networks fetch him for the morning TV talk shows. All of a sudden this emergency room physician, who happens to have a law degree and is working on a master's in public health, is the focus of international attention" (Costello, 2002a).

Journalists quantified reaction to the Ninth Circuit's ruling by focusing on the hatred and disgust expressed by some toward Newdow and the Ninth Circuit's ruling. This tendency took the form in their stories of angry messages left on Newdow's home answering machine. Newdow invited reporters to use messages in their stories. Consider this excerpt from a story by NBC News reporter George Lewis (Brokaw, 2002b):

> LEWIS: Since the court's ruling yesterday on the Pledge, Newdow has moved his daughter to an undisclosed location as angry, threatening messages pile up on his answering machine. Today, he played some of those messages for reporters.
> UNIDENTIFIED WOMAN: You (unintelligible) communist bastard.
> UNIDENTIFIED MAN #1: Shame on you. Shame on you.

> UNIDENTIFIED MAN #2: I'm going to be in your neighborhood today and I'm going to look you up and I'm going to beat your (word censored by station).

Instead of exploring further the depths of their anger, or perhaps expressing at least some concern for Newdow's safety, Lewis turned quickly to a member of the Elk Grove School District, who continued the theme of disbelief at the Ninth Circuit's ruling: "Never in my life did I ever think I would see a headline that said that the Pledge of Allegiance was unconstitutional" (Brokaw, 2002b). Elk Grove superintendent David Gordon, perhaps unknowingly fueling the journalist's love of conflict, said that while Newdow should be able to challenge something he believes to be unconstitutional, "we get, in return, to fight him in court."

CNN ran similar comments from those opposed to Newdow. A reporter for a CNN affiliate said that the calls came from "people who think he is wrong and ought to change his ways" (Costello, 2002b). The final quote was quite angry: "Michael, what in the hell is wrong with you, you dumb son of a bitch (deleted by CNN). I say, you're a dead man walking, man. Somebody is going to kill you, not me, but somebody will." A colleague noted the powerful irony of defenders of Christianity using obscene language and making death threats.

Thus, Newdow's impact was diminished by the suggestion that he was under siege, and by questions about whether he had gone into hiding as a result of the backlash to his suit. How could he sustain his challenge to the Pledge if he was too busy fending off death threats? "He is fearful for his daughter, who is 8 years old," reported CNN's James Hattori. "She, I believe, is no longer in the area, and he is taking those threats very seriously, more so for her than his own personal safety" (Costello, 2002b). Despite Newdow's repeated assertions that he was trying to keep his daughter out of the media spotlight, reporters could not resist playing armchair psychologist. The controversy may not center on her, suggested CBS anchor Josh Binswanger (2002), "but unfortunately, by association, they can be drawn into situations like this."

Conclusions

Instead of trying to encourage intelligent debate on the issues raised in Newdow's suit, journalists reduced his challenge and the Ninth Circuit's decision to an opportunity for jingoistic chest-thumping and pathological name-calling. It should be noted that Newdow claims that he was not pushing for the elimination of the Pledge, nor was he attacking anyone else's patriotism. "I think that the ultimate in patriotism is upholding the Constitution," he told a CBS news anchor (Clayson, 2002). Newdow claimed that he wanted to "strengthen the Constitution" (Couric, 2002).

The conduct of reporters is eerily similar to their conduct as they covered Japanese-Americans during the days after Pearl Harbor. Only here, Newdow did not get the chance to prove his patriotism before the news media began to marginalize him. He was forced to defend his patriotism, and watch as journalists for the most part ignored that defense. And while the journalists I spoke to about the case insist that Newdow's atheism did not color their reporting on Newdow, it seems like he was the wrong nonconformist at the wrong place at the wrong time, to paraphrase 2004 presidential candidate John Kerry. We'll explore this further in the next chapter.

Broadcast journalists, now firmly entrenched in the "guard dog's" role, were defending America's honor. Newdow was now the embodiment of our most recent spate of manufactured post–9/11 fear. Journalists made an example of Newdow—"He's a guitar picking, harmonica playing atheist," noted CNN's James Hattori (Costello, 2002b)—and suggested that he was reckless, selfish, and starved for publicity. Journalists had, for the moment, cleared the perimeter, so to speak, of threats to our values, and to the government's position on the Ninth Circuit ruling. They had also boiled down some fairly complex constitutional arguments into a simple narrative: "Newdow bad, Pledge good. Atheism bad, Christianity good." These reporters treated atheism as deviant behavior, while failing to acknowledge the zealousness that produced some of the bizarre reactions to the Ninth Circuit's ruling. Missing was even a passing acknowledgment that freedom of religion does in fact mean freedom *from* religion. Journalists rarely take issue with individuals in this country who choose to fervently worship God. As a former newspaper editor, I instructed my reporters that it was our obligation as journalists to cover religion as an important social issue, but not in a way that excluded those who might not practice religion, or who might not believe in God.

Chapter 5

Their Own Little World

In this chapter, I turn our attention to these questions: Did print journalists provide a more accurate, less inflammatory picture of Newdow? Did they leap as readily as their broadcast colleagues into the role of "guard dog?" What central storylines emerged from their coverage of the controversy? Did print reporters go beyond simply portraying Newdow as a *scapegoat*? Did they continue to use the frames discussed in chapter 3 (holy war, hands over hearts, still under attack, ceremonial deism, and outside the mainstream)? Did new frames emerge?

Holy War

Like broadcast journalists, print reporters struggled to make sense of the Ninth Circuit's ruling, at least in part because Newdow snuck up on them. One reporter whom I interviewed recalled writing a profile of Newdow that focused on family law claims in his suit, but for the most part, print reporters did not see "a significant legal controversy" (B. Egelko, e-mail interview, June 27, 2004) until the Ninth Circuit ruled on June 26, 2002. This may explain why print coverage of the decision, while much more detailed than broadcast coverage, still suffered from some of the misconceptions discussed earlier. For example, Evelyn Nieves (2002a) of the *New York Times* wrote on June 27 that the decision came from "the nation's most liberal appeals court," which we've learned isn't exactly accurate.

Rather than suggest that Newdow's claims might have merit, Nieves, like many of her colleagues, assured readers that the ruling "will certainly be appealed." And consider the *Times* headline: "Judges Ban Pledge of

Allegiance From Schools, Citing 'Under God.'" This reads like the court had created an instant educational crisis in the nation's schools. It is not an accurate characterization of the court's ruling, as Judge Goodwin pointed out in an interview. Framing the story in this way also creates a smokescreen for the real problems plaguing public schools: lack of funding and overemphasis on testing, just to name two.

To be fair, the urgency in the *Times* headline comes from the realization by journalists that Newdow's victory was now a significant news story—a "big deal," in the words of a reporter for the *San Francisco Chronicle* (B. Egelko, personal interview, July 1, 2004). Warren Richey (2004), a reporter for the *Christian Science Monitor*, said his coverage of the suit began once it became clear that the Supreme Court might take the case. Claire Cooper of the *Sacramento Bee*, the newspaper that serves Newdow's hometown and Elk Grove, California, said the Ninth Circuit's ruling "might have been the lead story even if the parties were from Timbuktu" (e-mail interview, July 2, 2004).

And when journalists made this determination, they began to frame the story as a conflict between Newdow and angry public officials devoted to protecting American citizens from his dangerous intrusion into their lives. The conflict did not quite reach the level of a "holy war," as was seen in early broadcast coverage, but Newdow's victory was cast as a struggle to sustain America's values. And there were tinges of anticipated feelings of victimization on the part of Christian conservatives. Lyle Denniston of the *Boston Globe* observed that the Ninth Circuit's ruling "is expected to open a new front in the ongoing cultural war over religious expressions in public life" (2002, p. A2).

USA Today quoted Reverend Louis Sheldon, who heads the Traditional Values Coalition, a conservative Christian lobbying group, as saying that if the Pledge is unconstitutional, "so then also is the Declaration of Independence. It has many references to God and the Scriptures" (Vanden Brook, 2002, p. 4A). The *New York Times*' Nieves quoted a law professor who said the Ninth Circuit panel had issued "a well-reasoned opinion that is certain to enrage the Christian right" (2002a, p. A1). But there was not the sense of the helplessness that marked early broadcast coverage, especially the coverage provided by CNN. Instead, Nieves, like most of her print colleagues, focused on the range of reaction to the ruling.

Negative reaction to the ruling was swift, and came from folks "across the political spectrum" (Nieves, 2002a, p. A1). We learned that the Ninth Circuit's ruling was both "stunning" ("Appeals Court Rules," 2002) and "baffling" (Hayward, 2002, p. 6; Holland, 2002) to the nation's politicians. It unleashed "a flurry of denunciations by public figures" (Dolan, 2002, p. A1). Jerry Falwell called the ruling "appalling" (Nieves, 2002a, p. A20). Some even "thumbed their noses" (Chase, 2002) at the ruling. Those critical of the ruling were "flabbergasted" (Hayward, 2002, p. 6; Hulse, 2002). Others "denounced" (Brassfield, 2002, p. 1A) the opinion.

Missouri senator Kit Bond called it "the worst kind of political correctness run amok" (Kasindorf, 2002, p. 1A). Two *San Francisco Chronicle* reporters said the impact of the ruling was felt "from the G-8 summit (in Canada, where President Bush was when the ruling came down) to suburban Sacramento." You would have thought the Ninth Circuit panel "had banned apple pie, motherhood, and Chevrolets all at once" (Salladay & Coile, 2002, p. A1). The *Cleveland Plain Dealer* called the decision "a triumph of foolishness" ("God and the Pledge," 2002, p. H2).

At stake were all religious references—from the recitation of "so help me God" in the presidential inaugural oath to the song "God Bless America." Unlike their broadcast colleagues, who looked for assurances from their sources that Newdow would not succeed as he continued his quest, print reporters enabled our elected leaders to reassure citizens that decisive action would be taken. There was no need for print journalists to ask Newdow about how far he would go, as several broadcast journalists had. Even staunch liberals like Senator Edward Kennedy had questions about the ruling: "It is not clear to me that the 'under God' phrase of the Pledge of Allegiance violates our freedom of religion" (Hayward, 2002, p. 6).

Whatever its ideological flavor, reporters writing in the days after the decision all tended to support one major assertion: the Pledge "as local school children [*sic*] know it is not going anywhere, at least for now" (Eaton, 2002, p. A1). There was no time for panic, even if panic was the furthest thing from the minds of readers. The nation had several months to get its ideological act together before the ruling took effect. This would "allow for appeals that are sure to come," wrote Debera Harrell and Margo Horner (2002, p. A1) in the *Seattle Post-Intelligencer*.

Reporters described nearly universal support for keeping the Pledge as it is. After nearly a year of commiseration about the 9/11 attacks, we were pissed off. It was time to take a stand. We had, in the words of *Los Angeles* Times columnist Steve Lopez, rediscovered "our sense of national purpose" (2002, sec. 2, p. 1). We would continue to say the Pledge—with the allegedly offending words. "I think the general feeling is to continue to say the Pledge," said a school district official. "Looking at our general population, just about everybody believes in God." Said a school official from a neighboring district: "In these times, it's ludicrous to argue about semantics" (Eaton, 2002, p. A1).

Reporters suggested that we were not going to allow activist judges to attack the Pledge—even though they had not, in this case, struck down the entire thing—and put our children in the same atheistic boat as children in the states served by the Ninth Circuit. Reporters gave us more than ample space to display our patriotism. "This isn't about liberal or conservative but being American," said a disabled Vietnam veteran interviewed by Harrell and Horner (2002, p. A1).

"This decision does not sit well with the American people," said former presidential press secretary Ari Fleischer in his first postdecision interview (Holland, 2002). Fleischer was probably correct, but not a single reporter asked him to verify his assessment. A Vietnam veteran told two *Seattle Post-Intelligencer* reporters that he was "all for personal freedom, but let's get reasonable—this is getting out of hand. I think this would cause a serious backlash among the majority of people in this county" (Harrell & Horner, 2002, p. A1).

At least a special education teacher in Minnesota tried a more scientific approach. He circulated a petition to support the Pledge ("Appeals Court Rules," 2002) and found that "[o]ne hundred percent of the people I've talked to were against the court ruling that came down today." But much of the time, readers had to be satisfied with vague reads on public opinion, like this one from the legislative director for the Christian Coalition of America: "the ordinary man on the street is just not going to understand this, especially after Sept. 11" (Vanden Brook, 2002, p. 4A). And this from the *San Diego Union-Tribune*: "we suspect most Americans—religious and not so—find the appeals court's ruling too extreme to their liking" ("Insult to All," 2002, p. B-12).

We were told that this threat to our governmental and ideological structure was serious, but it would inevitably be quashed. Reporters looked to the Supreme Court for guidance. The high court had noted on several occasions that the Pledge was constitutional, and was not an endorsement of religion. We would be fine. Most of the experts interviewed by reporters expressed their firm belief that the Supreme Court would step in and right the ship. "I'm quite confident it's going to be reversed," said a University of California law professor (Egelko, 2004b, p. A1).

Reporters could have explored the shock of public officials a bit more extensively—after all, Establishment Clause cases are not exceedingly rare. But journalists rarely looked behind the "autopilot" nature of this shock. The Supreme Court has issued a number of significant church–state rulings in the last decade, but has only indirectly commented on the Pledge. And while these early stories identified Newdow, and discussed his main claim, he was seen as being on the defensive—caught up in a "media storm" of his own creation. But he claimed that he did not intend to "provoke a national furor," as he told one Associated Press reporter. "Many people who are upset about this are people who just don't understand" (Frith, 2002). Reporters writing the day after the decision tended to boil down Newdow's arguments to: "People have to consider what if they were in the minority religion and the majority religion was overpowering them" and "Congress never intended to force people to worship a religion that they don't believe in" (Frith, 2002).

Hands Over Hearts

Soon, people were knocking each other over in our legislative halls to recite the Pledge, motivated by the inaccurate idea that schoolchildren could never again say the Pledge. They were carried by the "patriotic fury" unleashed after the Ninth Circuit's ruling ("Court Rules," 2002, p. A1). School officials in Texas, whose state was not affected by the opinion, promised that the Ninth Circuit's action would not "block recitation of the hand-over-heart exercise at schools and public meetings" (Eaton, 2002, p. A1). Legislators in Delaware even kicked around the idea of starting impeachment proceedings against the Ninth Circuit panel.

Veteran senator Robert Byrd, a Democrat from West Virginia, even threatened to withhold a promotion from Judge Goodwin: "I hope his name never comes before this body for any promotion, because he will be remembered," Senator Byrd told the Associated Press (Holland, 2002). Members of Congress tried to outdenigrate each other. "There may have been a more senseless, ridiculous decision issued by a court at some time, but I don't remember it," said Connecticut senator Joseph Lieberman in a *San Diego Union-Tribune* editorial ("Insult to All," 2002, p. B-12).

Opponents of the ruling were given ample room to bluster and fulminate about the decision. Ed Hayward of the *Boston Herald* led his June 27, 2002, story by telling readers that the Ninth Circuit's ruling was a shock to "Constitution experts and patriotic parents alike." What about the folks who don't belong to either of those groups? Are these the only people who get to register an opinion about the moral direction of the country? Several states had taken, or were preparing to take, decisive steps to counter the Ninth Circuit's ruling. A city council member from the state of Washington said the body would ignore the decision altogether—"and if someone doesn't agree, they can step outside the chambers during that part of the agenda," warned reporters from the *Seattle Post-Intelligencer* (Harrell & Horner, 2002, p. A1). A California state legislator, Mike Briggs, said he would ask Congress to bring impeachment proceedings against Judges Goodwin and Reinhardt (Olvera & Leddy,

2002, p. A1). A month before the June 26 decision, Virginia governor Mark Warner signed into law a bill that required every school in the state to display a poster with the words "In God We Trust, the National Motto, enacted in 1956" on it (Helderman & Samuels, 2002, p. B1). Sure that the Ninth Circuit would be reversed, school officials were ready to begin hanging the posters. "Unless something comes down the pipe that tells us to do differently, we'll go ahead and do it," said one official quoted by the *Washington Post* (Helderman & Samuels, 2002, p. B1).

Print reporters highlighted the decisive action taken by Congress and state officials: immediate passage of Senate and House resolutions "denouncing" (Holland, 2002) the Ninth Circuit's ruling—with members of the Senate voting from their desks (a rare occurrence); the call by Senators Joseph Lieberman and John Warner for a constitutional amendment that would guarantee "under God" would stay in the Pledge ("Let's not wait for the Supreme Court to act on this," said Warner [Holland, 2002]); and reassurances by leaders in many states—including, ironically, states that were not affected by the Ninth Circuit's ruling—that the decision by a bunch of West Coast liberals would not get in the way of saying the Pledge in their public schools and at public meetings. The ruling was "outrageous and reprehensible," said Texas governor Rick Perry in a statement quoted by the *Corpus Christi Times*. "Though not applicable in Texas, I still hope it is appealed to the U.S. Supreme Court and overturned quickly" (Eaton, 2002, p. A1).

Colorado officials were a bit kinder, and reminded readers of the *Rocky Mountain News* that schoolchildren were not required under state law (at the time) to recite the Pledge. Still, they were "bracing for the case to be taken to the Supreme Court" (Gutierrez, 2002, p. 46A). A day later, the state's attorney general announced he would join the appeal of the ruling. "The pledge [*sic*] is a ceremonial procedure; it's not an improper promotion of religion," said a state deputy attorney general (Mooney, 2002, p. A2). Meanwhile, legislators in other states would have to be content with introducing, or breathing new life into, bills that would require students to say the pledge. Said a Missouri legislator, "I think my bill is even more important now. It is important as symbolism and it is important as substance" ("Court Rules," 2002, p. A1).

So even where there was no tangible impact, it was still somehow felt. Our patriotism would see us through what was largely a manufactured crisis. The system, as Jamieson and Waldman (2003) would argue, would somehow recover. After all, as Lloyd Neal, the mayor of Corpus Christi, Texas, told a reporter, "I think we as a nation believe in God. Whether that God is the same person we all worship is not important" (Eaton, 2002, p. A1). The government was on the case. On June 27, John

Ashcroft announced the Department of Justice challenge to the Pledge, saying "The Justice Department will defend the ability of our nation's children to pledge allegiance to the American flag" (Liptak, 2002, p. A14; Von Drehle, 2002, p. A6). Ashcroft was joined by ousted California governor Gray Davis, who said he was "personally offended" by the ruling, and had directed lawyers for the state to "take decisive action to overturn" it, as if it were that simple. But decisive action is what we apparently were demanding: "This issue is not over legally, politically, or emotionally for many citizens," said Washington attorney general Christine Gregoire (Harrell & Horner, 2002, p. A1). Our hope lay with the Supreme Court, which would certainly take the case, since it rules on appeals from the federal government about three-quarters of the time, noted Ken Foskett (2002, p. 1A).

Still Under Attack

Our public officials would not stand idly by and let the Pledge be attacked. "Now more than ever," said a GOP official, "Americans feel a longing to rally around the flag" (Harrell & Horner, 2002, p. A1). In the months between the 9/11 attacks and the Ninth Circuit's ruling, Newdow's suit had been transformed from an example "of the kind of minor pique that a lazy, litigious society had the leisure to entertain" to an unwelcome burst of "aggressive atheism" for which "an angry, sorrowful public" had no patience ("A Higher Authority," 2002, p. N4).

Commenting on the Ninth Circuit's decision, a GOP official from the state of Washington said that "the timing couldn't have been worse. We're about to celebrate our first Independence Day since the Sept. 11 attacks" (Harrell & Horner, 2002, p. 1). The presence of troops in Iraq added to the sense of urgency. The Pledge is even more important "at a time when our troops are overseas in harm's way and our nation is under attack," said a member of Congress from New York (Hulse, 2002, p. 27). The mayor of Corpus Christi, Texas, said that the presence of God in the Pledge "shows the rest of the world that America is united and answers to a higher power, and that is especially important as the nation continues its war on terrorism" (Eaton, 2002, p. A1).

Even that ethical stalwart, former House majority leader Tom DeLay, chimed in: "It is sad at a time when our nation is coming together, this court is driving a wedge between us with their absurd ruling" (Jackson, 2002, p. A23). The Senate voted unanimously—"with what was lightning speed for their chamber"—to oppose the decision and to authorize the Senate counsel to intervene (Hulse, 2002). Senators would stand and recite the Pledge, bowing their heads as they uttered the words, "one nation under God."

The House of Representatives would quickly follow, voting 416–3 on June 27, to approve a resolution harshly criticizing the Ninth Circuit ruling. Then Senate minority leader Tom Daschle, who called the decision "just nuts," said that God was helping the nation heal, if slowly, from the 9/11 attacks. "We have been drawn together in the face of tremendous tragedy in the last nine months and in part that healing process has come by our belief in a supreme being," Daschle said in the third paragraph of a *New York Times* story by Carl Hulse (2002). And there was no way, suggested Foskett, that the Supreme Court would rule the Pledge unconstitutional "especially after the patriotic fervor across the nation since the Sept. 11 terrorist attacks" (2002, p. 1A).

I'm no legal scholar, but I'm sure that "patriotic fervor" isn't (or shouldn't be) on the list of criteria followed by Supreme Court justices when they consider cases. Such is the kind of comment that passed for perspective in the days after the Ninth Circuit's ruling—and it raises a key point: the court did not declare the Pledge unconstitutional—no matter what the president, Tom DeLay, and members of Congress claim. As Judge Goodwin pointed out in a June 30, 2005, e-mail, writing that the Pledge was in danger was a better fit for "bumper strip" headlines.

> It was several days before the print media began to explain what the court had decided, that a state supported educational system could not, consistently with the federal Constitution, compel children to participate in a patriotic exercise that included the assertion that theirs was "one nation, under God, indivisible."

Meanwhile, everything that had God in it—from our money to our "most treasured patriotic songs" (Dolan, 2002, p. A1) had been rendered "vulnerable" by the Ninth Circuit's ruling. "And what about that oppressive song 'God Bless America' that the entire Congress sang on government property after Sept. 11?" asked a *Los Angeles Times* editorial. "Then there's the problem of U.S. currency, which may now be unconstitutional because it says, 'In God We Trust.'" The paper called for an appeal to "come swiftly. God willing, it will" ("A Godforsaken Ruling," 2002, p. 14).

It was not clear who members of Congress believed was masterminding this new attack. Some Senate republicans were quick to point out that this kind of liberal decision is what the nation gets when the government appoints activist judges. Journalists allowed them to test their arguments, crafted to resemble concern for the Pledge. "This highlights what the fight over federal judges is all about," Mississippi senator Trent Lott told the *Times*. Lott reminded readers that Democrats were responsible for putting judges like Goodwin on the federal appellate bench. "We do need to put judges on there that wouldn't render this kind of decision," he said. President Bush also weighed in: the decision "points up the fact that we need common-sense [*sic*] judges who understand that our rights were derived from God" (Von Drehle, 2002, p. A6; see also Dolan & Gerstanzang, 2002, p. A1).

So we (or our elected leaders) were not being narrow-minded or overreacting out of needless fear; it was the fault of those darned activist judges—judges who would continue to write "goofy" opinions, in the words of one conservative activist, if congressional democrats "keep bottling up the President's nominations of dozens of judicial appointments" (Von Drehle, 2002, p. A6). Journalists at first did not comment on this spurt of political opportunism. "The American people have not lost their way. Some of our judges have," Senator Joseph Lieberman told the *San Francisco Chronicle* (Epstein, May, & Kim, 2002, p. A12).

Republican antipathy toward alleged Democratic obstructionism even found its way into a memo issued by a Republican campaign organization and sent to the nation's school boards in which the group urged school officials to ignore the Ninth Circuit's ruling. The memo also conveniently reminded these officials that Senator Daschle and his Democratic cohorts were blocking President Bush's judicial nominees (Hulse, 2002).

Ceremonial Deism

The core of the Elk Grove School District's argument was that the Pledge of Allegiance was an affirmation of patriotism, not an endorsement of religion, and that the Pledge serves a legitimate secular purpose, as suggested by Justice William Brennan—"a noted liberal," as one newspaper pointed out ("God and Country," 2002, p. A14). It is, in short, an example of "ceremonial deism"—a patriotic ceremony (see "God and Country," 2002, p. A14). The words "under God" carry "a very generic kind of meaning that is intended to encompass all kinds of beliefs" (Salladay & Coile, 2002, p. A1).

Print reporters, like their broadcast colleagues, accepted this frame, almost without exception. In the first *New York Times* story about the ruling, Nieves (2002a) noted that liberal Supreme Court justices had found that references to God, like "In God We Trust," had lost their religious flavor after decades of repetition. The *Times* called the reference to

God "a rote civic exercise" ("One Nation," 2002, p. A28) in a June 27 editorial, but one still imbued with immense symbolic force. America "never forgets that there is a 'supreme judge of the world' . . . who holds men and women responsible for their deeds. To them, awareness of God was not optional—not if American liberty and republican government were to succeed," wrote Jeff Jacoby (2002, p. A11) in the *Boston Globe*.

Several reporters (e.g., Egelko, 2002a, p. A1) quoted Ari Fleischer, then the president's press secretary, as saying the ruling was "ridiculous," and that our day-to-day secular life—and the lives of public officials—is replete with benign religious references—from "In God We Trust" on our money to several references to God in the Declaration of Independence to the Supreme Court ritual of starting each session by saying "God save the United States and this honorable court."

Then attorney general John Ashcroft, whose Department of Justice would on June 27 mount a legal challenge to the ruling, said the Ninth Circuit's decision was clearly "contrary to two centuries of American tradition" (Denniston, 2002, p. A2; Egelko, 2002a, p. A1). All of these references "have long been an integral part of everyday American life—honest to God," quipped an editorial writer for the *Los Angeles Times* ("A Godforsaken Ruling," 2002, p. 14). For more than a half century, Americans have recited the Pledge "with few, if any, enforcement problems over which words someone mumbles, or skips."

A key theme offered by government officials and fitted by reporters within this frame is the suggestion made by a few reporters that Newdow's motivations were superficial. "We can't take a radical sense of discomfort so far that we prevent any legitimate and reasonable broad expression of religion in the public square," said Matthew Spalding, director of the Center for American Studies, an organization sponsored by the conservative Heritage Foundation (Adams, 2002, p. A3).

In the majority of cases, reporters simply missed the point: Newdow didn't want to do away with the Pledge, just the reference to God *in* the Pledge. Few reporters caught the nuance (e.g., "Taking the Pledge," 2002, p. C12). This is to be expected when the goal is to protect "our civic religion," as a *Pittsburgh Post-Gazette* editorial explained. "Without it, our society has no philosophical underpinnings" ("A Higher Authority," 2002, p. N4).

School officials would do their best to make sure that these underpinnings were sustained. Like their broadcast colleagues, print reporters brought readers numerous examples of schools where students and their teachers bravely continued to recite the Pledge in the face of the threat posed by Newdow. Their parents, for the most part, supported the government's read on the Ninth Circuit's decision. At first, the ruling confused school officials. "I'm kind of dumbfounded," said a California schools superintendent. "To me, the Pledge isn't about God, it's about patriotism." A few school officials said the Pledge had "fallen out of fashion" (Epstein et al., 2002, p. A12), but reporters reassured readers that in most districts, the Pledge was alive and well. Students could decide not to recite it, and it was up to teachers (but not in all districts) to decide if recitation would be part of their morning routines. "It's not like (saying the pledge [*sic*]) is a graded activity," said a Colorado school district spokesperson. "If students want to stand up and say nothing, it's their prerogative" (Mooney, 2002, p. A2).

For every description of discretion, reporters offered rousing displays of patriotism. From the *Los Angeles Times* (Gold, 2002, p. A1): "With as much pomp and circumstance as can be mustered at a sixth-grade graduation, the children strode into the gym. The youngster in the Fat Albert shirt smiled as proudly as the girl in the Mary Janes. Parents bent their necks like flamingoes for the perfect snapshot." When the crowd rose to recite the Pledge, Scott Gold wrote, "a little slice of Americana turned into a big slab of patriotism."

Students would not sit by and allow the Pledge to be taken from them. "Kenny Carson never thought a national debate would be waged over words he and other students learned before they could read or write," wrote Javier Olvera and Matt Leedy in the *Fresno Bee* (2002, p. A1). Since 9/11, Kenny and his classmates have put "more heart into" their recitation of the Pledge, held near their school's flagpole. "If you don't believe in our God, you can stop right before you say the word and insert the name of who you believe in," Kenny told the reporters. "There's no reason it needs to be changed"—especially when journalists framed it as the most compelling example of *ceremonial deism*. "I think it shows that you love America," said another student. Saying the Pledge made her think "that it's great to be an American. It shows our country is strong and American can last forever."

Outside the Mainstream—A Lonely Quest

Print reporters reminded readers of the Ninth Circuit's alleged liberal streak, and reassured readers that the Supreme Court would almost certainly rule to keep "under God" in the Pledge. But reporters took the *outside the mainstream* frame in a slightly different direction by isolating Newdow and the Ninth Circuit. In their coverage, they secured places for Newdow and the court in the "Sphere of Deviance" suggested by Daniel Hallin (1986). The court shared a place on the margins with Newdow; one reporter (Egelko, 2002a, p. A1) wrote that the Ninth Circuit "was something of an outsider in the judicial community." Perhaps a better name for this frame, then, comes from the unsuccessful Kerry–Edwards 2004 presidential campaign: *Help is on the way*—in this case, to correct a ruling written by what Senator Robert Byrd called an "atheist lawyer" (Holland, 2002). A Tennessee lawmaker told the *Chattanooga Times* that he would "eagerly await the scathing opinions that will come from the Supreme Court putting those judges back in their place" (Riddell, 2002, p. A1).

A GOP official quoted in a *Seattle Post-Intelligencer* story took on the whole panel; he called the ruling "a typical piece of liberal absurdity from the Ninth Circuit Court" (Harrell & Horner, 2002, p. A1). Yes, this is the court that often decides to rule on cases that "tend to challenge the status quo" (Adams, 2002, p. A3), and when it does rule, it typically makes "liberal, activist opinions" that are part of a "serious, anti-religious trend in the courts" (Epstein et al., 2002, p. A12).

The court has, claimed a *San Diego Union Tribune* editorial, "issued any number of outrageous rulings over the years" ("Insult to All," 2002, p. B-12). It was also suggested that they were lousy judges, too: a New York reporter wrote that the judges "failed to use common sense, much less consult what previous legal minds had to say on the subject, before issuing this wrongheaded ruling" ("God and Country," 2002, p. A14). Not to mention self-absorbed—they ruled for Newdow "first to draw attention to themselves and second to appease iconoclasts who like nothing better than tearing down our cherished patriotic traditions" (Canfield, 2002, p. B3).

Several reporters quoted well-known Harvard law professor Laurence Tribe to bolster this point. Tribe colorfully predicted a Supreme Court reversal. "I would bet an awful lot on that," he told one reporter ("Appeals Court Rules," 2002). There was no chance that the Ninth Circuit would be upheld: "I think the odds of that are about as great as an asteroid hitting Los Angeles tomorrow," he said (Dolan, 2002, p. A1). He dipped into the well of ceremonial deism to suggest that Supreme Court justices would "conclude that it's OK to pledge to 'one nation under God,' just as it is OK to begin their own sessions with 'Oye, oye, oye, God save the United States and this honorable court'" (Hayward, 2002, p. 6). Tribe's penchant for compelling quotes underscores the tendency of reporters to rely on familiar sources who are able to speak fluent "sound bite." These impressions typically offer little in the way of real information.

The court's eccentricity was just a reflection of the state in which it is based, suggested journalists. "What are they smoking out there?" asked a New York truck driver in the lead of a *Los Angeles Times* story (Getlin, 2002, p. A1). "This is typical for San Francisco, isn't it?" he asked in the next paragraph. "These people live in their own little world." California was clearly out of step—not just on the Pledge issue—with the rest of the nation. After all, it's where all those liberal movie stars who voted for Kerry in 2004 hang out. It's no wonder that it produced "a loopy ruling from a liberal West Coast court." And check out this headline from *USA Today*: "Critics Say Court was 'California Dreaming'" (Vanden Brook, 2002, p. 4A).

The *Times* reporter then made an amazingly awkward—and in my mind bigoted—leap of logic. It's no surprise, he wrote, that the decision came from the San Francisco–based court—after all, it's "just across the bay from Marin County, home of John Walker Lindh, the American who fought for the Taliban" (Getlin, 2002, p. A1). And home to Congresswoman Barbara Lee, the only member of Congress to vote against authorizing President Bush to go to war in Iraq. Let me see if I have this right: San Francisco, once home to all those pot-smoking hippies, now is the source of a nascent national insurgency? And if a member of Congress votes their conscience, and actually thinks about what they're doing (unlike when they voted on the Patriot Act, which few legislators actually read), they're allied with Al-Qaeda?

Gauging the media's reaction to the Ninth Circuit's ruling, Getlin called on a conservative talk show host from Los Angeles, who said the ruling was not a surprise since it came from "the People's Republic of San Francisco" (2002, p. A1). Getlin didn't call on a single liberal radio or television personality to balance the story. They do exist, even if the liberal Air America radio network, launched in 2004, is struggling to build a national audience.

Print journalists provided a more detailed description than their broadcast counterparts of what happens after an appeals court rules. They do not, for example, take effect right away. The parties have 45 days (in civil cases where the federal government is a party) to ask for a rehearing. The ruling doesn't become law until seven days after this deadline. Officials from the Ninth Circuit said that the stay was Judge Goodwin's way of clarifying that the ruling was not yet enforceable, and that further action would not be taken in any event for 60 days.

That didn't stop reporters from sniping at the judge's bravery and his convictions. A *New York Daily News* reporter stated that the judge had "shelved" his "contentious" ruling (Bazinet, 2002, p. 6). The *Washington Post* reported that he had "pushed the 'pause' button" on the ruling by issuing the stay ("Taking the Pledge," 2002, p. C12). The *Post* suggested that Judge Goodwin had "blocked his own ruling" (Von Drehle, 2002, p. A6) in the face of heated criticism. Even though the decision "changed nothing," according to a court spokesperson quoted by several reporters (e.g., Dolan & Gerstanzang, 2002, p. A1), much of the reporting suggested that Judge Goodwin had withered in the face of "a second round of denunciations of the ruling."

Let's expand this frame to talk about how reporters (and those individuals quoted in their stories) described atheism. A Texas law professor quoted by a Corpus Christi reporter in a front-page newspaper story about the Newdow ruling noted that suits like Newdow's "have ripple effects either way. There are groups—they are called the Committee for the Separation of Church and State—that attempt to keep the government out of matters religious" (Eaton, 2002, p. A1). The professor's decision to ignore the Constitution aside, his comment suggests that support of the separation of church and state is somehow unpatriotic.

And even when reporters and their sources were trying to be nice to Newdow, it came across as marginalization. A reporter for the *St. Petersburg Times* (Brassfield, 2002, p. 1A) wrote that the Ninth Circuit ruling "cheered atheists, agnostics, and church-state separatists." We're not talking the Shining Path from Peru, or the ETA, the Basque separatist group—we're talking about citizens of the United States who choose not to believe in God, or who work to keep God out of the public schools. In late June 2002, *Time* magazine named Newdow its "Person of the Week," but only for his ability to distract the country from more serious issues—"things that have lasting impact, like the financial meltdown of WorldCom." Newdow—that "plucky atheist"—caused the nation to hope that we could return to a pre–9/11 America, "when we had nothing better to do than bicker over really critical issues like which politician is the most patriotic, or who has the biggest flag on the block" (Reaves, 2002).

If this is "nice" treatment, what did negative treatment look like? "[I]f Newdow thinks the nation's Pledge of Allegiance was humiliating to the child, imagine how she feels having a nitwit for a father" (Ruth, 2002, p. 2). This comes from a column, not from a "hard news" story. But it neatly exemplifies the tendency of reporters to suggest that Newdow had made himself a nuisance, even if he had done so merely by exercising his constitutional rights.

Reporters added another wrinkle to the *outside the mainstream* frame in the days after the Ninth Circuit's ruling: Newdow as *professional litigant*. This is an offshoot of the "frivolous lawsuits by avaricious lawyers are damaging American businesses and driving up the cost of health care by forcing doctors to close their practices" theme that permeated coverage of the 2004 election. In fact, businesses file most of what are considered "frivolous" lawsuits. But wicked lawyers and money-hungry plaintiffs make more compelling characters than a corporate lawyer.

Reporters respectfully noted that Newdow is an emergency room physician and holds a law degree from the University of Michigan. Their respect, however, was often tempered by the suggestion that he was putting his legal training to use by bothering the U.S. Government with needless lawsuits. "He said he hasn't worked recently and 'fights the government' as a profession," wrote a *Los Angeles Times* reporter (Dolan, 2002, p. A1). Two *Times* reporters led their June 27 story on Newdow this way (Gold & Bailey, 2002, p. A1): "First things first: Michael A. Newdow says he is not a nut. He's an eccentric, for sure, an emergency room physician by training who says he has given up working to 'fight the government,' an envelope-pushing free thinker who equates believing in God with believing in Santa Claus."

And Newdow isn't alone, suggested the *New York Daily News* in a June 27 editorial. After attacking the ruling as a wayward attempt by the court to "set comfort levels for our children," the editorial writer mused that even the presidential oath of office, which concludes, "so help me God," would become a target of what he called "fanatical civil libertarians." "Don't be surprised if they've got a lawsuit floating around somewhere. And they shouldn't be surprised when the U.S. Supreme Court tosses it out, as should be done with yesterday's stupefyingly silly appeals court decision" ("Somebody Bless," 2002, p. 42). A *Los Angeles Times* editorial was only slightly more kind to the court; it called the ruling "fundamentally silly" ("A Godforsaken Ruling," 2002, p. 14).

What about the death threats? They were, noted one reporter, "the price Newdow pays for getting a staple of American life declared unconstitutional" ("Pledge Challenger," 2002, p. 10A). Despite the threats, Newdow remained "defiant and unrepentant," as if what he had done was some kind of sin (Gold, 2002, p. A1). *Time* reported that he was "quite unmoved by the ire of his fellow citizens." He wasn't in this to enlighten or educate, as the *Time* reporter suggested: "And then, as if he knew precisely how to annoy his new enemies most, he mused on Thursday's *Today* show, 'I believe I am strengthening the Constitution with my case'" (Reaves, 2002).

When Newdow was not cast as an angry ideologue, reporters suggested that he was a selfish parent in search of a hobby. Newdow, wrote James Gill (2002, p. 7) of the *New Orleans Times-Picayune*, "must have too much time on his hands, for listening to kids recite the Pledge of Allegiance is a brief ordeal that is unlikely to cause an unbeliever's offspring any lasting psychic trauma." The *San Diego Union-Tribune* suggested that Newdow's suit was part of a movement toward "Burger King democracy," whose adherents "insist that they, and they alone, have a constitutional right to have things their way" (Rowe, 2002, p. E1).

An editorial in the *New York Daily News* chided the Ninth Circuit decision: "So, now we're using the courts to set comfort levels for children?" ("Somebody Bless," 2002, p. 42). Josh Getlin of the *New York Times* (2002, p. A1) interviewed a woman whose criticism of Newdow was a bit more muted: "We've been saying [the Pledge] all our lives, and then suddenly some guy out there is worried about his daughter being exposed to something. I mean, don't you think all this is a little precious?"

Several reporters also suggested that Newdow rather suddenly came to the realization that God was infiltrating our lives. "[W]hile waiting in the checkout line, he noticed that his currency included the phrase 'In God We Trust,' and became concerned that having those words on government-issued bills violated the Constitution" (Sanchez, 2002, p. A6). A Knight-Ridder reporter ("Pledge Challenger," 2002, p. 10A) characterized the "vision" incident a bit differently: "It all started when Newdow, an atheist, had an epiphany buying soap in Florida six years ago. He looked down to see 'In God We Trust' on his money, got offended and started filing lawsuits against the government for injecting religion into public life."

Even if Newdow's inspiration was that sudden, oversimplifying his inspiration speeds the marginalization process—and it's a more effective plotline for the master narrative about Newdow. "My money pissed me off one day" is far more compelling than a three-page discussion about the evolution of Establishment Clause law. Further, journalists noted only "muted" support for Newdow and the Ninth Circuit and "harsh" criticism of the ruling from a wide range of individuals, including the Reverend Jerry Falwell, not known for being a paragon of tolerance. Newdow's presence in the article amounted to four (out of 33) paragraphs—one mention placed above a one-column photo of Newdow "showing some of his court papers," as a *New York Times* caption read (Nieves, 2002a, p. A1). Newdow sat in front of a tub filled with papers, looking for all the world like a litigious person. The last three paragraphs detailed Newdow's fear for his safety. "I could be dead tomorrow," he said in the story's concluding paragraph.

Was that a legitimate point for the *Times* reporter to make? Yes. But it doesn't say a lot for our country that someone becomes the subject of death threats for expressing an opinion, no matter how outside the mainstream it may be. His daughter was "in a safe place" after the ruling, Newdow told the Associated Press (Frith, 2002). Ending the article this way strengthens the impression that Newdow is an outcast, an outlaw on the run. In fact, he stood his ground, and stayed at home, despite the threats.

The Ninth Circuit's decision was hailed by atheists, as reported by the *Seattle Post-Intelligencer* (the only newspaper to mention this reaction early in a story), but was "vilified" by most God-fearing citizens, which of course includes President Bush (Harrell & Horner, 2002, p. A1). In fact, quotes from groups like the American Civil Liberties Union (ACLU) and Americans United for Separation of Church and State (AU) were fairly hard to find in the first wave of stories about the opinion.

In many early stories, those in favor of the ruling were allotted a few paragraphs and a short quote or two. For example, the June 27 *St. Petersburg Times* story on the ruling limited support for the ruling to a few paragraphs—two from an AU chapter president, who said "I think it's great," and two (the last two) from a law professor who said he was not surprised by the opinion, and asked why the nation, which "claims to protect liberty, freedom, and equality, feel[s] the need to require a Pledge of Allegiance in the first place" (Brassfield, 2002, p. 1A). But you had to read the entire story to find this view.

Late in a story by the *Seattle Post-Intelligencer*, readers learned of efforts by the ACLU of Washington to assist students who are disciplined or harassed for not standing to salute the flag. The chapter convinced school officials to change the flag salute announcement, and to drop a requirement that parents give written permission before a student is allowed to opt out. Before reverting to a discussion of how the Ninth Circuit's ruling might impact communities—and plans by officials to ignore it—the *Post-Intelligencer* reporters reminded readers that the ACLU's efforts "reflect the sentiments of only a small slice of the population" (Harrell & Horner, 2002, p. A1).

Perhaps the subtlest element of this frame was the tendency of reporters to quote either a legal expert or Newdow, but rarely both in the same article, or in close proximity. They did quote several legal experts (often law school professors) who agreed with the ruling, but their quotes typically did not include a mention of Newdow. Connecting source and subject in this way would take a bit of rhetorical steam out of the "lonely quest" narrative that reporters had so busily constructed in the days after the opinion.

Many of the professors approached for comment by reporters said the Ninth Circuit's ruling was not a surprise. Eugene Volokh of the University of California–Los Angeles said that "the majority decision is actually a very plausible reading of the Supreme Court precedents" (Dolan, 2002, p. A1). The ruling made sense, given the Supreme Court's track record. "The courts have had the tendency to rule against forced, overt references to God," said Michael Gibbons of the University of South Florida (Brassfield, 2002, p. 1A). Experts (e.g., Egelko, 2002a, p. A1) often tempered their conclusions by predicting that, despite the Ninth Circuit's reasoned analysis, the Supreme Court would almost certainly overturn the decision. In an interview with the *Washington Post*, Volokh suggested that the push to redact the Pledge may have gone too far: "There is still a credible argument that at some point you have to stop trying to relentlessly extirpate religious symbolism from the life of a country that is after all very religious" (Lane, 2002, p. A1).

Newdow was given credit for being dogged, and for being so skilled at seeking the spotlight. He was rarely connected to the ruling and to the arguments raised by both sides. His mastery of the law in this area was barely acknowledged by reporters—perhaps because pro se plaintiffs rarely win, and because he in fact lost at the district court level. Despite his passionate arguments, he was portrayed as just a lonely guy who writes songs about keeping God out of civic life.

Pick Your Battles

A number of reporters, and many of their sources, suggested that other issues in the church–state pantheon—prayer in schools, for example—were more important than a Pledge challenge, and that Newdow might have damaged the efforts of civil liberties groups in these areas by so doggedly making his case. Nadine Strossen, the president of the ACLU, said she hoped Newdow would not press on, because she knew politicians of all ideological stripes would clamor for a constitutional amendment supporting the Pledge in its current form. Such an amendment would have "sailed through." This was energy better spent on other church–state related issues, she said.

Coverage of reaction to the ruling suggested that those happy with the Ninth Circuit's actions might have been distancing themselves from Newdow. Reactions from well-known civil liberties groups ranged from the elated ("I think it's great," [Brassfield, 2002, p. 1A] said the president of a Florida chapter of AU) to the cautious and pragmatic—and readers saw more of the latter tack.

The *Washington Post* noted that "even the ACLU was nearly silent on the subject, saying the decision was 'correct' and hastening to add that the ACLU had nothing to do with the lawsuit" (Von Drehle, 2002, p. A6). "They didn't strike down the Pledge of Allegiance," noted Joe Conn of AU. "All they said was that Congress made a mistake when they added God to the Pledge" (Nieves, 2002a, p. A1). The ACLU noted that the ruling was "correct and consistent with recent (U.S.) Supreme Court rulings invalidating prayer at school events" (Harrell & Horner, 2002, p. A1).

Stronger sentiment came from groups representing atheists—but still without inclusion of Newdow. "We finally got a court to agree [with] what every atheist has always known—that God is a religious term," said the president of Minnesota Atheists ("Appeals Court," 2002). The last three paragraphs of a *USA Today* story dismissively noted that the Ninth Circuit ruling "did have defenders," as if that was a surprise. The reporter quoted the president of American Atheists as saying she supported the ruling "100 percent" and that "government should stay out of the business of telling people whether or not they should acknowledge a particular deity" (Vanden Brook, 2002, p. 4A).

Reporters for the *Houston Chronicle* took a similar thematic path; after writing that the ruling "found a supporter" in a Texas-based watchdog group, the reporters quoted the head of that group as saying that the climate created by reaction to the ruling "will be used as a rallying point to revive support for school prayer" (Villafranca, Masterson, & Henry, 2002, p. A1). The head of an atheist group in the state of Washington was a bit more pragmatic in his assessment of the ruling: "I hate to say it, but I don't think to the average citizen it's going to make much of a difference" (Harrell & Horner, 2002, p. A1).

This signaled a new strand in the coverage: the arduous struggle still ahead of Newdow. An official for AU had kind words for the Ninth Circuit's ruling, but cautioned that Newdow faced "a tough road ahead" (2002, p. A1). The executive director of the Boston chapter of the American Jewish Committee told the *Boston Herald* that saying the Pledge "never made me feel comfortable," but that this was "one of those instances where you feel it is not right, but you don't take a stand. It's like a sacred cow. There are so many other issues of compelling interest" (Hayward, 2002, p. 6). Columnist Marc Fisher of the *Washington Post* (2002, p. B-1) suggested that "there are real church–state abuses that require the vigilance and courage of judges and lawmakers to police—displays of the Ten Commandments in schools and courthouses, mandatory moments of silence, assemblies at some D.C. public schools that still include Christian prayer."

Steve Lopez (2002, sec. 2, p. 1) of the *Los Angeles Times* made a broader "pick your battles" argument, saying "there are a dozen better reasons to scream and yell and march in the streets," including subpar schools and inadequate health care. The war in Iraq would be launched soon. "I can actually see us starting World War III in the fall without anyone noticing," he said. "We'll be too busy debating the inappropriateness of singing *God Bless America* at high school football games." The *St. Petersburg Times* urged us to move on: "once this judicial silliness is resolved, maybe we can get back to the real dangers that threaten our democracy and our constitutional rights" ("God Save," 2002, p. 18A). In a guest column published by *Newsday*, author Susan Jacoby, whose book *Freethinkers* (2004) is one of my inspirations for writing this book, expressed her wish that "a more substantive issue than the Pledge were responsible for reigniting the passions of the religiously correct" (2002, p. A41).

Conclusions

Print journalists tried to explain Newdow by focusing on his zeal and his eccentricities. They suggested that he must be crazy to take on the Pledge—just as Judge Goodwin was crazy to write such a clearly misguided opinion. Reporters created a significant disconnect between Newdow and the legal support for his ruling—as well as between the Ninth Circuit panel and our nation's other circuit courts. He was a man without a country—and was working without the complete support of the nation's civil liberties groups. They wanted to save their political ammunition for more significant fights.

And even though several reporters later chided politicians for their opportunistic reaction to the Pledge ruling, reporters reassured readers that they would act quickly to right this judicial wrong. In the meantime, the nation's students—God-fearing, patriotic students—would continue to proudly say the Pledge. Students who didn't feel this 9/11-induced rush of patriotism were free to "opt out"—and reporters left it at that, without exploring the reality in many classrooms that students are ostracized for expressing dissenting views. Instead of exploring Newdow's ideas in a more than cursory, comical fashion, or talking about his love for his daughter, reporters brushed Newdow off as a quirky fanatic—not the "warm, funny person" Strossen discovered when the two first met. Readers deserved a more complete picture of a person who turned the nation on its collective head by mustering the courage to challenge the Pledge of Allegiance.

CHAPTER 6

The Good Mother

Think for a moment about the stories you tell to explain events in your life to others. For example, when you're late for an important meeting with someone because you've been sitting in jammed traffic, you typically don't launch into a 20-minute discussion of traffic flow patterns or the level of federal and state funding for highway projects in your area—you talk about your anger, how lousy the drivers around you were (with vivid examples that may or may not include a middle finger directed at them), and how all of this conspired against you to make you late. You construct a narrative.

A narrative is made up of "symbolic actions—words or deeds—that have meaning for those who live, create, or interpret them" (Fisher, 1987, p. 58). As the author Joan Didion (1990, p. 1) observed, "[W]e tell ourselves stories in order to live." We use narratives to help us create a sense of order "on the flow of experience so that we can make sense of events and actions in our lives," as Sonja Foss points out (1996, p. 399). When trying to describe a significant other, you probably would not rely on a bullet-pointed list of the characteristics that you admire, or that attracted you. You'd probably share a story about that person. If someone asks me what drew me to my beautiful wife, I'd probably recall how we met at my brother- and sister-in law's Christmas party. I'd tell them about how my now brother-in-law was my roommate in college in the early 1980s, and how we hadn't kept in touch, and when we finally reconnected, I got the chance to meet my wife, who is his wife's sister. . . . OK, it needs a little editing. But it also says a lot about us.

A good story, says Foss (1996), "provides clues to the subjectivity of individuals and to the values and meanings that characterize a culture" (p. 401). Stories are structured so that the person hearing the story can pick out logical reasons for the actions of the participants—and learn something about the storyteller along the way. To keep a reader or listener interested, a story has to hang together, and it has to ring true. The accuracy of the story is less important. Sometimes stories are downright incorrect—and annoying, like some of the stories your parents or loved ones tell about you. You know the story is wrong, or missing some important facts, but you typically sit, listen, and laugh—even though at times you would like to throttle the storyteller. An effective, resonant story needs clearly drawn characters with which we can easily identify—or, in Michael Newdow's case, dislike and distrust. As described by reporters, Newdow was the ultimate outsider, the perfect antagonist.

To personalize the issues raised by Newdow, and to make a complex constitutional question accessible to their audience, journalists had to personify the thousands of students—and elected officials—who reflexively saluted the flag in the wake of the Ninth Circuit's ruling, threatened legal action against the judges who, in the eyes of our elected officials, had the unmitigated audacity to rule the presence of "under God" in the Pledge unconstitutional. They had to find a true protagonist, a "white hat"—a hero.

Newdow's daughter, while a compelling character, was only an abstract presence in the story to this point, thanks to Newdow's ongoing insistence that the case revolved around him. Reporters had successfully isolated him—moved him to Daniel Hallin's (1986) "sphere of deviance." But they still needed someone to sustain their version of the story so that we, in turn, would use it to understand the Newdow controversy.

That's where Sandra Banning, the mother of Newdow's daughter, comes in. She gained full legal custody of their daughter in February 2002. To get a better handle on Banning's evolving role in the narrative, we return briefly to a key issue in the case: standing. The Ninth Circuit panel ruled in June 2002 that Newdow had standing to bring suit on behalf of his daughter. The school district had unfairly usurped Newdow's right to guide his daughter in matters of religion, said the court. In the initial wave of coverage of the panel's ruling, the standing issue received scant attention. It wasn't until July 1, 2002, that Evelyn Nieves of the *New York Times* pointed out that changing the Pledge "is hardly Mr. Newdow's only preoccupation" (2002b, p. A8). "More than anything," Nieves wrote, "Mr. Newdow, a father in the throes of a custody dispute, would like to change family law."

The Lonely Quest Continues

Nieves (2002b) highlighted Newdow's zealous pursuit of changes both to the Pledge and to the family law system. "Television reporters still looking for sound bites on the Pledge would be well advised to steer clear of asking about his real obsession," Nieves wrote. Rather than portray Newdow as a potentially effective advocate for family law reform, Nieves suggested that even the mere mention of the topic "raises his blood pressure, turns his words into angry jumble and makes him late for appointments" (p. A8). This is no surprise, given his "boundless appetite for legal challenges over the separation of church and state," as a *Sacramento Bee* editorial writer noted in October 2002 ("Leave the Kid Alone," 2002, p. E4).

Newdow claims that in the days after the decision, he practically begged reporters from various news media outlets to explore the injustices he experienced while losing custody of his daughter to Banning. His entreaties continued all the way to the steps of the Supreme Court, where he again asked someone—anyone—to look into a family law system that is, in his words, "completely inept, wrong, harmful." Newdow contended that the media's extensive exploration of the Establishment Clause issue might have caused him to lose what was, at its core, the extensive outgrowth of a fierce custody battle (personal interview, July 28, 2004).

Nieves (2002b) allowed Newdow to harshly criticize the news media's failure to cover the family court issue, but not to build a sound argument: "You want to do a real story? Do it on the family courts. They steal people's children based on absolutely nothing. They take the most important people in a child's life and make them go away," Newdow said. He ended the quote with "Do I sound passionate?" (p. A8).

This approach adds to the impression of Newdow as an inflexible zealot prone to rants, and at the same time makes him sound vain, as if he was constantly checking how well his arguments were playing with reporters. This impression is reinforced by the headline to Nieves's story: "'Under God' Iconoclast Looks to Next Targets" (2002b, p. A8). He's indefatigable, always on the lookout for another lawsuit and the chance to talk about it. Nowhere in the story is an acknowledgment that Newdow was merely exercising his right to free speech. Where he exercised it, and how often, seemed more important to the reporter. "He is even willing to debate on tabloid television shows"—that's how far he'd go, Nieves suggested.

Nieves's approach reinforces a theory shared with me a few years back by a former student: a story has stopped evolving, or exploration of the real issues ceases, when the media start covering themselves, or (my addendum) when they discuss how either (1) resourceful and dogged or (2) omnipresent and overly aggressive they are. So instead of being a zealot about one issue, Newdow was now a zealot about several issues—including his push to remove gender-specific pronouns from conversational English, described by journalists as being a bit off the wall. "Just before the interview was over, he reminded the reporter to remember his ideas for changing the English language," Nieves wrote. "Don't forget the re, rees, erm thing," Newdow told her. "Just make it a little aside. Our language would be so much richer" (2002b, p. A8). CNN's Paul Begala and his cohost, renowned columnist Robert Novak (2002), mounted a testier challenge to Newdow's efforts. Begala claimed that Newdow had embarked "on a crusade to neuter the English language." Newdow rejected their characterization, saying that he would "like to refer to people without relation to their gender."

Begala, suddenly consumed by a bout of machismo, retorted: "No we don't brother . . . we figured out boys and girls a long time ago—most of us." For Novak, these gender-neutral pronouns (considering that using the word "chick" to refer to young women has made a comeback, Newdow may be on to something) were conclusive evidence of Newdow's eccentricity. "Maybe your position on the Pledge is a little odd but your position on this makes you look like a real nut. Do you realize that?" he asked (Begala & Novak, 2002).

To some commentators, like conservative Pat Buchanan, Newdow was simply a dangerous man with a radical agenda. "This is your plan. It's your idea. You're carrying it forward in the court, the American way and all that, no matter if we disagree with you," he said to Newdow during a July 2002 interview on MSNBC's *Buchanan and Press* (Press, Buchanan, Jansen, & Aspell, 2002). Newdow's agenda was deflecting attention from more significant issues, as host Paul Begala (Begala & Novak, 2002) suggested in a lengthy preface to a question: "[M]y kids couldn't play outside in Washington, DC[,] today because the air was so polluted . . . corporate criminals are taking over these companies with insider trading deals . . . John Ashcroft is shredding the Constitution while he puts burkas on statues with naked women. Of all the things you could be upset about, why pick this?"

Newdow contended that he just filed suit—it was the rest of the country that went ballistic. A disingenuous stance? Perhaps. Newdow probably had at least an inkling that challenging the Pledge would draw public criticism. Still, the arguments he raised—scorn heaped on one group of people because they don't believe in God, the government's growing desire to move religion into the public sphere—are valid. Invoking that elusive consensus, Begala was convinced that the American people "are more worried about their jobs and their economic freedom" than they are about whether the Pledge includes a reference to God.

Novak (who has refused to acknowledge that revealing the name of CIA operative Valerie Plame in a column was anything more than his journalistic obligation), enlivened the *pick your battles* frame with the "get a life" theme. "Have you ever thought of spending your time watching basketball or something like that? It's better than spending 4,000 hours (a figure supplied by Newdow) on this ridiculous case," he said (Begala & Novak, 2002).

The Good Mother

Back to Sandra Banning: A little more than two weeks after the Ninth Circuit panel's ruling, Banning, who has legal custody of the girl, told reporters that their daughter "has no problem with reciting the Pledge at school." She expressed concern that "the American public would be led to believe that my daughter is an atheist or that she has been harmed by the reciting the Pledge of Allegiance." And, as if checking off criteria for her character (as envisioned by the Christian right) she told one reporter, "we are practicing Christians and are active in our church" ("Girl in Pledge Case," 2002, p. A22).

Unlike the news media's portrayal of a scattered, zealous Newdow, Banning was treated with deference. She was a mother on a mission—an easy to follow, uncontroversial mission. She entered the case "for a simple reason: to make it clear that her daughter is not an atheist," wrote a *San Francisco Chronicle* reporter (Egelko, 2002b, p. A15). Banning's biggest fear, said her attorney, was that her daughter "would be branded for the rest of her life as the girl who was the atheist in the Pledge case or the girl who didn't like the Pledge of Allegiance" (ibid.).

Their daughter stayed strong by whispering "one nation under God" when she and her classmates said the Pledge, despite the Ninth Circuit's ruling "so no one knows I'm breaking the law," as Banning told CBS *The Saturday Early Show* anchor Gretchen Carlson (2002). Banning told Fox News (Cosby, 2002) that her daughter had actually led the Pledge during the first day of her summer school program. "She was excited, because her girlfriends—her best friend was the door monitor that day, but she . . . she got to lead the Pledge," Banning gushed with pride. Her daughter was placing her hand over her heart for the whole country. Newdow claimed that his daughter had not been ostracized ("Litigant Explains," 2002) in the wake of the Ninth Circuit's ruling. In fact, he never claimed that his daughter was at all upset by having to recite the Pledge. Journalists overlooked Newdow's assertion.

Instead, they commiserated with Banning. She was being a *good mother*—one of the master myths identified by Jack Lule (2001). Journalists typically portray the "good mother" as nurturing, kind, and gentle. This myth, writes Lule, "nurtures and nourishes and offers people a model of goodness in times when goodness may seem in short supply" (p. 24). Newdow had seen to it that goodness, reflected in his calculated attempt to change the Pledge, was in short supply, at least in the eyes of some reporters. In the months that followed, reporters would lionize Banning for rushing to the aid of their daughter. Unlike the self-aggrandizing, overly contentious Newdow, her sole motivation was the strong love she felt for her daughter. Take a look at this exchange between Banning and Carlson (2002):

> CARLSON: And I think this is what's so troubling to so many people is that this is a little eight-year-old girl. She's only eight.
> BANNING: That's right.
> CARLSON: And yet she's in the middle of this huge controversy at this point.
> BANNING: Right. Right.
> CARLSON: This must be tearing you apart as a mother to know that she's in the middle of this.

Carlson noted the little girl's age four times in the course of the interview, reinforcing the notion that she was an unwitting victim of her father's misguided zealotry. Banning appeared on the *Today* show (Lauer & Couric, 2002) to correct the purported impression that her daughter was an atheist and that Newdow was accurately citing her thoughts on the suit. Banning told Carlson (and other reporters) that the picture of their life painted by Newdow was inaccurate. "We are Christians. We're practicing Christians. We attend church. She voluntarily goes to church. In fact, I teach Sunday school and she helps me in my Sunday school classes" (Carlson, 2002). Appearing on MSNBC's *Donahue* (2002), she was even more emphatic: "My daughter is not an atheist. I believe that Mr. Newdow's brief would lead the nation to believe that my daughter is a practicing atheist, and that's not the case."

Rita Cosby of Fox News said her July 2002 interview gave Banning the "chance to respond" to Newdow's assertions—"for the first time ever," even though Carlson had beaten her to the interview by one day, and Banning had not chosen to involve herself in the case until her motion to intervene. Here, Cosby makes it sound as though Banning had been denied the opportunity to speak about the suit. Instead, she simply waited until the Ninth Circuit issued its ruling.

But as Lule (2001) explains, the "good mother" myth "can confine and restrict, presenting rigid models of maternity and gender" (p. 24). Newdow claimed repeatedly that Banning was an unwitting pawn in an effort by the religious right to advance their position on the Pledge. But as we will see, that claim never gathered much steam with reporters, who seemed content to congratulate Banning for being such a wonderful parent. Newdow told the Fox News Channel's Bill O'Reilly (2002): "I think that the religious right woke up one morning and said, 'Look at this, we have the Constitution being upheld, and we don't have the ability now to have our God stuck in the middle—'" O'Reilly interrupted Newdow: "So you think the religious right broke into her house and forced her to file this brief?" Stories did include information about her legal representation, her defense fund (even though she wasn't charged with a crime), and her public relations team, but nowhere did journalists question why the "good mother" needed all of this help, or how it suddenly materialized.

Let me offer one quick example: in the headlines of stories about Banning's attempt to intervene in the case, she is called "mom" (e.g., Teichert, 2002, p. B2)—the *Sacramento Bee*, for example, ran a story with the headline "Mom Asks Court to Remove Daughter from Pledge Case." An August 6, 2002, story from the *San Francisco Chronicle* was headlined "Mom Wants Girl Out of Dad's Pledge Lawsuit" (Egelko, 2002c, p. A3). She ran "a small clerical and computer support business from her home in Elk Grove" (Egelko, 2002d, p. A3). During roughly the same period, Newdow was called the "Pledge foe" (Cooper, 2002, p. A6) and the "Pledge dad" (Egelko, 2002e, p. A15).

These headlines suggest again that Newdow thinks Pledge challenge first, his daughter second. On the other hand, Banning is in there fighting to protect her child. She would not allow her to watch television coverage of the suit, although she did see her dad on the *Today* show. Banning reportedly turned down more interview requests than she accepted. When she did agree to be interviewed, "it has been, you know, that mommy has a meeting," said Carolyn Malenick, head of Banning's defense fund (Lin, 2002).

In the coverage of Banning's motion to intervene, journalists suggested she was more civilized than Newdow—she "asked" the court to remove her daughter from the suit (e.g., Teichert, 2002, p. B2), whereas Newdow was busy striking back—always aggressive, always on the defensive. He attended an August 5, 2002, meeting of the Elk Grove School Board, where he "accused" officials of "wasting money by fighting the suit in court" (Werkman, 2002, p. N1).

Banning's decision to become involved in the dispute put Newdow's standing at risk, claimed several experts cited by reporters. Newdow countered, arguing the suit was about "his beliefs, not his daughter's" (Egelko, 2002b, p. A15). Newdow acknowledged in a CNN interview ("Litigant Explains," 2002) that he had named his daughter in the suit in order to ensure his standing. But the chipping away at this newly discovered aspect of Newdow's case had begun. "I think you have a very serious standing question, because he's not in a position to have that child raised as a professed atheist," said a University of California–Berkeley law professor in a *San Francisco Chronicle* article (Egelko, 2002b, p. A15).

Here, the professor conflates standing and a value judgment on the fitness of atheists to raise children. To my knowledge, it is not illegal for atheists to have children. At this point, it was still possible that the child's interests could be protected while at the same time allowing Newdow to proceed with his suit. Banning's attorney, Paul Sullivan, said she would be happy "that she has had the opportunity to get the information to the court . . . and to the American public" (Egelko, 2002b, p. A15)—even though, according to Newdow, he never alleged that his daughter had been harmed by saying the Pledge—all in the name of "clarification," as Banning's attorney put it (Lauer & Couric, 2002).

Head to Head

Finally, reporters had their conflict, one more clearly drawn than Newdow versus the government, or Newdow versus the flag. The "holy war" that once involved so many lawmakers and public officials now centered around two people. It was parent against parent, battling for the soul of their child. Banning and Newdow's daughter personified the fear and indignation supposedly felt by most Americans after Newdow's success at the Ninth Circuit, despite the fact that Banning told reporters she wasn't interested in convincing the full Ninth Circuit that the June 26 ruling was incorrect. It certainly didn't help Newdow when journalists reminded readers that the couple never married.

We no longer needed endless pictures and videos of people saying the Pledge: Banning embodied this patriotism—the *hands over hearts* frame discussed in the last chapter - which made journalists' lives a little easier. As Banning told Phil Donahue in an August 2002 interview, "he sued the United States, so, you know, we are all co-defendants here. And I think, you know, as a nation, we need to just speak up and let our voice be known"—even if it angrily drowns out the voice of someone whose voice is rarely heard, and is denigrated when it is heard.

Carolyn Malenick, head of Banning's defense fund and a former fund-raiser for Oliver North once investigated by the Federal Election Commission for campaign irregularities, repeated this assertion on CNN. Banning, she said, knew she had to act when she saw members of Congress recite the Pledge en masse the day after the Ninth Circuit ruled. What a patriot.

On August 5, 2002, Banning, now backed up by an impressive legal team that included Kenneth Starr, the government's special counsel in the Monica Lewinsky case, and assisted by a public relations firm, moved to intervene in the case in order to protect her daughter's legal and education interests. She asked the court to dismiss her daughter from the case if it rejected her motion.

Banning claimed that she knew nothing of Newdow's intent to challenge the phrase "under God" until the Ninth Circuit ruled in June 2002. Adding to the lack of seriousness with which journalists treated Newdow's legal action, Banning said she "blew it off as hobby litigation" (Egelko, 2002b, p. A3). When they were together, Banning told MSNBC's Phil Donahue (2002), "I was aware that he always had an interest in constitutional law. Initially, though, it was my understanding he wanted to remove 'In God We Trust' off our currency." Newdow disputed Banning's description of events, saying the two had discussed the suit "a million times."

Banning didn't ask the court to dismiss the case—she wanted the court to recognize that her right to guide her daughter's religious upbringing was more significant than Newdow's because she was awarded custody of the young girl in February 2002. "Newdow may view himself as prejudiced by losing the ability to represent his daughter's legal interests," Banning argued in her motion. "But that ability was taken from him already by the custody order." Without this ability, Banning claimed, Newdow no longer had standing to sue.

Further, both Banning and her daughter "approve of the words 'under God' in the Pledge and wish for her to be able to recite the Pledge at school exactly as it stands." The *Seattle Times* reported Banning's fear that her daughter would experience a "lifetime of public scorn" if she came to be known as the "little atheist girl that attacked the Pledge" ("Across the Nation," 2002, p. A4). Not possible with news media coverage that highlighted her daughter's clearly stated belief in God. The *San Francisco Chronicle* reported that Banning's motion came "because the child believes in 'one nation under God'" (Egelko, 2002c, p. A3).

The *Chronicle*'s Bob Egelko noted that Banning's "public emergence," combined with her claim that her daughter was "a churchgoing Christian" muddled an already murky situation. The Ninth Circuit was reaping a harvest of dissent. It was "inundated with pleas to reconsider the ruling" or to agree to rehear it en banc (2002c, p. A3).

Outside the Mainstream

But what about the other frames—did journalists continue to use them as the case unfolded? The short answer is: to varying degrees, and with minor amendments. Having marginalized Newdow and the Ninth Circuit, reporters continued to treat them as if they were *outside the mainstream*. Columnist Debra Saunders (2002, p. A25) of the *San Francisco Chronicle*, one of the few newspapers to treat Newdow's case in more than a cursory manner, poked fun at Newdow's legal approach. Naming President Clinton and the Sacramento School District was, in her view, inappropriate, as was including a list of folks who reportedly are (or were) atheists.

The court should have dismissed such an erratic argument out of hand. A former U.S. attorney quoted by Saunders (2002, p. A25) said the case belonged "in the general category of 'too silly.'" Nothing, wrote Saunders, was "too silly for this court," which syndicated columnist Robert Novak referred to in July 2002 as "the Left Wing Ninth Circuit U.S. Court of Appeals" (Begala & Novak, 2002). In a story headlined "The Court Conservatives Hate," *USA Today* reminded readers of the reaction to the Ninth Circuit's ruling: "Another off-the-wall opinion from those wacko, liberal judges in San Francisco" (Kasindorf, 2003, p. 3A). Conservatives continued their push for "more judges who wouldn't be so quick to strike down laws that conservatives like." In fairness, the paper later noted that the Ninth Circuit might not be so liberal after all—it follows a "libertarian, Western spirit." Only 2 of 24 Ninth Circuit judges hear cases in San Francisco, and only 5 are liberal.

But it was Newdow who received most of the ideologically charged treatment from journalists during this period. He was silly, prone to acting hastily, and ignorant of the impact his actions were having on others—in particular, on his daughter. "When you brought this case, I wonder if you wanted the ramifications that are going to happen," began NBC reporter David Bloom. "In 10 days some 10 million public school kids in nine states across the western United States are not going to be able to recite the Pledge of Allegiance. Is that what you wanted?" Newdow corrected Bloom's error, explaining that students would not be able to cite the Pledge "as it now stands. They can certainly recite it that it's 'one nation indivisible,' which is what it's supposed to be" (Bloom & O'Brien, 2003). Few, if any, broadcast journalists took the time to explain this distinction to their viewers.

Further, Newdow was a coward, "an atheist heel who used his Pledge-loving daughter to quash speech he cherishes." Saunders (2002) used a quote from Elk Grove superintendent David Gordon—"It's a wonderful country because this man has the right to push his argument, and we have a right to defend it"—and to launch a final barb against Newdow, and tie in the Ninth Circuit panel: "In a free country, a 'free thinker' is free to hide behind his second-grade daughter in his quest to outlaw speech which he has decided he has a right not to hear" (p. A25).

Reporters tended to accept, without asking for clarification, Sandra Banning's claim that Newdow was just using his daughter to propel his case, despite Newdow's repeated assertion that he brought this case on his own behalf. "I believe he's used her as a vehicle to get—to gain sympathy from the court," Banning told Phil Donahue (2002). A clip of Banning making the identical statement was shown by CNN before its August 10, 2002, interview with Newdow.

When told that his daughter reportedly wanted to say the Pledge, Newdow told CNN's Carol Lin (2002), "I don't talk about my daughter. She's not the key of this lawsuit. And I've kept her out of this since the beginning." The *Sacramento Bee* didn't get this memo. In an October 20, 2002, editorial, the paper noted derisively that "the kid sure came in handy in Newdow's quest to excise 'under God' from the Pledge of allegiance" ("Leave the Kid Alone," 2002, p. E4). Newdow suggested that folks from the religious right had taken Banning on "as a puppet" and arranged countless television interviews for her "so that she can announce her name to the world, and therefore tell her how much that she's concerned about protecting her."

Lin did not follow up on Newdow's assertion. Journalists tended not to challenge claims by Newdow's opponents—even veiled claims—that he had filed suit to stroke his own ego, and that his was not an ego easily satiated. "Well, I can't say it's ego," said Banning advocate Carolyn Malenick. "Mr. Newdow would have to answer that, but I would say that he has a desire . . . whether we want to say it's unpatriotic views or whether it's a desire to remove 'one nation under God' or 'in God we trust'" (Lin, 2002).

Malenick reminded CNN's Carol Lin (2002) that "this is the same gentleman . . . who had challenged congressional resolutions that included the words 'under God.'" Vituperative talk show host Sean Hannity went Malenick one better, suggesting that Newdow misled the court by not revealing in his original suit that he had lost custody of his daughter. Hannity (Hannity & Colmes, 2002b) didn't want to hear that Newdow actually had custody of his daughter when the suit was first filed. "I would like to know, and you can explain to this audience, why you used your daughter for your political views," Hannity announced near the end of a September 4, 2002, interview with Newdow.

It probably won't shock you to learn that Hannity's ideological sidekick, controversial Fox News Channel host Bill O'Reilly (2002), continued the assault on Newdow's motives in an interview held three months later. "So would you say that you were using the little girl to drive your lawsuit?" O'Reilly asked to open the interview. Newdow once again said that he had not tried to protect his daughter's privacy, "but, you know, politicians use their children all the time to gain elected office and power. I used my child, I guess, to uphold the Constitution."

On CNN, *Crossfire* host Robert Novak declared to Newdow you "knew you wasted 4,000 hours and you really injured your daughter" (Begala & Novak, 2002). Broadcast journalists and commentators never allowed Newdow and Banning to confront each other during the interviews that have been discussed in this chapter. This is a continuation of the "he said/she said" style of reporting recently criticized by some veteran journalists and by journalism scholars. We get what reads like a tennis match—often between more than two people—without much exploration by the reporter as to whether the information gleaned at the tennis match is true.

And if he wasn't a coward, or consumed by his own ego, he was a fame hound. The *Sacramento Bee* described an August 2002 meeting of the Elk Grove School Board at which Newdow chastised school officials for "wasting money we could spend on students, helping them get educated" (Werkman, 2002, p. N1). Superintendent David Gordon politely refused to debate the Pledge issue, but a board member was quoted by the paper as asking Newdow, "haven't you had your 15 minutes of fame?" The *Bee* reporter noted that the board picks a worthy school volunteer to lead the board in the Pledge at the start of each meeting. Charmaine Kuss, honored at the August meeting, told officials "it was a pleasure to be here tonight and say the Pledge of Allegiance."

For his part, Newdow claimed that Banning waited too long to become involved in the case. In his opposition to her motion, Newdow claimed that he and his daughter had endured nearly three years of "theistic dogma" (*Newdow v. The Congress*, 2002, p. 3). "Neither should be forced to endure more of this constitutionally outlandish conduct," he claimed. Allowing Banning to intervene so late in the case "will do nothing but delay" a decision on these extremely significant issues.

Newdow also rejected Banning's contention that she was only "vaguely aware" that Newdow was challenging the Pledge. Banning had asked the court to prevent Newdow from bringing his daughter to oral arguments. In supporting her claim, she told the court that Newdow would be trying to convince the court to remove "under God" from the Pledge. She knew about the original lawsuit, filed in Florida, and that Newdow wanted to enroll their daughter in public school so that he would have standing to sue in that state. "This was more than three years ago!" Newdow argued. Banning was fully aware of the incident involving the Pledge at the heart of the complaint, and attended a conference with school officials to discuss the incident.

And by rejecting Newdow's contention that recitation of the Pledge had injured their daughter, Banning had failed to show that she had suffered what is known as a "protectable injury." Banning, wrote Newdow, "contends it is 'imperative' that she intervene in order to "protect her daughter." This notion is completely illusory. If the Pledge is unconstitutional, then—according to the Supreme Court—there is harm" (*Newdow v. The Congress*, 2002, p. 6).

But the heart of Newdow's argument was that by becoming involved in the suit, Banning had tipped off the country to their daughter's identity—he told Claire Cooper of the *Sacramento Bee* (2002, p. A6) that it was part of Banning's "well-publicized campaign to intervene" in the case. Newdow claimed that he had gone to great lengths to not discuss his daughter. He did not respond to Banning's allegations about her made during interviews with reporters. But two weeks after the Ninth Circuit's ruling, we learned her name. Remember Banning's claim that she didn't want her daughter to go through life being known as the "atheist child who hated the Pledge?" According to Newdow, "Banning cannot create an injury and then move—especially at this late date—to intervene in order to protect her child against the harm she, herself, has created."

Banning had gone from claiming that their daughter was unprepared to grapple with the question of whether God exists to claiming that she was now regularly attending church—an example of what Newdow called "her typical opportunism" (*Newdow v. The Congress*, 2002, p. 7). Banning, he wrote, "would never have been worried about her child being known as 'the Christian child who hated the Pledge.' But what if the child decides to be an atheist as she grows older?" Keeping "under God" in the Pledge will sustain the government's policy of discriminating against atheists, Newdow claimed, "thus forcing the child to suffer the very harm Banning acknowledges" (p. 9).

Newdow reminded the court that he was trying to have the Establishment Clause upheld, while Banning's action, if successful, would ensure that their daughter would "continue to be indoctrinated by the government, which the Supreme Court has repeatedly stated is improper" (p. 10). A parent is free to involve a child in religious activities unless those activities cause harm, Newdow noted. Here, it was Banning's decision to publicize her daughter's name, not the fact that Newdow is an atheist that harmed the girl. She was "completely anonymous until Banning decided to broadcast her name so that—by some bizarre twist of logic—she could somehow show how her involvement is necessary to protect her," Newdow said (p. 15).

And while a California Superior Court judge ruled in September 2002 that Newdow's daughter could not be listed as a plaintiff in his suit, nothing prevented him from suing on her behalf. Even Banning had acknowledged in court filings that "there are few, if any, rights more significant than a parent's right to represent their child" (quoted on p. 13)—even if the parent does not have full custody of the child, Newdow claimed.

In the *San Francisco Chronicle*'s stories on Banning's motion, she became known as the "church-going mother," while Newdow was referred to as "[t]he Sacramento atheist" (Egelko, 2002e, p. A15; 2002f, p. A9). Significant constitutional issues were treated like a professional wrestling match. In the third paragraph of the September 28, 2002, story on Newdow's objection to Banning's motion, the *Chronicle*'s Bob Egelko noted that Newdow "returned" to the Ninth Circuit seeking denial of the motion (2002e, p. A15). This suggests to readers that Newdow is no stranger to the court, and to litigation.

Banning was quoted as saying that she alone had the right to represent their daughter. She "described the girl as a Christian who wants to recite 'under God' and was saddened by the ruling" (Egelko, 2002e, p. A15). The pugilistic Newdow "struck back"—or "lashe[d] back," according to the story's headline—arguing that he "had no choice in light of Banning's assertions" to reveal that his daughter mentioned that she does not believe in God. Newdow placed little weight on the comment, but noted that three weeks after the Ninth Circuit's ruling, his daughter told a friend, "I hope he wins. That's what the Constitution says."

Still Under Attack

Meanwhile, federal and state officials were making sure the nation knew they were acting decisively to stop Newdow—a harkening to our *still under attack* frame. City officials in Cherokee County, Georgia—another state not affected by the Ninth Circuit's ruling—"made a formal stand" against the decision (Reinolds, 2002, p. 1JQ); in Woodstock, Georgia, a proclamation was issued, codifying the town's support for the Pledge; and in Holly Springs, Georgia, a resolution was passed that did essentially the same thing. "As community leaders, we need to stand up for what's right," said a Holly Springs, Georgia, city councilman (ibid.).

The U.S. Department of Justice and President Bush in August 2002 sought an en banc review of the Ninth Circuit's June 2002 ruling—they "formally weighed in," as the *San Francisco Chronicle* explained (Egelko, 2002d, p. A3). Journalists were reminding readers that their elected officials were taking aggressive action to stop this threat to the Pledge. They were joined by the Elk Grove School District and the state of California, whose attorney general, Bill Lockyer, claimed that the "depth and breadth of public outcry at the panel's decision should leave little doubt that the Pledge, as it is recited today, serves the secular purpose of fostering patriotism and a sense of unity as Americans" ("State Appeals Ruling," 2002, p. A22). Later, a congressman from Idaho would propose removing Idaho, Washington, Oregon, Montana, Alaska, and Hawaii from the Ninth Circuit to create a new circuit court "that presumably would be more amenable to conservative views" (Kasindorf, 2003, p. 3A).

The heart of the government's argument was that the words "one nation under God" were "a secular reference to the nation's religious heritage, not a government endorsement of religion." Journalists continued to deploy the *ceremonial deism* frame that emerged in earlier coverage of the case. The *San Francisco Chronicle* reported that while the Supreme Court had never definitively ruled on whether the post–1954 Pledge was constitutional, it had on several occasions noted "the Pledge was a ceremonial reference to the importance of religion in American life, like the phrase 'In God We Trust' on coins" (Egelko, 2002d, p. A3). Now even these references were under attack. CNN host Robert Novak suggested to viewers that Newdow was making intentionally incendiary, but half-assed, arguments. "I just wonder how far you plan to go if you've thought that out," he said during a July 2002 interview with Newdow (Begala & Novak, 2002).

Novak then listed ceremonial references to God: on currency, in congressional mottos, in the use of chaplains by governmental bodies and the military, the inaugural oath. "Pretty horrible for an atheist, don't you think?" was Newdow's reply. "Are you going to bring suit about all of those things?" Novak asked. When Newdow said yes, Novak used what had become a frequent response by journalists to Newdow's suit: "most of us didn't like it. We're not asking you to Pledge allegiance to the flag," said Novak, now acting as an advocate rather than a journalist. "It's a free country. You're saying that the 84 percent (of Americans) who want to—who enjoy saying 'under God'—are not permitted to" (Begala & Novak, 2002). Novak had already pronounced that Newdow should have felt "embarrassment" for leading the nation through this ideological minefield.

In its petition for rehearing, the government contended that the Ninth Circuit panel failed to follow the Supreme Court's observations in *Lynch v. Donnelly*, 465 U.S. 668 (1994)—in which the justices noted that "ceremonial acknowledgments" of the role of religion in the nation's founding do not "establish a religion or religious faith, or tend to do so"—and in *County of Allegheny v. Greater Pittsburgh ACLU*, 492 U.S. 573 (1989), in which the justices endorsed the idea (stated in *Lynch)* that the Pledge was "consistent with the proposition that government may not communicate an endorsement of religious belief" (pp. 6–7). In these cases, the government claimed, the Supreme Court was using its endorsement of the Pledge "as a baseline with which to adjudicate the constitutionality of other government actions" (p. 8). The words "under God" were "an integral part of a systematic development of constitutional doctrine," a development that the Ninth Circuit simply did not observe in reaching its decision.

While the Ninth Circuit panel applied the endorsement, *Lemon v. Kurtzman*, 463 U.S. 783 (1971), and coercion tests in evaluating the religious content of the Pledge, it failed to apply the "historical" test first used by the Supreme Court in *Marsh v. Chambers*, 463 U.S. 783 (1983), in which the justices upheld the state of Nebraska's policy of having members of the clergy offer prayers at the start of every session of the state legislature. "To support that holding," the government argued, "the Court relied exclusively upon what history reveals about the original understanding of the Establishment Clause, and declined to apply any of the Establishment Clause tests the Court has used in other contexts" (p. 9). And in *Lynch*, the Court applied only this test in reaching its decision. The Ninth Circuit panel was wrong to "reject *Lynch's* approval of the Pledge of Allegiance because of the panel's apparent disapproval of that test" (p. 10).

The government also claimed that the panel incorrectly found Newdow's daughter was coerced into saying the Pledge. In the seminal case on this issue, *Engel v. Vitale*, 370 U.S. 421 (1962), the Court ruled that while a New York public school's policy requiring students to recite a "government-composed prayer" each day did violate the Establishment Clause, that ruling in no way meant that students could not be "officially encouraged to express love for our country by reciting historical documents such as the Declaration of Independence which contain references to the Deity or by singing officially espoused anthems which include the composer's professions of faith in a Supreme Being" (p. 13).

The Pledge falls into the "historical document" category, the government argued—a line of reasoning accepted by reporters. Reciting the Pledge is simply "not an act of religious devotion" (p. 13). Justice Brennan made this clear in *Abington School District v. Schempp*, 374 U.S. 203 (1963), when he observed that readings or recitations from "documents of our heritage of liberty" do not threaten the "religious liberties of any members of the community" or chip away at the separation between church and state.

Finally, feeling like an "outsider" is not an injury severe enough to allow Newdow to claim standing. Just amending the Pledge in 1954 did not "cause Mr. Newdow the kind of individualized, direct, and concrete injury" required to establish standing. The government suggested that Newdow might lack standing since Banning moved to intervene in the case, and because at the time she had sole custody of their daughter, who stated that she was comfortable reciting the Pledge (p. 17).

Conclusions

As the parties waited for a ruling, Newdow appeared in November 2002 at a Washington, DC, rally organized by "atheists and other 'Godless

Americans,'" as the *Washington Post* put it, to "raise their profile in Washington." The *Post* reporter, Edward Epstein (2002, p. A2), led his story with a "now I've seen everything" flair, as if atheists are unknown to the rest of us: "As the nation's capital, Washington has witnessed marches for civil rights and women's rights, against war, for Israel and for Palestine, for slavery reparations and for evangelical Christians' agenda."

Atheists headed to Washington to press legislators and the president to stop further Establishment Clause breaches. "Any time we have any kind of attention, we pick up support," said the head of the Bay Area chapter of American Atheists, for what Epstein called their "underdog cause." Epstein noted that Newdow would speak at the rally, and reminded readers of the Ninth Circuit ruling, which was "widely expected to be reversed on appeal" (p. A2). Epstein's tone also suggests that atheists might be, in one sense, finally coming around; they were going to explore ways to properly package their ideas—ways that the single-minded Newdow had not considered. It was as though Epstein was intimating "now you're getting it." Going through the proper channels—channels that journalists have turned into frames through which they cover politics—might help them achieve their goal; for example, they should establish "a permanent lobbying presence" on the Beltway. It was okay for atheists to have an agenda—to hold this kind of "mass coming out party" for "the community of reason." So long as they politely marched in Washington, and made their demands from the steps of the U.S. Capitol—now a popular set for pronouncements of conviction—they would be treated with more respect. Newdow's path—a court-clogging, ideologically driven lawsuit—was not the way to go.

By reporting favorably on the more traditional direction taken by "nonbelievers," as Epstein's colleague, Caryle Murphy, referred to them, reporters could keep them where they could see them. Murphy wrote that the more than 2,000 "atheists and nonbelievers" who traveled to Washington "comprise a significant part of the population that needs to be taken seriously" (2002, p. C3)—so long as they were out in the open, and not sneaking around behind our backs, filing suit to challenge God.

Protest signs with provocative slogans ("God is a Fairy Tale," for example), speeches by officials ("Ladies and gentlemen, I see a sleeping giant that is waking up and is ready to assert its political and cultural influence," said American Atheists president Ellen Johnson), and appearances by nearly 100 members of the military are easy for journalists to digest, and easy for readers to understand. But by reporting that atheists have such a varied agenda, journalists create an impression that there is too much on the group's plate. They want too much; they want everything—which means they'll make little progress. Sure, atheists could try to come out of the closet, as one rally attendee told Murphy, but in so doing they shouldn't cause real trouble—only talk in political samplers.

Newdow appeared at the rally and led the attendees in a recitation of the Pledge (the sole mention of him in Murphy's story). In December, he ended the year by debating Cliff Knecthle, a pastor from Connecticut, about whether God exists. The debate was broadcast live from a church in California to listeners across the country by the Church Communication Network (Spinner, 2002, p. 8). This wasn't a political event, wrote Erika Chavez (2002, p. B1) of the *Sacramento Bee*; it did not "involve politicians jockeying for votes and the best sound bite"—an approach that, according to Epstein (2002, p. A2), might have helped Newdow. Also working against him was the fact that he was an atheistic Daniel entering the lion's den—a church and a broadcast set up by a Christian group.

Still, the debate provided a more familiar, and less threatening (for those who favored keeping the Pledge as it is), venue. The audience applauded Newdow, and listened "as he explained why he believes Christianity is 'mythology.'" Newdow apologized for "his lack of knowledge in areas like philosophy and theology" and adopted an "unswerving scientific approach" in debating Knechtle. "He equated believing in God to believing in UFOs or miracle weight loss pills," Chavez noted.

Chavez also noted Newdow's assertion that he would be unbiased, then undercut him by quoting his apology for lack of preparedness, and concluded with a pithy comparison. Chavez also offered markedly different descriptions of their body language. While Newdow "stood behind the lectern and rarely raised his voice," the pastor "strode around the stage, crouching, gesturing, and raising and lowering his voice for dramatic effect" (p. B1). The pastor challenged Newdow's characterization of himself as an atheist, and said Newdow had foolishly adopted "a skeptical scientific approach" in evaluating these issues. Dismissing Knechtle's assessment, Newdow posed questions for which he had received no satisfactory answers, including: "Why doesn't God appear?" and "If God is good, why do we have famine?" The audience laughed when Newdow asked, "Why is Conan O'Brien on late night TV?"

Those in attendance said that while it was great to have this kind of discussion, they remained steadfast in their views. "I wanted to give equal time to both sides even though I'm a solid Christian," said a business student from a nearby college (Chavez, 2002, p. B1). There you have it: it is easy to say you encourage debate when you set the terms of the debate, arrange a nationwide broadcast through a faith-based organization, hold the debate in a church, and fill the hall largely with people who agree with you, and aren't about to change their minds.

Reporters performed the same service for Banning. They underplayed the dismissal of her motion to intervene by the Ninth Circuit on December 4, 2002. They continued to burnish the portrait of Banning as victimized mother looking out for her daughter's interests. In its ruling, the Ninth Circuit found that Newdow had the right to challenge the Pledge even though Banning had sole custody of their daughter. "Non-custodial parents maintain the right to expose and educate their children to their individual religious views, even if those views contradict those of the custodial parent or offend her," Judge Alfred Goodwin wrote (Egelko, 2002f, p. A9).

The heck with all of that—we now had a lively protagonist, a victim with which to identify. We were all right there with her—the president, Congress, most elected officials, and the public—as she prepared for the next stage of the battle.

Chapter 7

On to the Supreme Court

To what could best be described as mixed reviews, the full Ninth Circuit on February 28, 2003, denied the government's motion to reconsider their colleagues' controversial June 2002 ruling. Some observers felt that the 15 judges who voted not to rehear the case wanted the Supreme Court to issue a definitive ruling, or were indicating that they in fact agreed with their colleagues' controversial June 2002 ruling. Still others felt that the judges were trying to sidestep a Supreme Court review.

But perhaps an even bigger surprise was the combined length of the panel's ruling and concurring and dissenting opinions. As Adam Liptak of the *New York Times* explained rulings on petitions for rehearing en banc are usually brief—"dry one- or two-sentence affairs" (2003, p. A1). Courts frequently revise earlier rulings, wrote Lyle Denniston of the *Boston Globe* (2003, p. A3), but the revisions are limited. "It is very unusual to reshape an entire opinion, and especially to drop completely a finding that a law is unconstitutional," he wrote. The appeals court's 18-page amended opinion was followed by Judge Stephen Reinhardt's 8-page concurring opinion, a stinging 18-page dissent by Judge Diarmiud O'Scannlain, and a short dissent by four other circuit judges.

The court chose not to reexamine Newdow's contention that the 1954 federal law that brought about the addition of "under God" to the Pledge was unconstitutional. The Ninth Circuit panel in June 2002 had ruled that the 1954 act's "affirmation of a 'belief in the sovereignty of God' and its recognition of 'the guidance of God'" were clearly "endorsements by the government of religious beliefs" (p. 9128). Crafters of the change did not intend for the words "to sit passively in the federal code unbeknownst to the public" (p. 9118). Their goal was to require the "recitation of the words 'under God' in school classrooms throughout the land on a daily basis." The Pledge, as amended in 1954, interfered with Newdow's right to shape his daughter's religious education.

The court simply decided not to revisit this issue. Recall that Judge Peter Nowinski did not explore whether the 1954 act was unconstitutional, having ruled that the Elk Grove Pledge policy did not, as Newdow had claimed, violate the First Amendment. Since the Ninth Circuit rejected Judge Nowinski's finding, it was required to "consider whether to grant Newdow's claim for declaratory relief as to the Act" (p. 18a). Judge Alfred Goodwin explained that declaratory judgments like the one sought by Newdow are "left to the discretion" of the district court. "We doubt that, given the relief, to which we decide Newdow is entitled," the judge wrote, the lower court would have decided to rule on his claim regarding the 1954 act. The Ninth Circuit panel did, however, uphold its earlier finding that the Elk Grove School District's Pledge policy was unconstitutional.

Judge Goodwin explained that he and his colleagues restricted their analysis "to the specific question of the constitutionality of imposing this recitation on minorities who may or may not subscribe to majority religious dogma" (e-mail interview, June 30, 2005). Such an approach was warranted, the judge said, since "it is not considered prudent judicial practice to decide anything not actually presented in the pending case." As much as reporters wanted to make the dispute about Newdow's quest to eliminate as many references to God as possible from public life, "the global constitutionality" of these ideas "was not really before the court."

Judge Goodwin noted that there are many Christians who aren't thrilled with what they see as "the exploitation of liturgical references to God in political polemics." Consumers of news rarely read about or see these individuals, however. The "political polemics" to which Judge Goodwin refers is a tried and true news frame. As for the religious component of his comment, I argue that religious zealots are simply more attractive to news directors and editors than individuals who keep their religious beliefs to themselves and who do not use religion as a springboard to political access. Judge Goodwin's explanation of the court's rationale in reaching its February 28 decision seems quite clear. However, it is not the explanation that found its way into news media coverage of the ruling.

In his concurring opinion, Judge Reinhardt explained that the power to order an en banc ruling is discretionary. It is not enough that a case deals with an issue of "exceptional importance" (p. 2776); there also must be a significant error in a lower court's ruling. "A decision may warrant correction because a three-judge panel has reached a decision or adopted a legal rule or principle that conflicts with our current circuit law or that the majority of our court believes is incorrect and needs further review," he wrote. Unless an appellant has shown that a significant error has been made, an en banc review is not necessary (p. 2777).

If an appeals court reheard cases en banc only because the cases dealt with important issues, courts would be inundated with hearings; such an approach would create "an impractical and crushing burden on what should otherwise be . . . an exceptional occurrence," Judge Reinhardt wrote. Decisions by appellate panels are not, the judge added, "measures of 'rough justice,' later to be refined by the en banc court" (pp. 2777–2778). Perhaps more significant was Judge Reinhardt's reaction to the dissenting opinion by Judge O'Scannlain, in which he harshly criticized the panel's decision not to reconsider the original ruling. Reciting the Pledge is not a profession of religious faith, Judge O'Scannlain argued. If it is, as the Ninth Circuit suggested in June 2002, "then so is the recitation of the Constitution itself, the Declaration of Independence, the Gettysburg Address, the National Motto, or the singing of the national anthem."

What troubled Judge Reinhardt was the belief of his colleague that the original panel should have considered the intense "public and political reaction" to the first Ninth Circuit ruling in reaching its decision about an en banc hearing. "Any suggestion, whenever or wherever made, that federal judges should be encouraged by the majority or deterred by popular disfavor is fundamentally inconsistent with the Constitution and should be firmly rejected," he wrote.

Lyle Denniston, writing in the *Boston Globe*, incorrectly took Judge O'Scannlain's finger on the public pulse as an indication that the entire appeals court had been "stung by the wave of resentment over its earlier decision" (2003, p. A3). They first stayed the ruling, then made significant changes to it because we were so angry about it. Such an assessment ignores Judge Reinhardt's plea to keep public sentiment out of judicial deliberations.

It was Judge O'Scannlain who took a similar view in a 1997 Ninth Circuit affirmative action case (*Coalition for Economic Equity v. Wilson*, 122 F. 3d 692)—a decision that Judge Reinhardt argued *should* have been reviewed en banc. "A system which permits one judge to block with the stroke of a pen what 4,736,180 state residents voted to enact as law tests the integrity of our constitutional democracy," he wrote. The view endorsed by Judge O'Scannlain threatens our constitutionally guaranteed freedoms, Judge Reinhardt argued. The Bill of Rights was crafted to "protect the rights of those in the minority against the temporary passions of a majority which might wish to limit their freedoms or liberties" (p. 2778). Indeed, in *West Virginia State Board of Education v. Barnette*, 319 U.S. 624 (1943), Justice Robert Jackson declared that these freedoms "may not be submitted to vote; they depend on the outcome of no elections" (quoted on p. 2779). A federal judge's "highest calling," wrote Judge Reinhardt, is to apply the Constitution in order to reject laws that infringe on these rights—whether or not these laws "are adopted by legislatures or by popular vote."

The Constitution—specifically Article 3—ensures that federal judges are "insulated from the political pressures governing members of the other two branches of government." A lifetime appointment is supposed to mean that judges will decide "constitutional issues without regard to popular vote, political consequence, or the prospect of future career advancement" (p. 2779). They must be protected from what Alexander Hamilton called "those ill humors which the arts of designing men, or the influence of particular conjectures, sometimes disseminate among the people themselves" (quoted on p. 2779). It is hoped that in time, people will gather accurate information and reflect on what has transpired; still, these "conjectures" often "occasion dangerous innovation in the government and serious oppressions of the minor party in the community."

Judge Reinhardt did not go so far as to say that judges must ignore public sentiment in reaching decisions. It is appropriate for federal judges to monitor "long-term societal trends" and factor that into decisions on what constitutes cruel and unusual punishment, for example. But this is different from "responding to particular immediate political pressures," the judge noted. "We may not—we must not—allow public sentiment or outcry to guide our decisions. It is particularly important that we understand the nature of our obligations and the strength of our constitutional principles in times of national crisis; it is then that our freedoms and our liberties are in the greatest peril."

Judge O'Scannlain, who was joined by five colleagues, dismissed Judge Reinhardt's claim that yielding to public pressure was the central argument in his dissent. The original Ninth Circuit majority misinterpreted the Constitution and Supreme Court precedent when it ruled in June 2002, the judge said. "It doesn't take an Article III judge to recognize that the voluntary recitation of the Pledge of Allegiance does not violate the First Amendment," he wrote (p. 2781).

In denying a rehearing, the Ninth Circuit failed to consider whether the 1954 change to the Pledge was constitutional. But more important, the court's June 2002 ruling had a sweeping impact on the lives of many Americans, the judge contended: "It bans the voluntary recitation of the Pledge of Allegiance in the public schools of the nine western states, thereby affecting over 9.6 million students, necessarily implies that both an Act of Congress and a California law (the Elk Grove Pledge policy) are unconstitutional, clearly conflicts with the Seventh Circuit's decision in *Sherman* . . . and threatens cash-strapped school districts and underpaid teachers with the specter of civil actions for money damages," the judge argued (pp. 2782–2783).

The panel's original error—ruling that recitation of the Pledge was a religious act—was still out there, the judge said. Affixing such a label to recitation of the Pledge and other essential, revered documents like the Constitution and the Declaration of Independence "would make hypocrites out of the Founders, and would have the effect of driving any and all references to our religious heritage out of our schools, and eventually out of our public life," Judge O'Scannlain wrote.

It is clear that recitation of a state-mandated prayer (the main issue in *Engel v. Vitale*, 370 U.S. 421 (1962)), requiring students to read verses from the Bible at the start of each school day (*Abington School District v. Schempp*, 374 U.S. 203 (1963)), a moment of silence "for meditation or voluntary prayer" (*Wallace v. Jeffree*, 472 U.S. 38 (1985)), and prayers offered by clergy at a graduation ceremony (*Lee v. Weisman*, 505 U.S. 577 (1992)) are all religious exercises, even if students are not required to take part. The most significant factor, wrote the judge, "was the nature of the exercise in which the students were asked to participate" (p. 2799).

The judge reminded his colleagues of Justice William Brennan's concurring opinion in *Schempp* in which he noted that "not every involvement of religion in public life violates the Establishment Clause" (quoted on p. 2787). Mentioning God in the Pledge simply recognizes "the historical fact that our nation was believed to have been founded 'under God'" (p. 2787). The judge contended his colleagues failed to appreciate the difference between "patriotic invocations of God" and "unquestioned religious exercises."

If it is found that a policy requires a religious exercise, courts determine if students would feel coerced into taking part in it. *Lee v. Weisman* sets the standard here; if the government requires that students take part in a religious exercise "in such a way as to oblige the participation of the objectors," Judge O'Scannlain wrote, then the policy is coercive, and, thus, unconstitutional. The original ruling in Newdow "is a case study, an advertisement, for why it is that the Supreme Court has anchored coercion analysis only to those situations where 'formal religious exercises' take place in our public schools," the judge argued (p. 2796).

Until the Ninth Circuit's original ruling, Supreme Court precedents in school prayer cases had never been applied "outside a context of state-sanctioned religious observances." But Judge O'Scannlain said his colleagues' ruling "finesses all that." Their "sleight of hand" is actually obvious: "obfuscate the nature of the exercise at issue and emphasize indirect coercion" (p. 2791)—this clearly contradicts the Supreme Court. Put simply, the Pledge is a patriotic act. "Whatever one thinks of the normative values underlying the Pledge, they are unquestionably patriotic in nature," the judge stressed. When one prays, on the other hand, one talks "directly to God, with bowed head, on bended knee, or some other reverent disposition. It is a solemn and humble approach to the divine in order to give thanks, to petition, to praise, to supplicate, or to ask for guidance" (p. 2792). Judge O'Scannlain noted that the Declaration of Independence "would seem to be the better candidate for the chopping block than the Pledge, since the Pledge does not require anyone to acknowledge the *personal* relationship with God to which the Declaration speaks," he wrote.

Finally, the judge argued that Newdow should not be allowed to impose his views on the rest of us—which is precisely what Newdow had claimed, only with the government in charge of the imposing. "[A]lmost *every* cultural practice is bound to offend *someone's* sensibilities," Judge O'Scannlain wrote. Thanks to the Ninth Circuit panel, atheism now enjoys a "favored status," while those who practice religion must now endure bias. This caused Judge O'Scannlain to wonder: "does atheism become the default religion protected by the Establishment Clause?" (p. 2798).

Backing Off

Carrying forward the outside the mainstream frame suggested by Judge O'Scannlain's dissent, reporters implied that the Ninth Circuit had acted erratically, almost cowardly, as it evaluated Newdow's appeal and the government's motion for rehearing. Consider the verbs used to describe the February 28, 2003, ruling: Adam Liptak (2003, p. A1) of the *New York Times* and Howard Mintz of Knight-Ridder News Service (2003, p. 1A) wrote that the court "refused" to take another look at its June 2002 ruling. They were joined in this characterization by then network news anchors Tom Brokaw (2003) and Dan Rather (2003). Lyle Denniston (2003, p. A3), a respected legal affairs reporter for the *Boston Globe*, said that the court "backed off its controversial ruling" about the words "under God" in the Pledge. Judge Alfred Goodwin firmly rejected Denniston's characterization (e-mail interview, June 30, 2005).

Other news organizations offered only slightly more accurate descriptions of the decision. *USA Today* reported that the court "rewrote" its "highly criticized" opinion in order to "narrow its scope." The court had "toss[ed] out earlier language invalidating the 1954 Act." But the scope referred to by the *USA Today* reporters had already been narrowed by the lower court—if I have accurately characterized Judge Goodwin's comments. But the paper concluded that this act of narrowing would "complicate the legal picture" (Kasindorf & Biskupic, 2003, p. 3A).

Charles Lane (2003, p. A1) of the *Washington Post* was less derisive, writing that the court "voted to let stand its much-criticized ruling banning teacher-led recitation" of the Pledge. He, like several of his print and broadcast colleagues, assured readers that the court's action, even with the change to its opinion, would "set the stage for a possible battle in the Supreme Court over patriotism and religion." Lane wrote that the court's decision "stops short" of declaring the 1954 law unconstitutional. Lane's characterization stops short of complete accuracy, at least in Judge Goodwin's estimation. The court was simply evaluating the issues that were properly before it at the time.

The words "backed off"—like Lane's description that the court "did take one step back" in its amended ruling—are particularly important. It's not clear that the court did back down, or back away, or give up the fight. While reporters accurately described the difference between ruling that the 1954 act was unconstitutional and the Elk Grove policy was coercive, the court's rationale for its later ruling was not clearly explained.

On the March 1, 2003, *Saturday Today*, the late David Bloom (Bloom & O'Brien, 2003) told viewers that the Ninth Circuit would stand by "its controversial ruling declaring that reciting the Pledge is unconstitutional." For the most part, reporters clearly and accurately drew the distinction between declaring "under God" unconstitutional—which still was not treated as the Ninth Circuit's finest hour—and declaring the entire Pledge unconstitutional. Still, it wasn't an "omission" by the appeals court, as Denniston (2003) and others reported.

Lane referred to the February 28 ruling as "altered," and the appeals court's decision not to revisit the constitutionality of the 1954 act as an "adjustment," which still isn't quite what the judges had in mind. Adam Liptak of the *Times* reassured readers that the amended opinion "makes the decision less sweeping," in that "it may now not apply by implication to reciting the Pledge in other official settings" (2003, p. A1). In contrast, Bob Egelko of the *San Francisco Chronicle* wrote that the court "slightly amended" the June 2002 ruling. Kinder words, perhaps, but in his story's next paragraph, Egelko noted the contention of the dissenting judges that the June ruling "confers a favored status on atheism in our public life." He followed with Judge O'Scannlain's claim that the ruling would in effect outlaw "all references to our religious heritage" (2003, p. A3).

Meanwhile the government, and most of the nation, was unimpressed by the amended opinion. Firmly ensconced once again in the still under attack frame, reporters reminded us that elected officials still had a war on terrorism to fight. As a result, Lane noted, "politicians of both parties have shown themselves eager to embrace traditional patriotic symbols and rituals" (2003, p. A1). The *Seattle Times* assuaged readers' fears by noting that "a host of politicians . . . have jumped into the fight" to save the Pledge ("Court Reaffirms Ban," 2003, p. A2). Conservative activist Jay Sekulow noted that we were "poised on the threshold of a possible war in Iraq" (Holt, 2003). But Sekulow took a path slightly different than most public officials who commented on Newdow's suit. There were simply more significant issues on America's plate; we didn't have the time or the emotional energy to deal with what really did not amount to a constitutional crisis, Sekulow suggested.

And some reporters still had not corrected the misimpression that schoolchildren in the states covered by the Ninth Circuit would soon no longer be able to say the Pledge. Had the case ended with the February 28 ruling, these kids would have been able to say the Pledge—they would simply have been required to leave out "under God"—or the opposite of what Mike Newdow and Sandra Banning's daughter was allegedly doing in class since the Ninth Circuit made its original ruling.

Several reporters offered their readers a countdown to the end of the Pledge as we knew it "unless opponents win a court order blocking" (Lane, 2003, p. A1) the Ninth Circuit's opinion. If nothing changed by Friday, March 8, 2003, reporters suggested, the lives of schoolchildren living in the Ninth Circuit would be forever changed, and not for the better. Atheism would inevitably insinuate itself into the minds of our children. This line of reasoning is reminiscent of the claim by conservatives that the work of homosexuals for tolerance and equal legal protection is actually a thinly disguised conversion campaign.

We certainly would not want Michael Newdow talking to our children, free to "impose his views on others," as Judge O'Scannlain had argued. Thus, the personalization of these issues by journalists continued. Newdow was a threat to our children. And what of those children? The Elk Grove School District prepared for life without "under God"; it would ask its 53,000 students to take part in a substitute patriotic exercise—a song, perhaps, or a poem. "We don't want to be at risk of anyone saying we violated the law," said district superintendent David Gordon (Egelko, 2003, p. A3). Barring additional appeals, the kids would be deprived of the Pledge—even though they could have just been asked to say the Pledge without "under God"—beginning March 10, 2003.

Newdow's supporters tried to illustrate for reporters that their quarrel was not with the Pledge, but with the inclusion of "under God." AU executive director Barry Lynn told NPR's Tavis Smiley (2003): "I certainly hope people are still doing the Pledge of Allegiance, but I certainly hope they're doing it the way it was originally written, that is, as a secular affirmation of our commitment to the country." Public officials—and journalists—largely ignored this line of reasoning.

But saying the Pledge was a vital part of the students' education, suggested officials. "It's every day. It's consistent. It gives us that opportunity to be patriotic every day," Mike Gulden, a principal in the Elk Grove district, told the *Sacramento Bee* (Louey, 2003, p. B1). Even if a child did not want, for some reason, to be patriotic. Opting out, a feature of many state laws discussed extensively by reporters, is an inadequate option, claimed Lynn. Choosing not to participate in an expression of religion will almost always have negative consequences for the dissenting student. They will face ridicule and isolation, Lynn argued. Instead of continuing dialogue about this very real possibility, reporters instead allowed opponents of the Ninth Circuit's ruling to focus in their comments on ceremonial deism, and purported discrimination against folks who publicly express their religious beliefs. "I guess if Dr. King were to be the graduation speaker at a high school," commented Jay Sekulow, director of the American Center for Law and Justice, a conservative activist group, "he shouldn't invoke God's name, either, if he was still with us" (Smiley, 2003).

Celebrated conservative media personality Pat Buchanan took up the theme of deprivation in a March 3 interview with Lynn and Sekulow. "What this does, Barry," Buchanan said of the June 2002 ruling, "is it denies freedom of speech to 10 million children" (Holt, 2003). Why should "two federal judges dictate what we can and cannot say?" he asked, especially given that the 1954 amendment to the Pledge was overwhelmingly approved by Congress, signed by President Eisenhower, and backed by all but a handful of the American people (Holt, 2003).

Lynn fired back, saying the case had "nothing whatsoever to do with censorship." He reminded Buchanan and Sekulow that the pre–1954 Pledge "got us through World War I, World War II, out of the Great Depression." There is no need, Lynn said, "to mix religion and politics like we do." A perfectly reasonable view, but one that will almost always be pushed aside by a conflict-happy cable news host—a tendency Lynn was well aware of (personal interview, September 9, 2004). "The story on cable programs was the subject of more intense editorializing for some time," Lynn said. Newdow was treated like "any other temporary celebrity—get him on camera, get him on the air, get [his] quotes in the paper." For the most part, the treatment of Newdow by reporters was "incredibly nasty."

Returning to the activist judges theme, MSNBC host Lester Holt chimed in: "Who are these two judges to impose, really, the rule of the tiny minority on an entire nation that is supposed to be democratic?" Perhaps Holt forgot, for example, that most of the purportedly massive outrage at indecency on television comes from one group: the Parents Television Council whose members—maybe not a "tiny minority," but the group doesn't speak for most Americans—generated 99.8 percent of the indecency complaints fielded by the Federal Communications Commission (FCC) in 2003 (Berkowitz, 2005). Thanks largely to the group's high-pressure tactics, or so it believes, the FCC increased the fine for an instance of indecency from $32,500 to $325,000 (Crawford, 2004).

Surely the Supreme Court, our nation's most revered legal body, would correct the Ninth Circuit's error and restore order, suggested journalists. "It's up to the Supreme Court to bring some sense to this issue," argued the *Pittsburgh Post-Gazette* ("Taking the Pledge," 2003, p. E6). "It's the Supreme Court's mess, more than anyone else's, to clean up," said one legal scholar quoted by Mintz (2003, p. 1A). *USA Today* noted on March 3, 2003, that if the high court decided to review the Ninth Circuit's ruling, "there is a strong possibility it will view the Pledge more favorably" (Kasindorf & Biskupic, 2003, p. 3A) than the appeals court, suggesting that the appeals panel had acted with contempt and disregard for the Pledge.

The nine Ninth Circuit judges who so heroically tried to defend our children's right to say the Pledge in its current form were simply "outnumbered by the 14 judges who determined that there was no need for a fresh look" (Mintz, 2003, p. 1A) at the earlier decision. Their "vehement objections" were ignored (Liptak, 2003, p. A1). As suggested earlier in the chapter, it was the nation's children, all of who wanted to say the Pledge, who desperately needed their help. Why should 10 million schoolchildren in the Ninth Circuit be denied this expression of patriotism because "one kid won't be silent?" Pat Buchanan asked in a March 2003 MSNBC broadcast (Holt, 2003).

In truth, the only folks under attack in the months after the original ruling were Judges Goodwin and Reinhardt—by reporters, columnists, the public, and even by some of their own colleagues. The *Seattle Times* cited the dissenting opinion "denouncing" ("Court Reaffirms Ban," 2003, p. A2) the ruling. The Knight-Ridder News Service's Howard Mintz told readers that the appeals court was wracked by dissension; he called the court "badly splintered" (2003, p. 1A) and called the judges' actions "an extraordinary display of internal conflict."

In an editorial, the *San Diego Union-Tribune* noted that the Ninth Circuit had "refused to reconsider" the panel's "outrageous ruling," adding that the panel "clearly interpreted the First Amendment's 'establishment' clause (the paper's quotation marks, not mine) in ways the nation's founders hardly could have intended" ("No Pledge Allowed," 2003, p. B8). It was the court, not Newdow, who was moving the nation toward a time when all references to God would be removed from our lives, the paper claimed. Even the idea of opting out, endorsed by the Supreme Court in *Barnette* "was not good enough for the Ninth Circuit."

They simply refused to reconsider their "overly clever" decision, as the *Pittsburgh Post-Gazette* called it ("Taking the Pledge," 2003, p. E6).

Only the *Seattle Times* sided with Newdow and the court. "Reciting the Pledge is a small part of nurturing good citizens, but the court reminds us that not all good citizens believe in God," the paper noted in a March 9 editorial ("One Nation," 2003, p. C2). The authors of the editorial were among the very few journalists who contended that while children can choose in most states not to say the Pledge, they are "essentially a captive audience," as Newdow had claimed. Further, taking "under God" out of the Pledge was not a denigration of the importance of religious values or of faith. "This is about the constitutional rights of citizens with differing religious views and no beliefs at all."

The marginalization of Newdow, at least by print journalists, abated somewhat as reporters focused on the Ninth Circuit's decision denying rehearing en banc. He was not quoted in the *Times*, *Post*, and *Globe* stories on the ruling. Newdow's hometown paper, the *Sacramento Bee,* reported his prediction that the Supreme Court would uphold the Ninth Circuit's ruling. "It'll clarify once and for all the meaning of the establishment clause, and hopefully it'll recognize that it pertains to Americans of all religious beliefs," he said (Louey, 2003, p. B1).

The Trouble You've Caused

But Newdow was still the *scapegoat*—and he was, in the eyes of at least one journalist, unable to acknowledge the havoc he had wreaked. "When you brought this case," began NBC's David Bloom in a March 1, 2003, interview, "I wonder if you wanted the ramifications that are going to happen. In 10 days some 10 million public school kids in nine states across the western United States are not going to be able to recite the Pledge of Allegiance. Is that what you wanted?"

Newdow explained that kids could say the Pledge without the words "under God." They could "certainly recite it that its 'one nation indivisible,' which is what it's supposed to be" (Bloom & O'Brien, 2003). Barely breaking stride (while missing much of what Newdow said), Bloom rephrased his question. Students "can't say under God" because of Newdow's concern that his daughter "was essentially being coerced or having her religious liberty violated by being forced to say 'one nation under God'?" The failure of reporters to pick up this obvious distinction troubled supporters of Newdow like AU's Barry Lynn. "Even relatively sophisticated reporters," he said, continually stated that these students "could never say the Pledge again," which was an incorrect assertion.

Bloom noted the surprise of "a lot of legal scholars" at the Ninth Circuit's ruling, then promptly failed to mention any. Instead, he read Ashcroft's now familiar "The Justice Department will spare no effort" quote and reminded Newdow that the Bush administration would inevitably appeal the June 2002 ruling to the Supreme Court. Never lacking confidence, Newdow told Bloom that he expected the Supreme Court to rule in his favor.

Bloom then returned to key themes in the marginalization of Newdow: the threats to his life and the negative impact of the ruling on his daughter. Asked by Bloom about how his daughter had been treated by her classmates since the ruling, Newdow refused to talk about her, "except to say she's a great kid" (Bloom & O'Brien, 2003). And since the initial spate of threats and "nonstop vitriol," Newdow's life had calmed down. "I think people are starting to understand what the issue is, even though the Attorney General seems to have difficulty," he told Bloom.

Bloom then interviewed Utah senator Orrin Hatch, who revisited the idea that the Ninth Circuit's ruling was an act of judicial arrogance that could have been corrected long ago if the Democrats in the Senate would have confirmed more of President Bush's judicial nominees. As if running down a list of key elements in the frames discussed thus far, Hatch told Bloom that the Ninth Circuit is "one of the most liberal courts in the country." After all, President Clinton appointed 13 of its judges; they simply did not "realize what the Constitution says." If Newdow and his band of atheists had their way, "we're going to have take God off all the Federal buildings" and our currency. "We're going to have to just change the whole society because of a very, very distinct few people" who are ruining the unquestioning adherence to Judeo-Christian principles for all of us.

But instead of challenging Hatch, Bloom offered a list of his own: Supreme Court rulings that have pushed religion further and further out of the public sphere. "Couldn't they reach the same decision here?" Bloom asked. Hatch returned to the "having to deal with an angry, but suddenly powerful minority" line of reasoning. These folks cannot, he said, "tell all the rest of the people in this country what to do." It certainly would have been instructive—and perhaps entertaining—to allow Newdow to address the senator's claims. "This is a country that's a great country because we believe in God," he said. The solution? Confirm the president's nomination of strict constructionist judges—not a national dialogue on the issues raised by Newdow, but "better judges on the bench."

Newdow told the *San Francisco Chronicle* that the Ninth Circuit "upheld the Constitution, as they're supposed to do" (Egelko, 2003, p. A3). The *Milwaukee Journal-Sentinel* (Mintz, 2003, p. 1A) characterized Newdow's reaction as praise for the Ninth Circuit. One reporter noted that Newdow was still off on his "crusade" to change the Pledge ("Court Reaffirms Ban," 2003, p. A2). In a March 2003 interview with Elk Grove superintendent David Gordon, talk show host Bill O'Reilly (2003) concluded that Newdow was "a big star on the left. I mean they love him. He's gotten tremendous publicity from this. He's now well-known in this country."

This continues the depiction of students and school officials as victims of Newdow's litigiousness. They suffered while Newdow basked in his newfound publicity. Reporters were also creating the impression that the Ninth Circuit was unraveling, thanks to its erratic track record. Coverage continued to suggest that government officials, alerted by the news media to the threat posed by Newdow, stood ready to act. Former attorney general John Ashcroft continued to reassure the nation that he would "spare no effort to preserve the rights of all our citizens to Pledge allegiance to the American flag" (Lane, 2003; Liptak, 2003).

In November 2003, Congress passed, and President Bush signed, a law that "reaffirms the reference to God in the Pledge" (Denniston, 2003, p. A3). Our public officials were still on guard, protecting us from imagined ideological incursions. Even Elk Grove School District officials were taking action; the district's attorneys on March 3 asked the Ninth Circuit to stay its ruling while it prepared its appeal to the Supreme Court (Louey, 2003, p. B1). The court issued the stay. "One thing the district won't do," wrote the *Sacramento Bee*'s Sandy Louey, "is say the Pledge without the words 'under God.'" Reporters transformed a complex constitutional issue into a spate of infighting among judicial colleagues, but they also suggested that those judges who lodged "vehement objections" (Lane, 2003), a "lengthy protest" (Denniston, 2003, p. A3), and an "impassioned dissent (Egelko, 2003, p. A3) to the decision to deny a rehearing, were on our side, apparently because we all embraced the concept of ceremonial deism. The Pledge, noted the *Pittsburgh Post-Gazette*, "is a worthy patriotic exercise that poses no serious danger to the proverbial wall of separation of church and state" ("Taking the Pledge," 2003, p. E6). Note the use of the word "proverbial" here—it is as though the paper is suggesting that the Establishment Clause had lost validity—it was a dusty relic.

Several stories included Judge O'Scannlain's comment that the original ruling was "wrong, very wrong," which was usually followed by his idea that the Pledge "is a patriotic act. After the public and political reaction last summer, it is difficult to believe that anyone can continue to think otherwise" (quoted in Liptak, 2003, p. A1). Ironically, Adam

Liptak quoted the judge as saying that his dissent had "nothing to do with bending to the will an outraged populace"—but it was their will that seemed to be driving the frames deployed by reporters who covered the case.

Liptak of the *Times*, and several of his colleagues (e.g., Egelko, 2003, p. A3; Mintz, 2003, p. 1A), included a reminder from California governor Gray Davis, whose bid to intervene in the case was rejected, that both houses of Congress and the Supreme Court begin their sessions by invoking God's name. "Surely the Supreme Court will permit schoolchildren" to do the same. In a story appearing in the *Sacramento Bee*, Elk Grove superintendent David Gordon stressed "the phrase 'under God' does not push religion on children . . . but rather reflects the history of our country" (Louey, 2003, p. B1). In an appearance on MSNBC, Jay Sekulow of the American Center for Law and Justice reminded hosts Pat Buchanan and Bill Press that the inclusion of "under God" was inspired by the Gettysburg Address, in which Abraham Lincoln stated, "This nation under God shall have a new birth of freedom."

Appearing with AU's Barry Lynn, Sekulow said that the addition to the Pledge was a "tacit acknowledgement of our heritage, not any different than what's in our Declaration of Independence." Sekulow then touched (once again) on a by now familiar theme: that folks like Lynn and Newdow would stop at nothing in their effort to remove every reference to God from public life. Repeatedly hearing and reading this argument is a bit like watching a television commercial with the tagline *everything must go!* Lynn countered by offering an argument that received very little coverage during the Newdow controversy: parents should determine how and when their children are exposed to religious messages. "Now there's an affirmation every day that this is a nation under God, not under multiple gods, not under gods that care about the whole world, but that care about this country alone," he said (Holt, 2003).

Conclusions

While most folks support saying the Pledge of Allegiance, those who supported Newdow—or even rejected Newdow, but agreed with his claim—were not a visible part of these frames. Such an act of inclusion would require a true examination of the "social origins" of the issue, as Richard Campbell (1994) suggests, an examination that journalists chose not to undertake. Instead, as the ACLU's Nadine Strossen explained, reporters continued to portray Newdow as "kooky," as a "lone wolf" who would exploit his own daughter to shove his eccentric view of the Constitution down our throats (personal interview, August 26, 2004).

Ironically, Strossen admitted that she did not want to meet Newdow, so strong was her belief that "nothing good [could] come" of his lawsuit. Too much attention would be diverted from truly significant issues facing the ACLU and other civil liberties groups. But when Strossen did meet Newdow, she was "blown away" by how extensively Newdow had prepared, and by his devotion to the case—and to his daughter. "He's such a committed father. He loves his daughter," she said. In Strossen's view, Newdow "really should be looked on as the ultimate hero," an assessment completely absent from the coverage of the case.

Strossen's change of heart came after hearing Newdow speak at a meeting of the American Humanist Association, which honored him in 2002. Without notes, Newdow spoke for 45 minutes about how he was inspired to file suit. Yes, it did happen while he was standing in line at the store, looking at the inscriptions on his money. But according to Strossen, this revelation did not inspire months of fanatical devotion to ridding American culture of God; instead, Newdow simply saw something he believed was unjust, and thought "you can do something about it," Strossen recalled.

Strossen was so impressed with Newdow's extemporaneous talk that she now uses a videotape of the speech in her class in advanced constitutional law. Newdow "was a different person" than the one depicted in news reports—funny and self-deprecating; a far cry from the wild-eyed, out of his league, flippant windmill-tilter suggested by news coverage of his suit. Such a portrayal is not surprising, Strossen said, given our society's continued "demonization" of atheists.

As the case headed to the Supreme Court, reporters continued their defense of the Pledge, the flag, and the American way of life, even though their services as "sentry" were probably no longer required. Newdow was a scapegoat—a living object lesson in what happens to individuals who challenge our core beliefs and rituals. They enabled those who disapproved of the Ninth Circuit's ruling to blame Newdow for a laundry list of social ills—all of which could be corrected if Newdow would just go away and our political system were changed to allow the president to appoint "strict constructionist" judges. Add to that list the demise of liberalism and persecution of those who discriminate against very religious people.

And when Newdow's opponents recognized his right to file suit, they did so condescendingly, as if they were humoring an inquisitive child. David Gordon told Fox News' Bill O'Reilly (2003):

> "[O]ne of the reasons this is a great country is because an individual can bring an unpopular request to change a law that is very, very unpopular, but gets to have his say in court, and we don't fight in the streets, we don't imprison him, and we, in our turn, get to respond and fight it out up to the Supreme Court.

Thus, Newdow should be thankful he was not incarcerated for exercising his rights—and that the American people did not get even angrier at him for having the audacity to awaken us from our comfortable mental slumber by challenging the Pledge.

Chapter 8

Tepid and Diluted

When most folks go to court, unless the matter is minor, they retain the services of an attorney. And when you're headed for the Supreme Court, it strikes me that it's not a bad idea to hire a lawyer—a very good lawyer, with experience arguing cases at that level. Still, the number of folks who choose to represent themselves is on the rise. The American Judicature Society reports that more than 95 percent of court officials who responded to a 2003 survey saw an increase in the number of pro se plaintiffs they saw in their courtrooms. Twenty percent of these officials saw a "dramatic" increase. The largest jump has come in the area of family law (www.ncsconline.org).

While the National Center for State Courts acknowledges that most courts do not keep official statistics on the number of pro se plaintiffs, some of the data that is available points to their growing presence. For example, in California, at least one of the parties in more than two-thirds of domestic relations cases was "self-represented." The American Bar Association found in 1990 that nearly 90 percent of the divorce cases filed in Maricopa County, Arizona, included at least one pro se plaintiff. More than half the time, both sides were pro se. Data for federal appeals courts is a bit older, but it's still worth noting that between 1991 and 1993, the number of pro se plaintiffs rose by nearly 50 percent.

The rise in the number of pro se plaintiffs occurs against the backdrop of our fascination with the legal profession. We all read *To Kill a Mockingbird* in school. We cringe (some of us) at the gavel-to-gavel coverage of sensationalized trials offered by Court TV and overwrought commentary by CNN's Nancy Grace, but we've all seen *Erin Brockovich* and *A Few Good Men.* We talk about how wonderful it is when an individual, or small group of folks, takes on "the system," but we seem to like their chances better when there's a skilled attorney at their side—it makes for better television, at least. It's like our treatment of dissenters: we approve of the *concept* of dissent, but a surprisingly large number of us would prefer that dissenters dissented in a cordoned off, out of our line of sight fashion—so as not to run the risk of causing real dissension. Such was the reaction from the news media to Michael Newdow as his case wended its way to the Supreme Court.

Experienced journalists are quite skeptical of pro se plaintiffs. Nina Totenberg, who covers the Supreme Court for National Public Radio, recalled how she had "creamed" an individual who represented himself in a California case (personal interview, July 8, 2004). He was unprepared and unprofessional. In fact, many pro se plaintiffs are "simply dreadful," Totenberg said. Thus, not only was Newdow an atheist thumbing his nose at the Pledge of Allegiance during wartime, he was headed to the Supreme Court alone. One critic of Newdow said before oral arguments that the issue "cried out for the Supreme Court to address and correct it" (Naylor, 2004). Newdow acknowledged that "the country went berserk" after the Ninth Circuit's ruling (Cooper, 2004), speculation that had become gospel in the hands of reporters. As NPR's Brian Naylor (2004) opined, "to many, every word of the Pledge of Allegiance is—for want of a better word—sacred—and the backlash has brought this dispute all the way to the Supreme Court."

Even absent the news media's expression of hope, and its exaggeration of the "backlash," the Supreme Court is a tough audience, one that rarely turns over its stage to a pro se plaintiff. The justices would not easily take a new direction after years of somewhat muddled precedent on the presence of God in public schools. And after discussing the Supreme Court with skilled veteran attorneys, I came away with the impression that the high court is not a friendly place for a newcomer. "It is intense, frustrating, and exhilarating," said Erwin Chemerinsky of Duke University Law School. "It is an unbelievably intense and focused experience: facing nine superbly prepared Justices; dealing with issues of national importance; knowing it is on such a big stage" (e-mail interview, December 17, 2005).

Near the top of Chemerinsky's list of requirements for Supreme Court practice is having to make your case eloquently, but in a painfully short time. "My advice to lawyers arguing before the Court is to anticipate as many questions as possible, and to reduce all the answers to a sentence or two," said Douglas Laycock of the University of Texas Law School. "[T]hat is likely to be all they get to say before the next question comes." Make your most important points quickly. "Their first sentence or two may be their only chance to talk about what they want to talk about," Laycock said. "Don't waste that opportunity on introductions, but go straight to the heart of your view of the case" (e-mail interview, January 3, 2006).

Newdow had to try to accomplish all of this knowing that most of us did not want him to win. We liked the Pledge just the way it was. As Steve Aden of the conservative Center for Law and Religious Freedom said during an interview on National Public Radio (Naylor, 2004), Newdow had forced the nation to grapple with "one of those critical culture war issues" that purportedly keep many of us up at night, worrying about women who blithely decide to have abortions and homosexuals getting married so that they can set up recruiting outposts in our nation's schools. Others felt that the situation had deteriorated to the point that no matter what the Court decided, the country would not recover. Commenting in the same interview, Douglas Laycock said that the Court would most likely reject Newdow's argument. The result? "It's probably just going to produce a bad result and a bad opinion," Laycock said. But if the justices sided with Newdow, "it would produce a political volcano"—not what the nation needs as it continued its fight against terrorism.

But Newdow was quite prepared; he graduated from the University of Michigan's law school in 1988, and passed the California bar exam in 2002. The Supreme Court waived its rule that requires an attorney be in practice three years before arguing before it. He also practiced his arguments during several mock trials (or "moot courts") at Santa Clara University before appearing before the high court.

Journalists acknowledged Newdow's extensive preparation, but suggested to their readers and viewers that his chances of victory were slim, at best. And there were still lingering hints from reporters about his eccentricities. "Newdow might have been a pro se plaintiff," said *St. Petersburg Times* columnist Robyn Blumner (personal interview, December 20, 2005), "but he was still a lawyer. I think there was some surprise at his competence because . . . the media didn't have a lot of confidence in the man's stability."

The *San Francisco Chronicle*'s Greg Lucas took a different view; Newdow's decision to represent himself "create[d] an image of a lone voice howling in the wilderness; the plucky individual bucking the system" (e-mail interview, July 7, 2004). Warren Richey of the *Christian Science Monitor* said Newdow's decision might have enhanced his public image. "I don't know that a Supreme Court hired gun could have done better," Richey said (e-mail interview, July 8, 2004). "It was a better story that he argued it himself. He is articulate and knows what he's talking about." But could he change the "system?" CBS News reporter Wyatt Andrews surmised that Newdow's attempt to alter the Pledge "was one tough argument in a nation whose leaders pray to God all the time, in a nation that added that phrase back in the 1950's [*sic*]." Later, Pete Williams of NBC News would conclude that "few of the justices seem willing today to see the Pledge in his (Newdow's) absolute terms" (Seigenthaler, 2004).

The high court heard oral arguments in Newdow's case on March 24, 2004. Newdow once again jostled with several other major events for a slot on our agenda. On March 23, the 9/11 Commission issued its preliminary findings on the government's lack of preparedness for the terrorist attacks. President Bush was touting his record on the campaign trail, mostly to laudatory prescreened audiences (still a key tactic of his administration) while his minions, led by his presidential campaign architect Karl Rove, were offering indirect help to the Swift Boat Veterans for Truth, the discredited group that successfully turned John Kerry's heroism in the Vietnam War from a campaign strength to a detriment. Journalists gave the group a prominent place in the election dialogue, despite their widely acknowledged lack of credibility.

But despite the amount of coverage devoted to these events, Newdow still captured at least some of our attention. Journalists continued to temper his prominence by reverting to the frames we explored in earlier chapters. I will summarize the main points raised by the parties (and addressed by the justices), and then explore the broadcast news coverage of events before, during, and after oral arguments.

A Legally Protected Interest?

Leading off was Terence Cassidy, a top attorney from a Sacramento law firm that represented the Elk Grove School District. Cassidy argued that Newdow lacked standing and that the Pledge "is a patriotic exercise that is part of an unbroken history of official governmental acknowledgement of the role of religion in American life." Cassidy took issue with Newdow's attempt to "invoke the aid of a Federal court to override the state family law court in an ongoing custody dispute." It was Cassidy's belief that the justices "should not interfere with what amounts to the mother's rights and interests in the upbringing, educational upbringing, of the daughter." Newdow had claimed that he had a right under California law to exercise some influence on how his daughter was raised. Cassidy rejected that argument, arguing that Newdow lacked a "legally protected interest" in the case, not even as what the justices referred to as a "next friend" of his daughter.

Justice David Souter asked Cassidy if Newdow's "interest as a father" in ensuring that his daughter was "not subjected to . . . an unconstitutional religious interest or religious influence" gave Newdow personal standing. Cassidy said no, arguing that in cases like this, the school district has to look to a "single decision-maker"—here, Sandra Banning—for information on how the child is being raised. "Otherwise," Cassidy said later, "they couldn't function properly when there are disagreements with parents that are involved in custody disputes." California law prevents schools from seeking input from a parent "if it conflicts" with a valid custody ruling. Justice Souter steered the discussion back to Newdow, noting that Newdow was simply trying to "raise that question by virtue of [his] interest as a father," despite the fact that under state law he could not "control her presence or absence at school."

The school district and Banning were acting "in the best interest of the child"—the focus of any custody dispute. Justice Souter veered away from this characterization, stressing that he was not talking about "next friend" rights, but Newdow's role as a father, "admittedly with limited rights." Cassidy argued that these rights are more "abstract," and do not carry "a legally protectable interest." Justice Anthony Kennedy contended that California law "says otherwise." Newdow has the right, said the justice, "to have an equal shot at trying to influence and raise this child." That same state law gives courts the authority to decide which parent will make decisions for the child.

Justice John Paul Stevens pointed out that the family court judge did not direct Newdow to end his suit, nor did Banning ever ask Newdow to end it. The Ninth Circuit even suggested that Newdow's daughter "could go hear him argue the case" if she wanted to do so. The family court judge said she should not go, Cassidy noted, and once again stressed that federal courts must defer "to the state court's judgment as to what's ultimately in the best interest of the child."

Theodore Olson, then U.S. solicitor general, echoed Cassidy, noting that the family court—a court "with specialized expertise"—found that Banning should make decisions about the young girl's education. Justice Kennedy responded to Olson's claim: "He's saying, you may be right about that," but "I have my own rights. I have a right to . . . try to influence this child," the justice said. Olson reiterated that the family court focused on what was best for the child; Newdow did not have a legally protected right" to "challenge the conditions in the public school with respect to how the child shall be educated." Perhaps more pertinent is the finding by the federal district court that it was "unconscionable" to file suit in the first place, particularly since Newdow was aware it might harm his daughter.

Allowing Newdow to exercise this right "will have the effect of disturbing and upsetting the effect" of the family court's ruling. Federal courts lack jurisdiction to review state domestic relations cases. Justice

Souter then sought clarification of Olson's position. The government was asking the Court to consider state rulings on custody and on what is best for a child as it determined whether Newdow has "next friend" standing. When the Court moves on to look at whether Newdow has "individual" standing, the Court risks damaging these interests, which are protected by not finding that Newdow has "next friend" standing. "We've got to come to the same conclusion in each case," Justice Souter noted, "or we will undercut our conclusion on next friend standing if it's adverse."

Olson endorsed Justice Souter's characterization, arguing that it was consistent with the "domestic relations exception" described earlier. If the Court ruled in Newdow's favor, it would "collide" with the issues addressed by the family court—again, a court with "special expertise" in these cases.

A Ceremonial Expression of Patriotism

Olson turned to the Pledge. The Supreme Court "has repeatedly noted" that the Pledge is a ceremonial expression of patriotism. Justice Stevens cut Olson off. "Do you mean repeatedly held or repeatedly said?" he asked. Olson argued strenuously that the Court's comments were "more than dicta." Fourteen justices noted the difference between a religious exercise and a "ceremonial reference in solemn public occasions." Justice Stevens countered, "without benefit of brief or oral argument"—a suggestion that a complete ruling on the issue would carry more weight. Olson was undeterred. These justices highlighted "a major distinction" between prayers, for example, and saying the Pledge. Olson emphasized, however, that school districts must be required to enforce opt-out policies—this rises to the level of a constitutional right.

Then came a key question from the justices: do the words "under God" carry the same meaning today as they did when Congress and President Eisenhower approved their insertion into the Pledge in 1954? Olson's response—"yes and no"—drew laughter from those gathered to hear the arguments. The insertion is an acknowledgment that the framers of the Constitution were guided by their religious beliefs. They believed, Olson argued, "not only that the right to revolt, but that the right to vest power in the people to create a government . . . came as a result of religious principles." Repeated recitation of the Pledge—in ceremonial settings—would lead practically anyone to conclude that it was not a prayer, or an endorsement of religion, Olson claimed.

Olson's response led Justice Ruth Bader Ginsburg to ask if "a stronger case" could be made for keeping "under God" in the Pledge than could have been made in 1954. Congress' reconsideration of the Pledge's meaning after the Ninth Circuit's ruling in June 2002, although at least in part politically motivated, as news coverage of their reaction reveals, suggests that we were all nudged to explore "what the Pledge means, the context of the Pledge in its historical context, in the connection with its civic invocation" and "its ability to invoke certain principles that are certainly true," Olson contended. Olson also pointed out that Newdow was not directly challenging the Pledge—he was challenging the Elk Grove policy requiring that the Pledge be recited. And in its policy, the district defines the Pledge as a patriotic exercise.

Rejecting Newdow's contention that saying the Pledge in its current form is like requiring individuals to say "one nation under Jesus," Olson noted again that the framers repeatedly invoked God as they labored to create a new nation. Thomas Jefferson was the chief architect of the Act for Establishing Religious Freedom, enacted in his home state of Virginia. A motion was made to amend the act so that it would refer to the "holy author" (Jesus Christ). Jefferson later said the amendment was rejected because Virginia legislators wanted the act to apply to individuals from all religious sects, as well as nonbelievers. This would suggest that Jefferson was amenable to the inclusion of religious references in this piece of legislation.

In fact, as Nancy Jacoby explains (2004), Jefferson spearheaded the movement toward separation of church and state, and was the author of the act's first draft. Virginia became the only state with a law "meant to comprehend, within the mantle of its protection, the Jew and the Gentile, the Christian and Mahometan, the Hindoo, and infidel of every denomination" (quoted in Jacoby, 2004, p. 19). Emboldened by reports that the ideas on which the act was based were impacting individuals in Europe, Jefferson noted, "it is honorable for us, to have produced the first legislature who had the courage to declare, that the reason of man may be trusted with the formation of his own opinions" (quoted in Jacoby, 2004, p. 25).

The Framers could have based what would become the Constitution on ideas embodied in the constitutions in place in the states, as Jacoby suggests. These ideas bring to mind the mistreatment of atheists suggested by Newdow. In Massachusetts, only Christians enjoyed equal protection under the law, and only Christians could run for political office. Catholics who wanted to run for office had to reject the papacy in writing. Catholics were not permitted to hold public office in New York until 1806 (Jacoby, 2004, p. 26). In Maryland, Jews, freethinkers, and deists were denied civil rights under the state's constitution. Instead, the Framers borrowed liberally from Virginia's law, whose original author was, in Jacoby's words, "the nation's best known freethinker and deist"

(p. 43). As Jefferson wrote in 1784, "[I]t does me no injury for my neighbor to say there are twenty gods, or no God. It neither picks my pocket nor breaks my leg" (quoted in Jacoby, 2004, p. 42).

But to Olson, it was acknowledgment of religious heritage more than any other factor that caused the Framers "to say that they had the right to revolt and start a new country." God empowered them "to declare their independence when the king has not been living up to the unalienable principles given to them by God."

Is the Pledge a Prayer?

Newdow followed Olson to the lectern. The effect of the Elk Grove policy, he began, was to "affirm that ours is a nation under some particular religious entity, the appreciation of which is not accepted by numerous people, including myself." He announced to the Court that he was an atheist. "And every morning my child is asked to stand up, face that flag, put her hand over her heart, and say that her father is wrong."

Following Newdow's statement, Chief Justice William Rehnquist returned to the issue of standing. He reminded Newdow with a hint of condescension that laws on standing "aren't just technical rules that we lawyers are interested in." The "common sense component" of the dispute, said Justice Anthony Kennedy, is that Newdow had asked the Court to "exercise the extraordinary, the breathtaking power, to declare Federal law unconstitutional" to a situation that could only result in harm to his daughter. "She's going to face the public outcry, the public outrage," Rehnquist said.

At the heart of the law on standing is the idea that "when a citizen wants the courts to exercise this awful power . . . they take the consequences." Here, Newdow was simply redirecting these "consequences" toward his daughter. Justice Kennedy later pressed Newdow about his definition of coercion, noting that his daughter was not required to say the Pledge. "She's not required, but she is coerced. She is standing there," Newdow said, purportedly enduring the scorn of her peers. "Imagine you're the one atheist with 30 Christians there and you say to this child, let's all stand up, face the flag, say we are one nation under God." It is unfair to "impose on a small child . . . this immense amount of power, prestige and financial support." Cassidy pointed out in his short rebuttal argument that it is the parents who decide if the student says the Pledge. And in the classroom, teachers are required to "instruct the students about mutual respect, respect of other belief systems, of all persons' belief systems."

Newdow said it was unclear whether the fallout from his suit would damage his daughter; in fact, she's "going to be able to walk around and say that my father helped uphold the Constitution of the United States." Newdow emphasized, as he had in numerous interviews with reporters, that he was filing suit on his own behalf. But in building his case, Newdow began to describe how his daughter was subjected every school day to the religious reference in the Pledge. "It seems to me this case has to be about your right," said Rehnquist, "and you began this argument by talking about your daughter."

Newdow shifted gears, stressing his right to participate in his daughter's education. "That is an actual, concrete, discrete, particularized, individualized harm to me, which gives me standing," he told the justices. Simply being in the classroom while others recited the Pledge amounted to coercion, he continued, citing the Court's ruling in *Lee v. Weisman*. But that case revolved around a prayer, Justice Sandra Day O'Connor said. The Pledge, she said, is not a prayer.

But President Bush, cited by the group AU in its amicus curiae brief, has noted that "when we ask our citizens to Pledge allegiance to one nation under God," we are really asking them "to participate in an important American tradition of humbly seeking" God's "wisdom and blessing." Justice O'Connor evoked laughter from the audience when she suggested, "[W]e certainly don't take him as the final authority on this." She would later challenge Newdow to describe why he believed the recitation of the line "God save this honorable Court" did not cross the line. "Nobody's asked to stand up, place their hand on their heart, and affirm this belief," he responded. Newdow would go on to argue that it doesn't always take a full-fledged prayer to violate the Establishment Clause. The Court ruled in 2005 that posting the Ten Commandments in an Alabama state courthouse was a violation—but it wasn't a prayer. The school district's repeated references to religion—made in support of Banning's right to direct her daughter's religious training—prove that this case was about religion, Newdow said. "To suggest that this is merely historical or patriotic seems to me to be somewhat disingenuous," he added.

Newdow conceded that the Pledge does not start out as a prayer, but he rejected Olson's claim that the rest was simply descriptive, and ceremonial. The Court has ruled that the Pledge is an "affirmation of belief," Newdow argued. As such, it must be viewed in its entirety. "It says under God. That's as purely religious as you can get," Newdow contended, adding that a child reciting the Pledge does not stop and think about its origins or the intent of the Framers.

Chief Justice Rehnquist posed a hypothetical question: what if students were required to sing "God Bless America," a song that we can all agree is an expression of patriotism, instead of reciting the Pledge. Would that strengthen Newdow's argument? If students had to face the flag, place their hands over their hearts, and sing the song, then it would be an Establishment Clause violation, Newdow said.

God or Supreme Being?

For Justice Stephen Breyer, the use of the words "under God" was inclusive—"many people who are not religious nonetheless have a set of beliefs which occupy the same place that religious beliefs occupy" in the minds of folks who adhere to a particular religion. In 1965, the Court ruled in *U.S. v. Seeger*, 380 U.S. 163, that conscientious objectors seeking to leave the military were required to show that it was their "religious training and belief" that led them to seek dismissal. As part of the Universal Military Service and Training Act, Congress defined "religious training and belief" as "an individual's belief in a relation to a Supreme Being involving duties superior to those arising from any human relation, but [not including] essentially political, sociological, or philosophical views or a merely personal moral code" (www.findlaw.com).

Three soldiers challenged the provision, claiming that it unfairly failed to exempt nonreligious conscientious objectors, and that it discriminated against some forms of religious expression. One of the soldiers claimed, for example, that he believed in a "supreme reality," while another argued that his stance against the war stemmed "from his acceptance of the existence of a universal power beyond that of man." The latter soldier told the Court that his "acceptance in fact constitutes belief in a Supreme Being."

But by using the phrase "Supreme Being," the Court ruled, Congress was only trying to clarify "the meaning of religious training and belief so as to embrace all religions and to exclude essentially political, sociological, or philosophical views." The test of a person's beliefs "is whether a given belief that is sincere and meaningful occupies a place in the life of its possessor parallel to that filled by the orthodox belief in God of one who clearly qualifies for the exemption." Newdow rejected Justice Breyer's application of *Seeger*. The Court was evaluating Seeger's ideas and beliefs, not imposing a religious belief. "[T]here's a crucial difference," Newdow argued, "between government speech endorsing religion, which the Establishment Clause forbids, and . . . private speech endorsing religion," which is protected by the First Amendment.

Justice Breyer pushed on, arguing that when one uses a broad definition of religion "in a civic context, it really doesn't violate the Establishment Clause because it's meant to include virtually everybody, and the few whom it doesn't include don't have to take the Pledge." The use of "under God," the justice said, was an example of "this kind of very comprehensive supreme being, Seeger-type thing."

To Newdow, "under God" could not possibly mean "no God." This kind of broad, vague definition "seems like the Government is imposing what it wants me think of in terms of religion, which it may not do." Justice David Souter used the words "tepid" and "diluted" to describe inclusion of "under God." In its current form, it is so far "beneath the constitutional radar" that it amounts to ceremonial deism—that the religious content of these words is lost as we go about our lives. Allowing the government to determine what is "inconsequential or unimportant" is an "arrogant pretension," Newdow retorted, citing James Madison. Every glance at the flag produces the feeling that "I'm getting slapped in the face," Newdow said, as if the government was saying his beliefs were invalid. His daughter's exposure to other religions was a positive thing, but "I want my religious belief system to be given the same weight as anybody else's"—a happening made unlikely by the government's endorsement of religion in the Pledge.

Justice Breyer acknowledged that some individuals do feel left out, or offended, but suggested that Newdow might have overstated the divisiveness caused by the addition of "under God" to the Pledge. "It's not perfect, but it serves a purpose of unification at the price of offending a small number of people like you," the justice said. Newdow explained that the Pledge had more than adequately served the purpose mentioned by Breyer for more than 60 years without an affirmation of religion. "It didn't include some religious dogma that separated out some—and I don't think there's anything in the Constitution that says what percentage of people get separated out." He challenged Justice Breyer's divisiveness estimate.

As oral arguments wound down, Chief Justice Rehnquist asked if the country was divided by the push to change the Pledge in 1954. The vote in Congress was unanimous, Newdow conceded. "That doesn't sound divisive," said the chief justice. Newdow quickly replied, "[T]hat's only because no atheist can be elected to public office in this country." Loud applause filled the courtroom, which angered the chief justice. "The courtroom will be cleared if there is any more clapping," he said.

Constitutions in eight states include provisions that require candidates to profess a belief in a Supreme Being. Legislators have made no attempt to excise these provisions, for fear that they would not be reelected, Newdow argued. Under Article 6, Section 3 of the Constitution, which prevents the government from administering tests of religious faith to candidates, these provisions are null and void, but "they still exist," Newdow said. In the end, Newdow said, the dispute came down to the "quintessential religious question: does there exist a God?" By endorsing affirmations of religion like the Pledge, the government has answered "yes."

Holding His Own?

Perhaps not surprisingly, the attorneys who argued against Newdow before the justices were not exactly gushing in their praise of his performance. Terence Cassidy, the attorney who represented the Elk Grove School District, said that Newdow actually benefited from the news media's tendency to treat him as an "underdog." Contradicting much of my analysis to this point, Cassidy said that reporters covered the story as if Newdow was "taking on Capitol Hill" (personal interview, June 1, 2004).

Despite his exhaustive preparation, Newdow repeated himself and did not respond directly to some of the justices' questions, Cassidy said. In fact, some of Newdow's responses during the discussion with the justices about the standing issue helped the school district and the government make their case. His insistence on telling the justices that the case was not primarily about the impact of the controversy on his daughter, but was solely about his rejection of the district's policy, "kind of backfired," Cassidy said.

Still, Cassidy acknowledged that "the sophistication level" of Newdow's arguments and presentation rose as the case made its way to the Supreme Court. Newdow's supporters offered glowing assessments of his arguments before the Court. "He strides up there, by himself," said Barry Lynn, executive director of AU, and "launches into a moving, passionate argument," one that was based on a complete command of the facts (personal interview, September 9, 2004). Douglas Laycock of the University of Texas said that the depth of Newdow's passion hurt him. "His problem was not inexperience or lack of ability," Laycock said. "His problem was that he's a true believer; he generally took the hard line on every question, and had no interest in helping them [the justices] find a softer way to rule for him" (e-mail interview, December 20, 2005).

Some praise for Newdow did come from those who argued against him. Brian Chilton, an attorney on Sandra Banning's legal team, prefaced his assessment by noting the justices "are not out to make someone look bad," and that, in fact, some, like Justice Antonin Scalia, who recused himself from Newdow's case after saying during a public appearance that he believed the Ninth Circuit's decision was incorrect, have questioned whether oral arguments are at all necessary. The briefs from the parties help the justices form their opinions, Chilton noted; their views rarely change, even after a compelling oral argument (personal interview, June 27, 2005).

To be sure, the justices would not have barraged Newdow with "hardball questions," Chilton said. "Any competent attorney should be able to deal with [them]." It was clear that Newdow understood the issues at the heart of the case better than most of the attorneys who handle a great deal of similar litigation. "This guy knows what he's doing," Chilton acknowledged.

David Gordon, superintendent of the Elk Grove School District, said that as an experience, the oral arguments before the Supreme Court were "far and away the most thrilling of my career." Gordon viewed the case as one grand educational experience for his students, so much so that the district ran an essay contest in which students were invited to write about the case—all points of view were welcomed. District officials "picked one on each side of the question" as the winners, Gordon recalled; later, teachers led a lengthy discussion of the suit (personal interview, August 1, 2004).

Gordon noted that the attorneys representing the district took Newdow were well aware of how much he had practiced his arguments. "This was his obsession," Gordon recalled. "He didn't do anything else." Gordon suggested that Newdow's obsession at times pushed him toward anger. "He was prone to lose it when [the justices] came at him on the custody issue," Gordon recalled. "They tried to bait him, but he checked himself."

But it was Newdow's ego, Gordon suggested, that derailed his attempt to drive awareness of the discrimination felt by atheists. Changing people's minds, he said, requires the presentation of data that shows "a pattern of discrimination." Newdow chose instead to couch evidence of discrimination in the story of his challenge to the Pledge. And at least one reporter, Nina Totenberg of NPR, was impressed by his approach, an assessment repeated by many legal scholars and journalists in news coverage of oral arguments. "If you had seen the other pro se litigants that we all have," she said, "you would know why we all were amazed" by Newdow's performance (personal interview, July 8, 2004).

Newdow admitted in 2004 that even indirectly causing so much attention to be focused on his daughter might have been his most significant error in managing his case even though he had not used her name in his original complaint. He recalled that Justice Anthony Kennedy, in particular, tried to ram home the point that Newdow's daughter would "bear the brunt" of the fallout from the lawsuit. "She's a separate entity," Newdow insisted, but he later acknowledged that he could have done more to show the justices that "I was a good father" (personal interview, July 28, 2004).

Chapter 9

Nice Try, Young Man

Several newspaper articles that appeared in the weeks leading up to oral arguments before the Supreme Court complimented Newdow on the depth of his preparation. Lyle Denniston of the *Boston Globe* led his March 22, 2004, story by noting that Newdow would have "gone through 11 practice sessions" before heading off for the Supreme Court. With help from a group of advisers, many of whom have argued in front of the justices, Newdow would soon be ready to fly solo. Denniston suggested that Newdow was confident; he quoted Newdow as saying, "I'm looking for 8–0"—meaning a unanimous verdict in his favor. Despite clear, unyielding opposition from nearly every public official in the country—not to mention most of the country—Newdow took strength from the belief that he had "the law and the Constitution on [his] side."

Newdow thrived on the opposition, suggested the *Atlanta Journal-Constitution*. Even though he was now "the most reviled atheist since Madalyn Murray O'Hair," Newdow had earned the grudging respect of some opponents for getting his case this far, suggested Cox Newspapers reporter Bob Keefe (2004). "Winning a case before a federal appeals court—even the often overruled 9th Circuit—is impressive enough for any lawyer," wrote Keefe. In the first 15 minutes of a moot court presentation at Santa Clara University, Newdow "already has challenged the religious references in the Declaration of Independence, "America the Beautiful," and the Gettysburg Address." Keefe's March 22 article lacked the now requisite derisive references to Newdow's eccentricities. Where other reporters wrote about Newdow playing selections from his CD to raise money for his case, Keefe noted that Newdow had tapped out his savings, much of it earned as an emergency room doctor, to finance his legal quest.

In short, Keefe wrote, "Michael Newdow is on a roll." For the moment, at least, he was not the zealous atheist bent on driving God from public life. Instead, he was "a concerned citizen, an atheist—and a father." Keefe was also nonjudgmental in describing Newdow's lifelong skepticism of religious institutions, and didn't sneer when describing Newdow's ordination in the Universal Life Church. He was one of the few journalists to accurately characterize Newdow's profession of his patriotism. "He says his journey . . . has given him a better understanding of the Constitution, its drafters and colonial history, and a better appreciation for the freedom that comes with living in America," Keefe wrote.

Not that Keefe's story was completely free of "Newdow as eccentric" references; he concluded by recounting that Newdow "picked up the wrong suit" before heading to moot court practice, and ended up standing before the mock justices "in a coat, tie—and shorts and bare feet" (2004, p. 1A). In the days leading up to oral arguments, Robyn Blumner (2004, p. 7P), a columnist for the *St. Petersburg Times*, went Newdow one better: she advocated the abolition of the Pledge of Allegiance altogether. "Daily oaths and Pledges of allegiance are for nations that don't have as much to be proud of as ours. We have freedom; we don't need a Pledge," she wrote. Chest-thumping, still, but at least on the right track. The American people should acknowledge, Blumner wrote, that the words "under God" were added "as an overt statement of religious belief," but we should also acknowledge that a ruling for Newdow would cause "the passage of a 'Pledge protection' constitutional amendment faster than you could say Tom DeLay." Blumner restated her position, "If Newdow succeeds . . . I fear that the Christian Right will take the opportunity to mount an effort to undermine the Establishment Clause through constitutional amendment. The results will not be pretty" (e-mail interview, December 20, 2005).

While I am tempted to endorse Blumner's prediction, I think it is based on two faulty assumptions sometimes made by reporters. First, the audience is stupid, or at least malleable. I challenge the position of many news executives that readers and viewers want to be entertained, not educated; where, as retired CBS reporter Tom Fenton (2005) explains, these same executives use news to "insulate viewers in a feelgood [*sic*] fantasy just to sell commercials" (p. 200). Vikram Amar, a Hastings College of Law professor who served as one of Newdow's advisers, argued that reporters "are far better able to understand the nuances in a case than they are confident that their readers will similarly be able to appreciate their complexity" (e-mail interview, January 3, 2005). But this "contempt for the audience's attention span," as Fenton (2005) calls it, is a cop-out. I have to believe that we would want to be educated, if only news executives would remove their heads from their rear ends and entertain, even for a moment, the notion that challenging content might be profitable.

Blumner's second faulty assumption: the Christian Right is a growing, powerful, ominous force, wreaking narrow-minded, biblically literal havoc on American culture. Growing? Yes. Powerful? Sure. Ominous? Absolutely—but it's also the "force of choice" among journalists who often haven't the time or inclination to go beyond the ridiculously inadequate "red states/blue states" rubric and take a more thorough look at the country. Our cultural landscape is dotted (some would say cluttered) with references to God, prayer, healing, the Pope—even Armageddon. News stories offer positive descriptions of nearly everything religious—from the power of prayer to cure illness to the theft of a sticky bun that purportedly held the face of Mary. But this shift is at least in part born of fear on the part of television network executives (and news directors and editors) that they will be inundated with invective from what amounts to an agitated fraction of the population every time they try to put something even mildly controversial or provocative on the air, or if they write stories critical of religious institutions.

An incident described by Blumner in our interview offers hope that this fear has not overtaken everyone. After revealing that she, like Newdow (and I) is an atheist, Blumner received 500 e-mails from readers—all positive; all from folks "relieved to see their viewpoint represented in the mainstream press." The mainstream press must wean itself from oversimplified descriptions of our ideological makeup; they must provide information free of regurgitated spin and overheated stereotype. Otherwise, as one CBS news executive told Tom Fenton (2005, p. 160), "the less people know about the things they need to know, the less they will make informed choices when it comes to what they want to know."

Not all of the print coverage of Newdow's pre-oral argument preparation was positive. Maura Dolan of the *Los Angeles Times* (2004) painted a different picture of a Newdow moot court session. "Things were not going well," she wrote. Newdow asked a person pretending to be Justice Ruth Bader Ginsburg how she would feel "having to say 'Jesus' instead of 'God'?" Beginning a portrayal of Newdow as rough around the edges, Dolan wrote, "no, no, no, his advisors warned him. Do not bring up the justices' personal religious views." Another member of the moot court panel asked Newdow if references to God should be removed from our money. When Newdow said yes, Dolan again relayed his advisers' displeasure with his response: "No, no, no . . . stick to the narrow facts of the case: that minor children in public schools should not be led in recitation of a Pledge that invokes religion" (p. A1).

To that point, Dolan said, Newdow's performance had "not inspired confidence." Advisers were quite concerned that he was a "neophyte" and that he was "combative and unpredictable, with a tendency to vent obsessively about what he perceives as unjust" (p. A1). This approach would not sit well with the justices, who prefer a "low-key and nonrhetorical approach," said Pamela Karlan of Stanford Law School. Unlike his "ideological allies who have fewer quirks and know how to argue in court," Newdow leads a church called The First Amendmist Church of True Science, keeps a picture of the Supreme Court justices in his attic office, complete with their religious affiliations, is "consumed" by the custody question, and spends nearly all of his time on litigation (ibid.).

Dolan paraphrased a comment about Newdow's zealousness by Sacramento Superior Court judge James Mize, who earlier in March 2004 ruled that Newdow's daughter could not attend oral arguments. "Newdow is the kind of person who, upon coming to a brick wall, tries to go through it rather than around it, the judge said," Dolan wrote (p. A1). Not only did Dolan revisit the zealousness mentioned so often by journalists in earlier coverage of Newdow, she reintroduced the "flake" theme. Near the end of the article, she finds herself riding with Newdow in his SUV. Newdow, "an amateur folk singer," plays one of his CD's during the ride. "The song interspersed his lyrics with threats left on his home telephone number on the day the 9th Circuit ruled for him," Dolan explained. "My life is shattered," he told Dolan later. "I get up, and I am furious all the time." But he does it all for his daughter—what Dolan called his "absorption" with her earlier in the piece (ibid.).

But at least Dolan and Keefe informed their readers that Newdow earned his law degree in order to reform the nation's creaky family law system—David Kravets of the Associated Press (2004) wrote that the law degree was simply a tool used by Newdow "to sue doctors."

Outside the Mainstream

Most of the stories written by print journalists about oral arguments followed the same formula: a "rookie lawyer" (Connor, 2004, p. 2) takes his quest to purge "under God" from the Pledge to the Supreme Court. Protestors—for and against him—awaited Newdow outside the Court. He tells the justices he doesn't believe in God. He is upset that his daughter is made to feel that her father is wrong. The government argues that the Pledge is an expression of patriotism, not an endorsement of religion. They worry (as do the justices) that Newdow will next seek to remove God from our currency. Attorneys for the government and school district argue that only Banning has the right to make decisions about their daughter's education. Banning tells reporters that the young girl now freely says the Pledge; she even volunteers to lead the Pledge in class.

Though skeptical of Newdow's legal arguments, the justices are impressed with his preparation, his demeanor, and his pertinent questions. Justice Sandra Day O'Connor tells Newdow she believes that most of us do not view the Pledge as a prayer. Justice David Souter notes that the religious effect of the words "under God" is "so tepid, so diluted, so far from compulsory prayer that it is beneath the constitutional radar" (quoted in Savage, 2004a, p. A12). Justice Stephen Breyer diminishes Newdow's feelings of unease. "It's not perfect, but it serves a purpose of unification and has the small price of offending a few people like you," he said (quoted in Coile, 2004, p. A1).

Justice Anthony Kennedy questions whether Newdow has standing, and worries that his daughter will be affected by the case, no matter the outcome. Justice Ruth Bader Ginsburg focuses on the opt-out provision of the Elk Grove policy. "There's an option here. The child does not have to say it at all," she notes (quoted in Savage, 2004a, p. A12). Finally, reporters recount Chief Justice William Rehnquist's assertion that the 1954 amendment to the Pledge was made unanimously, an act that lacked the divisiveness cited by Newdow. Newdow's reply—"that's only because no atheists can get elected to office"—draws rancorous applause from the audience—it was an "amazing reaction," said NPR's Nina Totenberg (Siegel & Norris, 2004). Angered by the applause, the chief justice threatened to "clear the courtroom if anyone applauds again," a warning heeded by those in attendance. This kind of "back and forth," as Dahlia Lithwick noted, between a party and a justice is rare. "Everyone in the press room was buzzing because it was a very emotional, very passionate day in an otherwise pretty staid court," she said (Chadwick, 2004).

Let's look beyond the formula. It was clear from the reporting by many journalists on oral arguments that, even with his preparation and pluck, Newdow was still far outside the mainstream. Broadcast journalists suggested that he had simply run into some good luck at the Ninth Circuit. One Newdow critic explained that he "found" judges that would agree with him, as if he stumbled upon them, and as if these judges—the liberal justices in a circuit that "leans a little to the left," as this same critic said on NPR (Naylor, 2004)—are otherwise hidden from public view. Thalia Assuras of CBS News (McGinnis, 2004) commented that these judges "backed" Newdow, as if he were running for public office. Journalists were absolutely clear that he did not represent a mainstream view, despite statistics suggesting that most Americans favor a clear separation of church and state. Journalists were quick to point out that these same Americans—around 90 percent of them, according to polls cited in several oral argument stories—believed that "under God" should stay in the Pledge.

Broadcast journalists were not alone in treating Newdow's case like a misbegotten quest. An editorial writer for the *San Diego Union-Tribune* chided Newdow, "who has made a cottage industry of filing federal lawsuits challenging any public references to a deity" ("One Nation, Under God," 2004, p. B-8). Noted for its conservative bent, the *Union-Tribune* warned its readers that Newdow, called the "complaining atheist" by William Safire of the *New York Times* (2004, p. A-21), was "seeking to impose his atheistic views upon schoolchildren throughout the land." Newdow was out to convert us all. The Supreme Court must not, the *Union-Tribune* editorial concluded, "allow him, or others who share his hostility to religion, to banish God entirely from the public square"—again, not exactly what Newdow was after. He had help in this effort, wrote Safire, from well-known groups like the ACLU as well as from "assorted iconoclasts."

On *The Abrams Report*, which airs on MSNBC, host Dan Abrams (2004), an attorney with a law degree from Columbia University, drew on several of the frames we have explored in a segment on Newdow that ran the night before oral arguments: "Can something that has been a tradition for half a century *(ceremonial deism)*, which enjoys overwhelming support by the American people (*who Newdow insists on attacking with frivolous litigation)* be banned by a man's mission (*a mission that's clearly outside the mainstream*)?"

Like Joe Scarborough, his MSNBC colleague, Abrams suggested that Newdow was on a "crusade" to force the removal of "any reference to deity from the daily Pledge." Scarborough (2004)—a former congressman who poses as a journalist, especially during hurricanes—reminded viewers on March 24 that Newdow (an atheist) was on a "crusade to oust God." Over at NBC, anchor Tom Brokaw (2004a) warned viewers that the Pledge was about to be "put to the ultimate legal test." Newdow was back on the offensive.

Diminishing Newdow's arguments further, Abrams (2004) suggested that Newdow should have at least some reverence for "words that he himself recited as a child." Like so many of his colleagues, Abrams also reverted to the idea that Newdow would not rest until God was driven from all walks of public life. "I'm not asking for no God. I'm not asking for God. I'm not asking for Jesus. I'm not asking for anything," Newdow told an ABC reporter (Vargas, 2004). "I'm asking for government [to] just stay out of this business." Newdow repeated this contention in nearly every interview conducted during this—and every—phase of the case. But broadcast journalists ignored it.

Newdow noted that while reading money while spending it is optional, saying the Pledge really was not. "We're putting children in a position where they feel odd," Abrams (2004) replied, "but you use money a lot more often than you do recite the Pledge . . . kids look around, they look down at their money." Missing Newdow's attempt at making this distinction, Abrams concluded that taking "under God" out of the Pledge means "you also have to take the position we've got to eliminate it from everything." Abrams then suggested that Newdow had not chosen to argue that position because it would be "a loser"—a hint to his readers that Newdow was more than a zealot—he was an *opportunistic* zealot.

Abrams was not alone in his inability to grasp the nuances of Newdow's position. Describing the oral arguments in a report for NPR, Dahlia Lithwick said, "as you would expect there was a lot of concern that if Newdow objects to the words 'under God' in the Pledge, does he also want to get rid of coins?" (Chadwick, 2004). Journalists later might have been pleased at their prognostication; Newdow filed suit in November 2005, seeking to do just that. Newdow clearly restated the distinction at the heart of his lawsuit: "If it's the government acting in terms of religion, it's forbidden. If it's people, individuals, groups, acting in terms of religion, it's absolutely protected." Over at NPR, reporter Nina Totenberg incorrectly stated that Newdow was out to eliminate the Elk Grove policy "of having teachers lead willing students in the recitation of the Pledge every day" (Edwards, 2004).

Like many of her colleagues, Totenberg made use of quotes from religious organizations that had filed amicus curiae or "friend of the court" briefs in support of the government's position on the Pledge. In one instance, John Seigenthaler (2004) of NBC mischaracterized the American Center for Law and Justice, a conservative watchdog group, as a "public interest law firm." Their contributions to the dialogue were mostly one-sided and in some cases inaccurate. Steve Aden of the Center for Law and Religious Freedom told NPR's Brian Naylor (2004) that the addition of "under God" to the Pledge "juxtaposed the American foundation for rights and for civil liberties against that of the socialist system, which begins from an atheistic presupposition."

Our real hang-up? We believed, said Aden, that the product of this "presupposition" would be a "wholesale disregard for human rights." The obvious political motivations of President Eisenhower and members of Congress in rushing the change through were not explored. And nowhere in the coverage of Newdow—from the Ninth Circuit's decision right through to the Supreme Court's eventual ruling and beyond—did a single journalist cite amicus curiae briefs filed on Newdow's behalf by organizations like American Atheists. This conveys the impression that groups like the Liberty Counsel are mainstream, when in fact, they are quite conservative, and typically advocate a far more robust presence of religion in our lives than the words in the Pledge.

Totenberg also noted that Sandra Banning had enlisted the aid of "some big-time Washington lawyers," including former independent counsel Kenneth Starr, to present her case to the justices. Both Banning and Newdow, she said, have "handled the case in their own idiosyncratic ways." But while Banning said she was counting on God to help her pay her mounting legal bills ("He's always taken care of me before, and there's no matter too great for him"), Newdow used unconventional means to make his point. "[H]e's eaten up almost all his savings and he's thrown his creative energies into his fight, including a CD with songs he's written and performed," Totenberg reported. She closed her story on the upcoming oral arguments with a clip of Newdow singing "They had those Pledge of Allegiance need-some-old religion blues" (Edwards, 2004).

Journalists at ABC's *Good Morning America* that morning seemed more concerned with suggesting that Newdow's refusal to end his lawsuit (CBS anchor Harry Smith referred to "two years of legal wrangling" [Smith, Storm, & Chen, 2004]) was a threat to our country. This was "an explosive issue." Even Newdow was still in danger; viewers were reminded that he had "received numerous death threats." His case threatened to tear apart the country's already fraying social fabric. And what was the big deal? We had been saying the Pledge this way for half a century.

Use by reporters of the *ceremonial deism* frame soon expanded to include a strong "what's the harm?" flavor. "The girl's school claims America's heritage is on its side," said Thalia Assuras of CBS News (McGinnis, 2004). Journalists also expressed skepticism about Newdow's claim that recitation of the Pledge amounted to coercion. Alan Wolfe, director of the Boisi Center for Religion and Public Life, told NPR's Brian Naylor (2004) that he had to sing Christmas carols and say prayers in school; this didn't make him uncomfortable, despite the fact that he is Jewish. "Personally I'm glad I learned the words of all those Christmas carols. I think it's made me a better person," he said. "I think if you're a person of your own convictions, you can withstand that kind of thing." And one reporter, Jack Torry (2004a, p. 1A) of the *Columbus Dispatch*, took a bolder step, reminding readers about the presence of God in our civic institutions, leading his March 25 story like this: "The U.S. Supreme Court, which opens every session with the words 'God save the United States and this honorable court.'"

If the Supreme Court ruled in Newdow's favor, suggested ABC News reporter Claire Shipman, "the rift in this culturally divided country could widen, adding more controversy to an increasingly heated political season" (Vargas, 2004). Once again, journalists were on the lookout for threats to our national institutions. They had allowed themselves to be led around by the nose as the government made its case for war, manufactured the "red/blue" cultural rift that most sociologists and political scientists argue is an overstatement, and now were telling viewers that Newdow—with the country rallying against him, and some of its less intelligent, more overzealous citizens sending him vile death threats—could bring down the country with a verdict in his favor. Somehow, we were *still under attack*.

Broadcast journalists at times allowed Newdow's opponents to deflect questions about coercion of students with simple reminders of the opt-out procedures. While journalists struggle valiantly in most cases to remove bias from their reporting, preconceived notions about how a story should transpire do creep through. They often spring from previous stories on the same topic, an editor's assessment of what readers or viewers want to read and see, and an acknowledgment that we expect the stories to unfold in this fashion. In 1999, I was interviewed by a reporter for the local NBC television affiliate for a story about the proposed construction of a new stadium for the Philadelphia Phillies. Residents were concerned that they, not the team or the city, would have to foot most of the bill for the new facility, which opened as Citizens Bank Park in 2004. City officials essentially toyed with residents for months, threatening at one point to build the new stadium in the heart of the city's heavily populated Chinatown section. Citizens Bank Park was constructed across the street from the Phillies old park, Veterans Stadium, which was imploded—an event always heavily covered by television reporters—in 2004.

The reporter had found a paper I had written that explored how sports stadium controversies almost always unfold as "social dramas"—a term coined by anthropologist Victor Turner. When a team threatens to move if they don't get a new stadium, city officials scramble to satisfy the team's demands; typically, they denigrate the existing stadium. Residents express some concern about who will pay for the stadium, but the news media focuses on their love of the team, and their anger at the city for letting the team move. At no point in the paper did I claim to provide expertise in describing the economic conditions that cause a team to think about moving, and a city to desperately stop the team from doing so—mostly because I have none. I quoted several noted authors, including noted economist Stephen Zimbalist, who argue that construction of a new stadium never produces the economic stimulation guaranteed by team and city officials in the hopes of preventing a team's exodus.

Yet there I was in my office (my colleague's office actually, since the station's equipment wouldn't fit in mine), answering a question from the WCAU-TV reporter about whether I believed the proposed plan to pay for the new stadium was "a tax" on residents of Philadelphia who already have to deal with an onerous city wage tax. The reporter did give me the chance to explain my thoughts about Turner, ritual, and social drama, but my stammering "I guess so" was all that ran on that evening's newscast. The reporter was perhaps more interested in my status as a university professor, and the fact that I had written a paper remotely connected to the topic at hand, than about the quality of information or perspective I could bring to the table.

To her credit, CNN's Soledad O'Brien pressed David Gordon on the "opt-out" issue, noting that in some cases, choosing not to say the Pledge "doesn't work, because with all of the peer pressure in schools, the kids feel pressured to do it anyway, regardless of what their parents have sort of authorized them to do" (Hemmer, O'Brien, Cafferty, King, & Stone, 2004). Gordon then inexplicably compared the treatment of students who decide not to recite the Pledge with the struggle faced by children with special needs. "In our schools for the last 25 years, we've made great efforts to include special education children," he said. "If you walk through our classrooms, you have many, many students with disabilities in the regular classroom."

Gordon continued: "Our teachers do a very, very good job of helping our students learn to embrace differences." He added that he was confident that "if a child simply didn't want to participate in the Pledge of Allegiance, that the teachers and our principals would help them to not feel ostracized at all." Not only is this an unrealistic scenario, it likens the desire to dissent as a disability—if you disagree with a policy, and refuse to abide by it, you are burdening your classmates and instructors, who must go outside their job descriptions—which I hope still include "encouraging robust discussion on important issues"—to try to accommodate your "handicap."

O'Brien didn't challenge Gordon's characterization.

The God People

Oral arguments began at 11:08 a.m. on March 24. Describing the scene outside the Supreme Court that morning, *Slate* writer Dahlia Lithwick told NPR's Alex Chadwick (2004) that the area was "packed out front with protestors, mostly which proves the lie that this case is not about religion." To be sure, she said, it is "very much about religion and out front; it's the atheists against the God people." The intense debate about the Pledge "could be felt outside the court, where about 150 Christian activists and about 75 Newdow supporters held raucous, dueling rallies," wrote Michael Hedges of the *Houston Chronicle* (2004, p. A1), as if every issue in today's allegedly polarized America has to be decided by who can shout their talking points the loudest. The pro-Newdow camp has its sign, "Democracy not Theocracy," and the pro-current Pledge folks had theirs; it read, "I support the Pledge"

Marcia Coyle, reporting for PBS (Lehrer, 2004), surmised "it was probably the largest group that had gathered on the court's steps this year." Gina Holland of the Associated Press (2004) saw a more secular, perhaps more civic-minded, scene: "Dozens of people camped outside the court on a cold night, bundled in layers and blankets, to be among the first in line to hear the historic case." Newdow's supporters, outnumbered four to one according to Holland, struggled to convey their message over recitation of the Pledge by its supporters.

But sometimes the "God people" got better billing. Anderson Cooper of CNN (2004), introducing a story by reporter Bob Franken about the opening of oral arguments, focused on the "demonstrators [who] defended under God." A few hours earlier, his CNN colleague, Daryn Kagan (2004) warned viewers that Newdow, a "self-proclaimed atheist"—don't folks from other religions "proclaim" their faith all the time these days?—was trying to "have the phrase purged from the lips of children." Kagan's colleague, Sean Callebs, noted that Newdow "was greeted by some support but more critics, many saying they are fearful of what the court can do." Later, a supporter of keeping "under God" in the Pledge approached Newdow and said "God loves you." Callebs explained that Newdow thanked the demonstrator and added, "you can say that; the government can't."

Newdow, the school district, and the government may have been debating *ceremonial deism*, Lithwick said, but "out there this case is very much about whether God is in or out of the classroom" (Edwards, 2004). Said CBS News reporter Thalia Assuras "they are two simple words . . . but the passions they arouse are not simple at all" (Chen, 2004). NPR's Nina Totenberg (2004) described the scene in much the same way. "The scene on the steps of the Supreme Court was raucous with ministers and atheists vying for the microphone," she said. Fox News Channel reporter Mike Emanuel saw "activists kneeled in prayer at the Supreme Court this morning to say the Pledge of Allegiance, and later, equally passionate atheists demanded that it be changed" (Hume, 2004).

Visiting the *hands over hearts* frame, Dan Abrams (2004) explained that while we had been saying the Pledge with "under God" for 50 years, Newdow had only spent 6 years on his quest. Newdow said the Pledge when he was a child, Abrams noted; why was he now trying to take the Pledge away from today's children? He asked Newdow what he planned to do when the Court began its session by saying "God save the United States and this honorable court." Newdow argued that one line read before the Court's session was different than reciting the Pledge in school. "It's an affirmation," he told Abrams. "People actually have to voice this."

CBS News reporter Wyatt Andrews included short clips of Presidents Bush, Reagan, and Eisenhower—all Republicans—concluding their oaths of office with the phrase "so help me God" (Roberts, 2004). Other reporters defended the laws in place to protect those who choose not to say the Pledge. "Now you well know that no child in the United States is actually compelled to say the Pledge, let alone the words 'under God' during the Pledge" said CBS host Harry Smith, as if almost scolding Newdow (Smith, Storm, & Chen, 2004). Before one such segment, ABC's Claire Shipman reminded viewers that Newdow would argue before the justices "the words 'under God' should be stripped from the Pledge of Allegiance" (Vargas, 2004).

Or risk putting yourself at the center of a *holy war*. As Newdow prepared to argue his case before the high court, several journalists suggested that the presence of religion in society—in our lives—was at stake, and that two ideologically disparate camps were pitted against each other—an extension of the "red/blue" description of the nation that gained national prominence (if not credibility) after President Bush was reelected in 2004. Several print reporters (e.g., Hedges, 2004, p. A1) described how many individuals on both sides of the issue had traveled to Washington, DC, to be a part of this historic, life-altering legal battle. The *San Francisco Chronicle*'s Bob Egelko explained that the "anti-Newdow folks were much more numerous, and, by and large, more vehement" than the individuals and groups who supported Newdow; they "tend to be somewhat quieter than, say Focus on the Family (a staunchly conservative group headed by Reverend James Dobson) or Senator Trent Lott" (e-mail interview, June, 29, 2004). Rarely did journalists make this distinction in their coverage; they noted that both sides offered their support aggressively.

Governments in other nations were attacking religious expression, CNN's Fredericka Whitfield (2004) explained in an interview with Newdow. "[I]n France, the government there is not allowing in public schools students to wear crosses, Jewish yarmulkes or even Muslim head dresses [*sic*]. Should that be the standard for the U.S.?" Perhaps lost amid the clamoring attempts by journalists to paint Newdow as a scapegoat was his rejection of this trend. "That's individuals doing what they want to do in terms of religion," he said. "If it's the government acting in terms of religion, it's forbidden. If it's people, it's individuals, groups acting in terms of religion, it's absolutely protected."

Rave Reviews

As he led off an interview with Newdow that aired the evening of March 24, MSNBC's Joe Scarborough reverted (2004) to a tactic used by journalists with increasing frequency, in part to avoid what they believe will be boring discussions of key issues: handicapping. "Do you think you prevailed on your argument?" he asked. "Do you think the Supreme Court is going to rule your way?" CNN's Fredericka Whitfield (2004) asked questions with a similar theme: "Do you feel you made the best case possible? Do you think you swayed any of the justices your way?"

While some journalists, like Whitfield, were still tapping into the "where will it end?" theme (Whitfield asked Newdow: "Is it every reference to God that you have a problem with in every public forum?"), much of what was heard from broadcast journalists amounted to a rousing "nice try, young man." Close—well, not even close—but no cigar. You get an "A" for effort, but you still lose. Newdow was prepared, all acknowledged, but he was arguing a suspect case.

"The one thing that was very interesting," reported CNN's Bob Franken, "was the performance of Newdow." He "has never practiced before the Supreme Court. He is a doctor with a law degree" (Blitzer, 2004a). A *Houston Chronicle* reporter (Hedges, 2004, p. A1) noted that Newdow "appeared confident and articulate in a setting that intimidates many veteran lawyers." Anne Gearan of the Associated Press (2004) noted that Newdow "withstood the justices' vigorous questions, and based on their smiles and glances, it seemed he had won their respect. Newdow, wrote a *New York Daily News* reporter (Connor, 2004, p. 2), "injected a dose of passion into the proceedings."

Linda Greenhouse, the *New York Times*' esteemed Supreme Court correspondent, noted in the second paragraph of her March 24, 2004, story that Newdow performed "with passion and precision." While most expected him to lose—or were trying to find "reasons he should lose," those who attended oral arguments would probably never "forget his spell-binding performance" (2004a, p. A-1).

Reuters reported that he "held his own against a barrage of fast-paced questions" ("Flap Over Pledge," 2004, p. A28). Despite his lack of experience, he "didn't appear intimidated by sharp questioning by the justices," wrote David Savage (2004a, p. A12) of the *Los Angeles Times*. Such a session "can reduce even the most experienced attorneys' arguments to rubble," suggested Jack Torry of the *Columbus Dispatch*, "but Newdow often appeared to control the debate" (2004a, p. 1A).

Gwen Ifill of the *The NewsHour With Jim Lehrer* (Lehrer, 2004) asked the *National Law Journal*'s Marcia Coyle if Newdow's decision to represent himself was "unusual," but then stressed that Newdow "had carried the case in the lower courts" and now, before the justices, had done "a super job." It was the sole assessment of Newdow that lacked a dismissive flavor. "He brought something to the court and to the argument that no hired lawyer could do," Coyle said. "He could stand up before the justices and say 'I am an atheist. I don't believe in God. Every time the Pledge is said, it feels like a slap in my face.'"

The Supreme Court had seen fit to allow Newdow to appear before it, and "by all accounts he did a very good job." Nina Totenberg of NPR reported that Newdow "gave what was widely viewed as a virtuoso performance" (Siegel & Norris, 2004). Even the Fox News Channel, not known for its kindness to liberals or their ideas, acknowledged the praise lavished on Newdow. "[A]lready Michael Newdow is getting rave reviews," noted Fox's Greta Van Susteren (2004a).

But even though Newdow withstood tough questioning from the justices, it was probably not enough, these broadcast journalists suggested, to convince the Court to rule in his favor. "The justices were very skeptical. They just peppered . . . peppered Newdow with questions," CNN's Bob Franken noted when asked by anchor Wolf Blitzer (2004a) about "which direction the majority seemed to be moving toward." Pete Williams of NBC (Brokaw, 2004a) said that the justices were "skeptical" of Newdow's claims, and hinted that they deftly deflected his attempts to back them "into a corner with their own rulings limiting religion in schools."

You're pretty cagey, Newdow, but we've been at this a lot longer than you have—this was my impression of Williams's comment. He noted Justice David Souter's comment that the Pledge was "so tepid and diluted" that it was "very different from a prayer." Williams ended his story with Justice Stephen Breyer's endorsement of the opt-out provision present in most Pledge laws. "It's not perfect, but it serves the purpose of national unification at the price of offending people like you."

It took quite a while for the justices to press Newdow on the constitutionality of "under God," Franken suggested (Blitzer, 2004a). Meanwhile, Newdow "calmly parried . . . the seemingly skeptical Supreme Court" (Cooper, 2004). Once they did, both sides restated what by now are familiar arguments: for the government, represented by then Solicitor General Ted Olson that the Pledge is a patriotic ritual, not a religious affirmation; and for Newdow, that the Pledge is an endorsement of religion, one that harms his daughter even though she is not required by the district policy to say it.

Justice Sandra Day O'Connor pressed Newdow on the question of whether "God" should be removed from our currency. The Elk Grove policy condoned a learning environment in which students were "psychologically coerced into believing in God," Newdow said. "If someone took a dime out of their pocket and made my daughter say 'I believe what this dime says' . . . then that would be the same case."

Several journalists turned to Jay Sekulow, chief counsel for the American Center for Law and Justice, a conservative group strongly opposed to Newdow's suit, to assess Newdow's performance. "I think he gets an A," Sekulow told Joe Scarborough (2004), but quickly predicted that not a single justice would vote to uphold the Ninth Circuit's ruling. Scarborough played the "liberal media" card, reminding Sekulow that the Court is a target of regular criticism from "the *New York Times* and others" for its conservative interpretation of the law.

Sekulow then breathed life into a new theme: the Court's recent Establishment Clause rulings "have been confusing, contradictory, no matter which side you're on." Is the phrase "legitimate secular purpose" unclear (as the Court ruled in *Lemon v. Kurtzman*)? Sekulow then claimed that not even the justices themselves are sure of where the Court stands on this issue. Maybe they needed more help from God, too. As Sean Callebs of CNN noted (Kagan, 2004), "remember, this is a court that time and time again has barred school-sponsored prayer in the classrooms, athletic fields, and school ceremonies."

It became clear to reporters that the high court might not fashion a conclusive answer to Newdow's claims, after all. Journalists blamed the fight over custody; it was the issue that "threatens to derail the entire case," wrote the Associated Press' David Kravets (2004). The Supreme Court was slowly made to seem less than heroic. Deciding that Newdow lacked standing would be "an easy out," Kravets wrote, one that would get in the way of the Court's affirming (for most of us) that the Pledge was not an unconstitutional endorsement of religion.

Was there a new front in the holy war? Was Newdow now being treated as a hero? Not quite. William Safire (2004, p. A-21) of the *New York Times* called Newdow a "time wasting pest," but acknowledged, as did famed columnist Ellen Goodman, that his challenge to the Pledge was valid. "Those of us who believe in God don't need to inject our faith into a patriotic affirmation and coerce all schoolchildren into going along," he wrote. Adding the words "under God" was a mistake, Safire said, but changing the Pledge would only inflame the "religious majority," by which (I argue) he meant the Christian Right. Safire expressed his hope that the Court would not "use the issue of standing to punt, thereby letting this divisive ruckus fester."

Dan Lungren, formerly California's attorney general, told the *San Francisco Chronicle* (Coile, 2004, p. A1) that the custody issue gave the Court a "fallback position." The *Milwaukee Journal-Sentinel* argued that "succumbing to the temptation to dodge the matter . . . would be a mistake (Franzen, 2004, p. 16A). "This is finally the case that everybody has been talking about for decades and it's almost a dare," Steven Aden told Brian Naylor of NPR (2004). "Will [the Court} say the nation's own Pledge, its own motto, violate[s] the Constitution?" It was clear that despite some leeway from reporters, Newdow was still treated as a scapegoat. A *Boston Herald* columnist called him a "secular militant" who was "waging unholy war on anything smacking of religion" (Fitzgerald, 2004a, p. 14).

Yet even Joe Fitzgerald gave Newdow "high marks" for his "perseverance and commitment to his cause," even as he hoped the Supreme Court would give Newdow a "comeuppance" that would include "a much-needed crash course in American history." By the end of his March 24, 2004, column, he had returned to the "zealot" theme, calling Newdow's suit "political correctness run amok." He hoped that the justices would "thank Dr. Newdow for his interest, then tell him to scram and wish him Godspeed." Columnist Ellen Goodman (2004, p. 13A) also took a "bigger fish to fry" angle in her column about oral arguments. "What a pain this Michael Newdow is. Who needs this in the middle of an election? Why stir up the culture wars? Why make such a big deal out of two words?"

"You know, I think they're going to keep it muddy," MSNBC's Joe Scarborough (2004) said. Along the way, the justices kept the case citations and references to precedent to a minimum during oral arguments, and focused on the question, stated by Sekulow, "well, gee, does this really harm anybody?"

Some reporters still cast Newdow as unpatriotic, despite his repeated protestations to the contrary. Introducing an interview with Newdow, CNN's Fredericka Whitfield (2004) asked "why does he think it (the Pledge) is so un-American?" At one point, Newdow told NBC's John Seigenthaler (2004), "I should be able to Pledge allegiance to my flag and join my fellow citizens without being confronted with religious dogma that I disagree with." As discussed in previous chapters, this sentiment was absent in much of the coverage of Newdow's suit.

The Good Mother Returns

One of Newdow's original intentions in filing suit back in 2000 was to call attention to what he believed is California's flawed, biased family court system. As Newdow's case headed to the Supreme Court, broadcast journalists paid limited attention to the question of whether Newdow had custody of his daughter (he regained partial custody in the months before oral argument, and can now spend 10 days a month with her). They continued to portray Sandra Banning, the young girl's mother, as being on a mission—a more culturally acceptable mission—to assure the nation that her daughter was comfortable saying the Pledge and the words "under God" and that she was not an atheist like her father.

"We attend church regularly and we are active in our church . . . and talk about God at home," she said. She was a "committed Christian," in the words of the *New York Times* columnist William Safire (2004, p. A-21). So much so, it seems, that she complimented Newdow on his performance in front of the justices. He "was very well-spoken," she said. "He showed as much passion in front of the Supreme Court today as he shows in family court" (Duin, 2004)

On the first day of school in September 2002, months after the Ninth Circuit ruling, the young girl "volunteered to lead her class" in the Pledge, Banning told ABC's Elizabeth Vargas (2004). Thalia Assuras (McGinnis, 2004) of CBS reminded viewers that immediately after the June 2002 ruling, the young girl allegedly told Banning, "Mom, I will still say 'under God' when I recite the Pledge of Allegiance. I'll just whisper it so no one knows I'm breaking the law." She came to epitomize the "rift" that movement away from God in public life is purportedly causing in America. In a brief interview with ABC News, she told a reporter that Americans "should be proud of our heritage and proud of our history and not succumb to popular culture" (Gibson, 2004). Of course, this "history" includes at least the perfunctory tolerance of dissent. Banning at least acknowledged that Newdow should be free to pursue "his own legal interests" (Smith et al., 2004).

Banning was a key element in coverage of oral arguments before the Supreme Court, but only to the extent the custody battle she fought with Newdow might lessen the high court's desire to address the question of whether "under God" violated the Constitution. Borrowing a page from their coverage of recent presidential elections, journalists imbued this strand of Pledge coverage with a marked "he said/she said" flavor. Clearly, Banning was still the nurturing mother, and Newdow the self-absorbed father.

Three weeks before oral arguments, James Mize, a California Superior Court judge, ruled that their daughter could not hear Newdow's argument before the justices (Lucas, 2004, p. A-13). Citing a state law that prohibits children from attending a custody hearing where their parents are the parties, the judge said attending oral arguments would be "dangerous." Banning contended that her daughter was not prepared to decide whether she should go. Newdow never actually decided if he would take her along. "I don't want her to be exposed to anything, either," he said.

But Bob Egelko of the *San Francisco Chronicle* recalled that when Banning announced to the news media that she would become part of the suit, she repeatedly said her daughter's name—"each time followed by a verbal 'oops.'" It was Banning, Egelko explained, "who brought the daughter into the case while insisting that she was intervening only to keep Newdow from getting the girl involved" (e-mail interview, June 29, 2004). Journalists did not explore this discrepancy. They might have learned that Newdow convinced the *National Enquirer* to keep her daughter's name out of a planned story on the case (personal interview, June 22, 2006).

CNN's Fredericka Whitfield (2004) editorialized that Banning "has done her job to try to recuse her daughter from her involvement." Not surprisingly, Starr agreed. Banning, he said, "has just been very thoughtful and careful about trying to allow this 9-year-old girl to be a 9-year-old girl, to play soccer . . . and to listen to Britney Spears." Only one reporter, Nina Totenberg of NPR, acknowledged that Banning and Newdow had tried to be civil to one another throughout the dispute. "Each says the other loves their daughter and both speak proudly and protectively of their daughter," she noted (Edwards, 2004).

Other journalists were not as equitable. Harry Smith of the *CBS Early Show* revisited a theme evident in earlier coverage by asking Newdow, "Do you have—have any feelings about—in terms of the emotional welfare of your daughter being sort of caught in this tug of war here?" Journalists permitted Banning more time to make her case—often invoking God—that her daughter had been damaged by the litigation, but was bearing up well, than they did to Newdow, whose assessment of his daughter was limited to "[S]he's doing fine. She knows that her mother is a Christian. She knows that her father is an atheist. She's raised in two households and she'll choose whatever she chooses to be when she gets older." Banning's inability to pay her well-known lawyers "is a matter that I keep before the Lord every day. He's always taken care of me before, and there's no matter that's too great for him" (Smith et al., 2004).

Fox's Greta Van Susteren (2004) asked Banning if her daughter understood the issues raised by her father's suit. "She understands it. She knows that she's the child involved in the case." What she did not understand were "the ramifications, and we've tried to keep it on her level and make her the focus." Several journalists gave Banning the chance to describe the broad public support for the Pledge and for them. "Are there any parents who are opposed to it, who sort of joined with the viewpoint of your child's father?" Van Susteren asked. "Apparently, there are, but I'm not aware of them," Banning responded, suggesting that these folks might be in hiding, or are at far from public view—scared, perhaps, to come out in support of Newdow.

The justices had commented on the harm that might come to the little girl. Dahlia Lithwick of salon.com noted Justice Anthony Kennedy's concern that "this child is going to be sort of suffering needlessly because Newdow doesn't like the Pledge" (Chadwick, 2004). Justice Kennedy was not sure if Newdow had in fact been harmed by the recitation of the

Pledge. But by watching television coverage of the case, one could get the impression that Newdow didn't care. Banning told CNN that her opposition to Newdow's suit stemmed from "the use of the child as a way to gain sympathy with the court [by] claiming that the child had been harmed" (Cooper, 2004).

ABC News reporter Claire Shipman suggested that the custody battle between Newdow and Sandra Banning, his daughter's mother, "could actually provide the Supreme Court with an easy out" as it evaluated the arguments from all sides (Vargas, 2004). Greta Van Susteren (2004), prefacing her March 24 interview with Banning, acknowledged that Newdow received "rave reviews from some corners" for his performance during oral arguments, but noted that his case might be "on shaky ground" as the Court turned to standing. Some legal scholars argue that the Court should have focused on the Pledge. Erwin Chemerinsky of Duke University School of Law contended in 2004 that the standing issue was "a red herring." Newdow, even with limited custody, "surely has an interest in his daughter's education and religious upbringing."

Conclusions

During coverage of oral arguments, journalists moved the narrative about Newdow a bit closer to the border between what Daniel Hallin (1986) has called the "sphere of legitimate controversy" and the "sphere of deviance." Coverage became more balanced than it had been in earlier stages of the controversy. Journalists were still playing the guard dog role—protecting our cultural institutions—but they began to paint a more complete, less neurotic picture of Newdow. He was still marginalized, but his portrayal by reporters was taking on more depth.

This was especially true for print journalists; on television, which, as Hallin notes, "forces much of news into the unity of a story line" (p. 121), Newdow was still seen as the publicity-obsessed zealot, bent on eradicating religion from our lives. Broadcast journalists, Hallin notes, are more apt to "condemn" or "celebrate" people than their print colleagues (p. 123). Subtlety is not a hallmark of television news coverage; obvious moralizing is, Hallin argues. Still, reporters acknowledged that Newdow had given it a worthy shot. His arguments would not carry the day, even if the Supreme Court gave up the opportunity to issue a conclusive ruling about the Pledge, but he had mastered the tactics for crafting an argument that, if nothing else, satisfied the journalist's expectations.

Newdow put aside the quirky behavior and his intransigence and performed admirably, in a way that journalists felt comfortable relaying to their readers and viewers. Even though they still did not challenge the government's position on the Pledge, they didn't seem as sure as before that Newdow was a threat to the country. They were bucking a little bit against the guard dog's leash held by elected officials. Thanks to his stellar performance at the Supreme Court, Newdow was, for the moment, a figure worthy of more balanced treatment. After nearly two years of portraying Newdow as a litigious eccentric, reporters now tried to reconcile the "eccentric" narrative with an emerging "underdog" narrative.

But before we revoke Newdow's charter membership in Hallin's "sphere of deviance," a few points: first, journalists still described him as a nuisance; he was distracting the country at a time when we should have been deep in thought about the upcoming election, and up to our necks in fear about the terrorist threat. Second, Banning was still the "good mother." Journalists failed to explore her true motives for becoming involved in the suit. David Remes, an attorney for AU, argued that reporters did not consider "the mobilization of the broad amicus effort to secure reversal of the Ninth Circuit's ruling," an effort that included "the arrangement, if not financing" of Banning's legal team (e-mail interview, August 16, 2004).

"The effort to set Banning up in opposition to Newdow, and to undercut publicly and in court his claim to be serving his daughter's best interests, deserved more attention than . . . it received," Remes said. Instead, she was still a patriotic pawn in Newdow's ego-fueled quest. Journalists gave Newdow more opportunities to profess his love for his daughter, and to describe his abilities as a father, but they continued to imply that he was still exploiting her. Banning would never do that.

Chapter 10

We're Saved—For Now

The suggestion by reporters during and after coverage of oral arguments that the Supreme Court might sidestep the question of whether the Pledge was an Establishment Clause violation gives us another chance to see the guard dog at work. It has long been President Bush's desire to weed out "activist judges"—those who, in the president's words (words he uses repeatedly), "legislate from the bench." The president favors judges who adhere strictly to the that Constitution. Recall both print and broadcast reporters repeatedly reminded us that the Ninth Circuit, in ruling for Newdow in June 2002, was an obvious example of the kind of overreaching purportedly abhorred by the president.

The day after the Supreme Court ruled against Newdow, a reporter for the *Boston Globe* (C. Savage, 2004) reached back to allow longtime Senator Orrin Hatch, a Republican from Utah, to voice his displeasure at the Ninth Circuit's "judicial activism and overreaching" in making its controversial ruling. A writer for the *Los Angeles Times* went one better, telling readers after the Court's ruling that it was "the liberal leaning majority" that had put a temporary end to Newdow's suit (D. Savage, 2004b, p. A1). Not only were they liberal, they were impudent. When the appeals court ruled, noted *The Oregonian* in a June 15 editorial, "you could almost see the mischievous glint in the appellate judges' eyes. They knew they had lobbed an early firecracker at the nation" ("The Firecracker," 2004, p. B8).

While an analysis of how reporters cover interpretations of the Constitution is not a part of our journey, I think it is fair to say that the tendency of journalists to accept the validity of the president's view stems, at least in part, from an unacknowledged tendency to ensure that our important institutions—Congress, the courts, the presidency, the flag—and ideals—patriotism, loyalty, gratitude for our freedoms—remain intact, safe from attacks by dissident voices, even those dissident American voices who make a coherent point.

So when the five of the eight Supreme Court justices held on June 14, 2004, that Michael Newdow indeed lacked standing to sue on behalf of his daughter—a "fractured ruling," in the words of the *Columbus Dispatch* (Torry, 2004b, p. 1A)—journalists began to engage in a rather emphatic round of "I told you so," directed at Newdow. But their hope that the Court would once and for all decide that the Pledge was not an endorsement of religion, but was instead a ceremonial expression of patriotism, was, for the time being anyway, dashed.

In the words of *USA Today* reporter Joan Biskupic (2004, p. 1A), the justices "left for another day—likely years away—any resolution" of the Establishment Clause question at the heart of Newdow's case. Thus, the issue that Erwin Chemerinsky of Duke University School of Law called a "red herring" had gotten in the way of a clear-cut affirmation of the pledge, much to the disappointment of more than one legal scholar on both sides of the issue (e-mail interview, December 17, 2005). At least one paper forecast what would have happened if Newdow had won: "it would have meant he could ride roughshod" over Banning's opinions about how to raise their daughter ("The Firecracker," 2004, p. B8). The nerve of Newdow—trying to act like the girl's father.

In an opinion written by Justice John Paul Stevens, the justices reminded us that domestic relations law is the purview of the state courts. Only if an issue raised in a case transcends family law will federal courts intervene, Justice Stevens wrote. Here, a California state court determined that Sandra Banning would make decisions about their upbringing of their daughter when she and Newdow disagreed. Neither Banning nor the school district had prevented Newdow from teaching his daughter about atheism.

And in the end, despite Newdow's claims to the contrary, it was his daughter who was at the center of the controversy. Not only does the case touch on Newdow's rights, and Banning's, "it implicates the interests of a young child who finds herself at the center of a highly public debate over her custody, the propriety of a widespread national ritual, and the meaning of our Constitution," Justice Stevens wrote. Newdow's claim of standing clearly was built on his relationship with his daughter. Their interests simply are not "parallel," the Court held. California law does not allow Newdow—or any parent in a similar situation—"to dictate to others what they may and may not say to his child respecting religion," the justices ruled. He was free to speak with his daughter about anything, the Court found; he could not, however, limit what others discuss with her.

Federal courts should not involve themselves in a case where standing "is founded on family law rights that are in dispute when prosecution of the lawsuit may have an adverse effect on the person who is the source of the plaintiff's claimed standing," Justice Stevens wrote. "When hard questions of domestic relations are sure to affect the outcome, the prudent course is for the federal court to stay its hand rather than reach out to resolve a weighty question of federal constitutional law."

In a concurring opinion, Chief Justice William Rehnquist chided the majority, calling their decision on standing an "ad hoc improvisation." The majority, he suggested, had gone to the trouble of developing a new doctrine of "prudential standing" in order to avoid ruling on the merits of the pledge. But Newdow was not asking the court to alter the terms of his custody arrangement with Banning. He had brought "a substantial federal question about the constitutionality of conducting the Pledge ceremony"—this was the source of the high court's jurisdiction. The relationship between Banning and Newdow had "nothing to do" with his Establishment Clause claim, Rehnquist argued. Therefore, the Court should not have refused to take on the question. Thus, the majority had raised the bar for how much a case has to "transcend" family law in order to gain the Court's attention.

Journalists covering the decision seemed to embrace Rehnquist's reasoning—some with a bit more ardor than others. To some, the justices were signaling their intent to steer clear of stirring up an already turbulent political landscape. Historian David Garrow said the decision "bears all the hallmarks" of a politically motivated decision (Henderson, 2004, p. A1), an assessment shared by, among other news organizations, the *Houston Chronicle* (Reinert, 2004, p. A1), which reported the decision "defused a potential election-year issue."

The *Seattle Post-Intelligencer*'s editorial board suggested that the ruling had the same effect: it essentially took the Pledge controversy off of the nation's agenda in time for the presidential election ("Church-State Issue," 2004). The *Christian Science Monitor* quoted Douglas Laycock of the University of Texas as saying that "it was politically impossible to strike it down, and legally impossible to uphold" the Pledge (Richey, 2004, p. 1). The *St. Petersburg Times* expanded on this theme, noting that the last thing we needed was another issue "that threatened to drive another wedge between Americans and divert us from more pressing matters" ("The Right Pledge," 2004, p. 14A). The *San Antonio Express-News* agreed; the election "will be divisive enough as it is ("Ruling Gives," 2004, p. 6B). At least one newspaper, the *Boston Herald*, saw an opportunity pass by: "so the Pledge stays untouched for now, and President Bush is denied a fast pitch over the center of the plate" ("'Under God' Fight," 2004, p. 36)

But to other journalists, the high court had simply passed up the chance to rule on the merits of the pledge. It "ducked a final ruling on the legality of the Pledge and its reference to God," wrote David Savage of the *Los Angeles Times* (2004b, p. A1). Steve Chapman (2004, p. 17A), a columnist for the *Chicago Tribune*, stressed that the ruling "turns on one of those annoying technicalities that seem to let the courts evade their duty to interpret our laws." So it's their *duty* when we want them to rule on something, and an overextension of their power when we don't want them to. Journalists repeatedly used words like "sidestepped," "dodged" and "technicality" in describing the ruling.

The *New York Times* called the ruling "inconclusive" (Greenhouse, 2004b). Bob Egelko (2004b, p. A1) of the *San Francisco Chronicle* said that the justices had "brought two years of pleadings and passion" to "a crashing anticlimax." Wrote Joe Fitzgerald in a *Boston Herald* column (2004b, p. 16): "As victories go, it was a shallow one, but at least the U.S. Supreme Court reached the right conclusion in telling Michael Newdow . . . to take a hike."

Perhaps the most compelling reason for a firm decision, suggested many of the nation's editorial writers, was that other individuals would inevitably mount new challenges to the pledge. Newdow told the *New York Times* that there were "fellow atheists waiting in the wings" (Greenhouse, 2004b) to mount new legal challenges to the Pledge. We would once again find ourselves *under attack*—one of the frames that has guided our discussion. It is a frame that has worked particularly well for the Bush administration, although a claim by the president in February 2006 that our national security apparatus had thwarted a possible 2002 attack by Al-Qaeda on Los Angeles was, as he scolded John Kerry in a 2004 debate, "one of those exaggerations."

Maybe the nation has finally had enough of empty and largely dishonest fear-mongering, but some journalists may need a bit more prodding. Joe Fitzgerald of the *Boston Herald* (2004, p. 16) emphatically predicted "they'll get another chance someday. You can bet on that." In a June 15 editorial, the *New York Daily News* said that while it was pleased the Pledge was "intact for now. Thank God," the right of children to "cheerily chirp their allegiance" to the flag "still could be taken away from them" ("The Pledge Is Safe," 2004, p. 40). The *Denver Post* also picked up on the "for now" theme ("'Under God' Preserved," 2004, p. B6), as did many other news organizations. Few journalists had the temerity to suggest that it was "the zealotry on both sides"—not just one—that would eventually push the issue back before the Court. The battle would start again someday, but it would be an atheist—another "scapegoat" ripe for the marginalizing—who would make the first move.

"We wish the high court had taken the opportunity to settle the issue on the merits because, odds are, it will keep coming back until it is settled," noted the *Milwaukee Journal-Sentinel* ("Pledge 'Issue,'" 2004, p. 12A). The newspaper intensified its language later in the same editorial, suggesting the justices had "decided to take a powder" on the Pledge. The high court's ruling, contended the *Seattle Post-Intelligencer*, turned a "long anticipated ruling" into "little more than a high-profile ruling in a custody dispute" ("Church-State Issue," 2004).

The tone of these editorials suggested that "real Americans," like Rehnquist, O'Connor, and Thomas wanted to finish the fight. They wanted to "settle the Pledge issue once and for all" ("Pledge Stands," 2004, p. B6). But instead, the Court had "spurned pleas" (Egelko, 2004a) from both the parties in the case as well as the news media, to make a definitive ruling. The *Cleveland Plain Dealer* announced three days after the Court's ruling that we would sit idly by and let this issue slip from the national consciousness. "America will not much longer allow it to go unresolved, because it is the national acknowledgement [*sic*] of God—on whose name the court calls for salvation each time it meets—is at its core" ("Under God, For Now," 2004, p. B8).

God Stays in the Picture

Broadcast journalists in particular reacted as though the nation had been saved from Newdow—even though the justices did not offer a lot of help. Newdow was now referred to by at least one journalist as a "devoted atheist" (Norris, 2004) rather than the much more discomfiting "avowed atheist" seen stirring up trouble previously. Calling to mind our *hand over hearts* frame, NBC's Tom Brokaw (2004b) opened the June 14 *NBC Nightly News* by reassuring the nation that the attack mounted by Newdow had been defeated: "In the nation's classrooms, just as in service club meetings, when Boy Scout troops gather and American Legion posts assemble, if the ceremony includes the Pledge of Allegiance, God stays in the picture." The *ceremonial deism* frame was clearly intact, as broadcast journalists joined their print colleagues in emphasizing opinions from the justices supporting the notion that some references to God are, as Justice Sandra Day O'Connor explained, "the inevitable consequence of the religious history that gave birth to our founding principles of liberty."

In introducing his story on the ruling, CNN's Bob Franken (Blitzer, 2004b) highlighted the fact that the decision came down on Flag Day. "Let me be the first, Wolf (Blitzer) to wish you a happy Flag Day—certainly a happy one on the 50th anniversary of the establishment of

Flag Day for those who would advocate leaving the words 'under God' in the Pledge of Allegiance."

Brokaw (2004b) told viewers that the Court "ducked the central question" in the Newdow case. NBC correspondent Pete Williams said that the Court agreed that Newdow "can teach his own child as he likes, but he cannot dictate to others what they may and may not say to his child about religion." One could detect dissatisfaction from these, and other journalists, that our system of government did not correct itself. It had not emerged unscathed from the Newdow threat. Harmony had not been reestablished.

Despite the direction of the Court's ruling, some of Newdow's opponents magically transformed the Court's reasoning into a resounding victory for the Pledge. Jay Sekulow said the ruling "freed up 10 million students on the West Coast that desired to say the Pledge of Allegiance," as if those children had been imprisoned—like so many "enemy combatants" or the 140,000 Japanese-Americans interned at the start of World War II. "A cloud has been removed that's been hanging over the school districts for a long time now," Sekulow said, a quote repeated in many of the stories written about the ruling.

This cloud seems a lot less threatening than the "lack of funding caused by the President's *No Child Left Behind* initiative" cloud, which has forced many states to cut already stretched education budgets and has caused teachers in schools across the country to worry more about ensuring that their students pass a standardized test than encouraging a real, ongoing love of learning.

But even an ardent anti-Newdow figure like Sekulow acknowledged that by not ruling on the constitutionality of the Pledge, the justices had left the door open for more suits—at least one would be filed in 2004 by Newdow himself, which would be upheld, at least in part, by a federal judge in Sacramento. District officials were not happy at this prospect, suggested Williams. Legal scholars quoted by Nina Totenberg agreed that the Court had taken advantage of what one called "a very attractive out."

It probably would not surprise you to know that Bill O'Reilly (2004a) of the Fox News Channel predicted that "the left wing loonies on the Ninth Circuit Court of Appeal" would be the ones holding the door open for the slew of new Pledge suits. "They will find another atheist to file a suit," he said in a June 14 interview with constitutional law expert Jonathan Turley.

So we were back to the "activist judge" argument—the Ninth Circuit would once again gladly act as advocates for the left-wingers and the atheists in its jurisdiction, allowing them to impose their views on everyone in the states in their charge. But the Supreme Court? It turns out the justices weren't activist enough—they were, to quote O'Reilly, "a little cowardly." O'Reilly's colleague at Fox, legal commentator Andrew Napolitano, said that the justices "punted" (J. Gibson, 2004). CNN senior legal analyst Jeffrey Toobin said the "case ends sort of with a whimper rather than a bang" (Blitzer, 2004b).

It would also probably not surprise you to know that O'Reilly was a one-person "trot out the other frames we've discussed" machine during this interview. He argued that Newdow was just using his daughter to score ideological points by bringing our hallowed institutions under attack. Perhaps previewing his tirade about our nation's anti–Christian-driven bias against Christmas, O'Reilly said that Newdow "encapsulated the Ninth Circuit court of appeals, the most anti-Christian court in the history of this country." I have no idea what he meant by "encapsulated," but I am relatively sure it had something to do with the Ninth Circuit not liking God, even if they were, as CNN's Toobin said, "out to lunch" when they ruled in June 2002.

The Ninth Circuit, or any other federal circuit for that matter, could expect a similar assault if it dared rule "under God" unconstitutional, Toobin suggested. They could expect another "sad day," using O'Reilly's words, if they tried to remove God from the Pledge (O'Reilly, 2004b). The high court's ruling, even though only three of the justices rejected the Ninth Circuit's decision, "was certainly a shot across the bow" of the appeals court.

O'Reilly spoke glowingly about the "good mother," Sandra Banning, claiming that she had nothing to do with the escalation of the controversy, and that she was "outraged" that Newdow had exploited the young girl for publicity's sake. He allowed Banning to express gratitude for her limited victory, and to once again let the nation know that her daughter was a God-fearing, Pledge-embracing Christian—and to reinforce the unsupported idea that Newdow had just used his daughter. "You know, whenever you present information to a court claiming that a child may be harmed, then you're going to gain sympathy from the court," she told O'Reilly.

Her comments reinforced the "we're glad it's over" theme, repeating, as she had for print journalists, that the young girl breathed "a sigh of relief" upon hearing the news. The young girl "wanted to avoid being put in any spotlight"—unlike her mother, who, with the aid of a formidable, well-paid legal team, embraced it. And lo and behold, Banning acknowledged that despite the attention—despite Newdow's alleged manipulation—the young girl was doing just fine. Manufactured crisis averted. "Kids are real resilient," O'Reilly said. "So I'm glad to hear that you don't think she's been damaged in any way"—an argument Banning and those opposed to Newdow had been making for nearly two years.

For his part, Turley echoed the concerns of other legal scholars in his contention that a father, "whether divorced or not, should have enough standing to be heard on an issue like this" (O'Reilly, 2004a).

The impact of the high court's ruling must have somehow persuaded Turley and Fox's Napolitano that Newdow and Banning were married; they were not. Napolitano erred again when he said that Newdow "has no relationship with his daughter." Even the staunchest opponent of Newdow would acknowledge that he does play a significant role in his daughter's life—and he has partial custody. This erroneous, but still nuanced view was lost in the din of O'Reilly's rabble-rousing, as so many views are. NPR's Nina Totenberg quoted Banning as saying that her daughter "actually had more of a sigh of relief that it was over more than an opinion of the case itself" (Norris, 2004).

Much like the Supreme Court.

Banning's comment underscores a significant new theme in coverage of Newdow's suit: we're just glad it's over. The Court's decision may have fallen short of the constitutional mark, and the justices may have mishandled the standing question, but journalists were content to tell America that the attack was over. We had been saved from Newdow's ranting and windmill-tilting. We could, for the moment at least, stand down.

The "bitter custody fight," as Fox News' Greta Van Susteren called it (2004a), continued to obscure, at least to Newdow the larger issue: the nation's "horrible family law system." Almost to a person, journalists applied the "battle" frame, pitting Banning and Newdow in a fight over the course of their daughter's upbringing, rather than explore in any detail the flaws in the system alleged by Newdow. Journalists, particularly those working for broadcast news organizations, tend to focus on the fallout from a single event, rather than explore organizational or systemic flaws.

Or perhaps they wanted to tell us to stand down, but couldn't, thanks to the Supreme Court's decision. Discussion by journalists of the likelihood of future suits took on the tone of a warning. "The day of legal reckoning has been postponed but in all likelihood not forever," suggested NPR's Nina Totenberg (2004). We could easily find ourselves *under attack* again by these crazy atheists. The Supreme Court is well aware, argued Fox's Napolitano, that significant issues like these should be decided. "They know it will come back," he said (J. Gibson, 2004). Napolitano's comment, like those of his colleagues, suggests that this is all just a giant bother, that the efforts of individuals like Newdow are illegitimate and misdirected.

In an interview with Newdow and David Gordon, Greta Van Susteren (2004b) suggested that the country would not want to endure another round of legal controversy. "I'm a little disappointed in the

Supreme Court because it didn't decide the issue; in some ways it's going to come right back up with some other litigants," she said. Ever the champion of our legal system, Gordon stressed that Newdow had fought the good fight—on an uneven playing field, perhaps—and had lost, fair and square. "[W]e had a legal dispute, we fought it through in the courts. If we're challenged again, we will fight it through again," he said. The system, in Gordon's view works just fine.

On Being a Dissenter in America

Just before President Bush was about to make his State of the Union address on January 31, 2006, Cindy Sheehan, the antiwar protestor whose son, Casey, died while serving in Iraq, was roughly ejected from the Senate gallery after U.S. Capitol Police became alarmed at the T-shirt she wore to the event. It read, "2245 Dead. How Many More?" Congresswoman Lynn Woolsey of California invited Sheehan to attend the address. Sheehan said she overcame her initial reluctance to attend as a courtesy to Woolsey. Sheehan had given her ticket to another antiwar activist, but reclaimed it when Woolsey told her she had already told journalists Sheehan would be there. At no time was Sheehan warned about the message on her shirt.

Screened twice by law enforcement officials before the speech, Sheehan removed her jacket as she sat down. "I wasn't boisterous. I didn't say anything. I just sat down," she said ("Police Apologize," 2006). At the sight of her shirt, a Capitol Police officer named Mike Weight reportedly shouted "protestor!" at her, removed her from her seat, and, in Sheehan's words, "shoved me up the stairs" (Sheehan, 2006). Weight handcuffed her and rushed her out of the gallery. As they hustled along, he urged Sheehan to be careful. "You didn't care about me being careful when you were dragging me up the stairs," she said. "That's because you were protesting," Weight reportedly said.

Sheehan was arrested—"after demonstrating in the spectators gallery of the House of Representatives," reported the *Washington Post* (Williams & Lengel, 2006)—charged with violating District of Columbia law, which bans disruptive conduct on Capitol grounds, then was released after being detained for four hours. After being fingerprinted, a Capitol Police sergeant shared some kind words about her shirt, telling Sheehan he had just returned from a tour of duty in Iraq. "I told him that my son died there. That's when the enormity of my loss hit me. I have lost my son. I have lost my First Amendment rights. I have lost the country that I love. Where did America go?" she said.

The *Post* apparently believed it was quickly falling into the hands of the protestors. It reported that Sheehan, who was "apparently" given a ticket by Woolsey, was the leader of a "band of banner-waving antiwar demonstrators" who "clustered outside the Capitol," waiting for Bush to begin so they could "let loose with an ear-splitting outburst of noise." Later, they would, the paper noted, sing "peace anthems of another day," including John Lennon's "Give Peace a Chance."

As Sheehan's supporters criticized the government for her arrest, the Capitol Police quickly concluded that its officers should not have confronted Sheehan and Beverly Young, wife of Congressman Bill Young of Florida, about their shirts. Young wore a shirt with a pro-troops message. But while Sheehan was arrested and hauled away, Young was asked to leave and was not arrested. Capitol police officials apologized to Sheehan, and vowed to revisit policies about protesting in the Capitol building ("Police Apologize," 2006).

Sheehan acknowledged that she was trying to make a statement by wearing the shirt. If she had wanted to disrupt the president's speech, however, she claims she would have taken her jacket off while he was talking. "I don't want to live in a country that prohibits any person, whether or not he/she has paid the ultimate price for that country, from wearing, saying, writing, or telephoning statements about the government," Sheehan said the day after Bush's speech. It is also worth noting that State of the Union guests do not receive instructions about what to wear to the speech.

The conduct of the Capitol Police underscores once more the lengths to which those with dissenting views have to go to have their views heard—and the lengths that law enforcement, and our state and federal governments, will go to prevent these voices from being heard, unless the hearing is happening in a predetermined area. The Sheehan incident also suggests that even respectful displays of dissenting opinion may be met with unnecessarily formidable shows of force.

So while it seems that the "little guy fighting city hall" theme that I tell my students to look for as they scour the streets for stories, isn't dead, it certainly has lost much of its mythic steam, thanks at least in part to the uneven work of print and broadcast journalists. I should acknowledge that I instruct my students to treat the stories offered by whistle-blowers with caution, since many do approach journalists with little more than axes to grind. Still, several of the journalists I interviewed for the book insisted that it was this quality that caused them to cover Newdow's case. I'm not convinced, though. I think we take this myth out of the attic from time to time. If we can take anything from Newdow's story, it is this: we must, as a nation, reintroduce ourselves to the notion that anyone can mount a challenge to a policy or a law that is perceived to be unjust or discriminatory. This reintroduction is especially important now, as we learn seemingly every day of the continued expansion of the powers exercised by elected leaders on all levels of government.

As I write this, the fallout intensifies from the revelation that President Bush authorized the National Security Agency to monitor international phone calls by American citizens. Bush has defended the policy as necessary in the fight against the ever-elusive "terror." The news media, which only recently shed some critical light on Bush's handling of the war, has thankfully continued, in increments anyway, the rediscovery of its watchdog function as it relates to these issues.

Journalists, especially those on the broadcast side, continue to misrepresent the NSA policy, largely to Bush's benefit. In fact, the *New York Times* agreed to hold off publishing its story about the wiretapping story for one year (after the 2004 election) at the White House's request. Bush administration officials claimed that running the article would damage ongoing terrorist investigations, and might tip terrorists off that the government was keeping tabs on them. The *Times* accepted at face value the claim by the government that the program did not run afoul of the law or threaten anyone's civil liberties. "It is not our place to pass judgment" on these issues, said *Times* executive editor Bill Keller ("The Scoop," 2006).

Let me see if I have this right: the nation's most revered newspaper now believes it is incapable of evaluating the veracity of official reasoning behind a program that is based on a very creaky interpretation of the Constitution. Instead of caving to the government, the *Times*, at the very least, should have brought in its own lawyers to assess the program. And it turns out that the *Times* might not have printed the story had it not been for the fact that James Risen, a *Times* reporter, was about to release a book about the NSA program.

Bottom line: we depend on the press to perform its watchdog function at our peril.

Those who disagree with Bush's war policies are given little time and space to share their views with the public—Sheehan, whose son, a soldier, was killed in Iraq and John Murtha, a decorated Vietnam veteran and Pennsylvania congressman, are two notable, very public exceptions. This is not to say that antiwar protests are never covered—they are, but with strict adherence to the frames discussed in this book. They are covered when they are large enough, and potentially destructive. The message, like the one on Sheehan's shirt, is secondary to reaffirming the idea that protestors are loud, boorish, selfish, and ultraorganized in a threatening (dare I say terroristic?) way.

Sheehan, criticized for purportedly political motivations by many commentators, took her fight directly to Bush's Crawford, Texas, ranch, where he was enjoying some of the vacation time he takes more of than any other American president. Murtha made his comments on the floor of the House of Representatives. A freshman colleague from Ohio, Joan Schmidt, essentially called him a coward, saying Marines (the branch of the military in which Murtha served) don't "cut and run." The news media provided extensive coverage of these expressions of dissent, but upon closer inspection, continue to treat Sheehan and Murtha like eccentric interlopers.

Thus, Newdow would have probably remained obscure had the Ninth Circuit not ruled in his favor. His claim that the Pledge of Allegiance includes an unconstitutional endorsement of religion would probably have been reduced to perhaps a line in our history books, or a news brief on a back page of a newspaper. Yet he forced his way onto our agenda—and affixed a target to his back. Despite what the "We Welcome Dissenters" brochure distributed by the country when we're children tells us, atheists, to borrow from the late comedian Rodney Dangerfield, don't get a lot of respect. Those who are passionate about their belief in God probably have atheists right up there with Janet Jackson, network television executives, and teachers who refuse to blindly espouse creationism on their "Those Who Are Leading Our Nation Down a Moral Sewer" list.

The 9/11 attacks (and later, the war in Iraq) and the attendant national swell of patriotism moved Newdow into the spotlight, or at least caused the spotlight to shine more harshly on him. Some journalists, and television commentators (in particular) highlighted Newdow's charter membership in the "sphere of deviance," as Daniel Hallin (1986) calls it. His ideas, until this point, were unworthy of being heard. The public demanded that he go back where he came from. If he refused, we would (with the help of journalists) turn him into Jack Lule's "scapegoat." He would serve as a reminder of what happens to those who have the temerity to challenge our hallowed cultural ideals and institutions.

The journalists with whom I spoke in researching this book to a person asserted that Newdow's atheism—and the patriotism roused by the war—in no way colored how they covered his case. Several noted that it was the "little guy" theme that caused them to cover Newdow in the first place. Still, I wonder if Newdow would have been treated differently—and his ideas received by the public differently—if he attended church regularly, or if he and Banning had at one time been married. Reporters may not have set out to marginalize Newdow, but by once again breathing life into the scapegoat myth, they did exactly that as the story unfolded.

My scholarly colleagues will probably read this and utter the question that strikes the most fear in the hearts of anyone engaged in extensive research: so what? (or maybe "no kidding"). *Of course* reporters marginalized Newdow, they would argue; he's the latest in a long line of radicals and dissenters whose ideas have been pushed to the margins by reporters. Central casting could not have sent reporters a more clearly defined villain: single father, not married, atheist, flaky, writes songs about his exploits that conveniently call to mind 1960s protest songs, brash, smart, obnoxious. The frames almost leap from his words. His dissent makes for a great story—one easily told, one that reinforces our dominant narratives about dissenters.

My response? First, I'm not thrilled with the possibility that we expect reporters to help the government identify potential threats to our minds and souls. I'm also not thrilled that those radicals who do find even a less than prime spot on the national agenda do so by packaging themselves, and carving up their ideas into easy-to-digest morsels—hell, even Newdow did that. It's a tough choice to make: suck up, de-emphasize the allegedly threatening parts of your personality, and attenuate your arguments or you'll continue to play at the margins, armed only with the fervent hope that someone will hear what you have to say in unexpurgated form.

In the end, then, what we've explored together is the establishment by reporters of the news media equivalent of a "protest zone," located on the border between Hallin's "sphere of deviance" and "sphere of legitimate controversy." Like its real-life equivalent, used with alarming frequency these days by public officials on all levels across the country, this handy device enables you to engage protestors at a safe distance—where they can't do any real harm, and where they must observe your conditions for entry: short, pithy messages, appropriately odd behavior. You can then say, for all the world to hear, that you have allowed them to exercise their rights. They are visible; they are allowed to speak—but at a distance.

When Newdow delivered what was by all accounts an outstanding performance at oral argument, reporters rushed back to the zone in which they had previously contained him, and conferred temporary legitimacy on his ideas. He had figured out a way to slide past the ideological checkpoints, and onto the national agenda; now, reporters, sensing conflict, were helping him along. Think of it as a "one-week pass" from the "sphere of deviance." They practically gushed about how he dealt with tough questions from the justices. A few reporters even suggested that he might have a point. He exceeded the standard of performance created by journalists to evaluate pro se plaintiffs. Yet when the Supreme Court ruled against him, they moved along—and then returned him to the sphere of deviance. He was no longer a valuable part of the narrative. Journalists have offered only sporadic coverage of Newdow's suits challenging the prayer recited by a chaplain at the presidential inauguration and his second attempt to have "under God" removed from the Pledge, even though a California federal court has cleared the way for him to pursue that claim further.

I also take issue with one of the criticisms of my analysis made by a colleague: that the media *should* treat as deviants—or at least as not credible—those individuals and groups who advance unsupported, discredited, or truly eccentric ideas. This colleague asked if there was any difference between Newdow and someone who denies that the Holocaust ever took place. This comment caused me to consider whether I cast Newdow in an overly positive light because I agree with the principle he advanced. Is he a whacko I happen to agree with?

If I asked for John Kerry's help with this question, I'm sure he would say that many journalists (especially those who work in television) have abdicated their responsibility for determining the veracity of someone's claims before presenting those claims in a story. The Swift Boat Veterans and the folks trying to persuade us that intelligent design is a valid theory with no religious overtones spring immediately to mind. The ideas offered by both groups have largely been discredited, yet the news media gave both groups more than ample time and space to make their points. And then consider this: CBS scrapped a planned docudrama about President Reagan because of complaints raised by Reagan's family and still very active (at least in terms of PR) coterie of advisers. Later, our hallowed television networks refused to run an issue ad from the group MoveOn.org—too political, they said. How about cable TV? Joe Scarborough, former republican congressman from Florida, holds court, as does the nation's favorite ill-informed blowhard, Bill O'Reilly. Who do they have on their programs when they need a little stroking? Ann Coulter? William Donahue? Jerry Falwell? I don't want to step on Eric Alterman's toes, but Al Gore—a prevaricating lunatic who can't decide if he wants a beard? I don't think so.

Bottom line? Only those deviants who support the status quo need apply.

Put it another way: Newdow made a strident, but cogent analysis of the Constitution and of the framers' intent—one, by the way, that came from a group of deists who wanted to keep religion and government separate. He was arguing in the hopes, perhaps, that we would see the true breadth of our freedoms. Yet he was branded, at least in the beginning, as a nut. It took most of 2004 for reporters to finally dissect and reject the claims made by the Swift Boat Veterans; until that time they were content to inundate us with reports about "the mere fact of the accusation" (quoted in Franken, 2005, p. 71) by a group with close ties to Bush adviser Karl Rove. Bonnie Anderson (2004), a former CNN journalist and producer, might argue that, like the correspondent who asked me whether a new stadium in Philadelphia was a "tax" on residents, reporters only looked for those facts that supported the accusations made against Kerry.

Why? My guess is based on my wife's idea that the nation elected George W. Bush because we like a president with high entertainment value. Or, as Jeffrey Toobin of CNN noted "[T]elevision does a better job of covering people than ideas (personal interview, January 20, 2006). News organizations concluded that the Swift Boat Veterans added spice to coverage of the election—they argued that Kerry, in essence, didn't deserve the three Purple Hearts he received for his service in Vietnam. The passion of those who supported the continued dissemination of intelligent design in the Dover, Pennsylvania, school system pressed the editor's "conflict" button. Once these folks are discredited, they should fall off a journalist's radar screen, or at the very least, they should merit only a two-second or one-line mention, for the sake of including all points of view. Even print journalists, who covered Newdow in a more balanced fashion than their broadcast counterparts, often steered readers toward the conflict between Newdow and Banning, and offered support for the idea that Newdow—and the Ninth Circuit—were beyond the mainstream.

Perhaps, then, reporters no longer have a "deviance" standard. Anyone with an idea, half-baked or otherwise, will find a voice, as long as that voice entertains us—and doesn't challenge God, the flag, or apple pie—or our presence in Iraq, or the World Trade Organization. In other words, you can dissent, as long as your dissent is quirky, and supports the wobbly frames that journalists have developed about us. Oh, and that voice should, if possible, support conservative politicians and causes. Otherwise, it's off to the sphere of deviance. Maybe the Supreme Court was correct, if only in one way: the decision did prevent, for the time being anyway, one more "divisive shouting match at a time when reasonable voices can barely be heard above the din," as an editorial in the *St. Petersburg Times* cautioned in June 2004 ("The Right Pledge Ruling," 2004, p. 14A). Creating din is all we do on the political stage. Reasonable people, like casual sports fans who don't buy foam fingers and paint their faces and torsos, are relegated to the kiddie table of policy discussion.

It's also disingenuous to suggest, as several journalists and editorial writers did in the days after the Supreme Court's ruling against Newdow, that our time would be better spent discussing "real problems instead of focusing on battles that have no significant impact on Americans' daily lives" ("Ruling Gives Americans," 2004, p. 6B). Excuse me? When did the right to free expression, and to be free, if one chooses, from the endorsement of religious expression by public officials—or by anyone, for that matter—become a secondary issue? I thought for a moment there that journalists had run out of ways to marginalize dissenting views, but I guess

I was wrong. They certainly did spend a lot of time and energy making sure that this "secondary issue" was framed as a "primary" issue, though.

By acting in this way, journalists truly are guard dogs. President Bush has told us that he welcomes dissent; that Americans have the right to disagree with his policies—as if we needed reminding (maybe we do). But his actions—from the carefully screened audiences at his events to forcefully ejecting dissenters who manage to sneak into those events to expanding the shroud of secrecy that obscures a skein of legally questionable actions by his administration—suggest a very low tolerance for ideas that don't reinforce his view of the world, even when they come from experienced military leaders.

What's at stake, you might ask? Truth. We're left to cling only to our myths, something we've always been quite good at. We simply have a hard time looking beyond the dominant narratives offered up by journalists. We want to see our politicians climb the steps of the Capitol and recite the Pledge—even though we know it's only patronizing theater. As Vikram Amar explained, reporters should have looked skeptically at Congress, rather then applaud its members, or make glib comments about strange bedfellows. Congress' reaction "was so swift and reflexive," Laycock said, "that it couldn't have been based on . . . careful consideration of what the Ninth Circuit actually said" (e-mail interview, January 3, 2003). And, as viewers of *Desperate Housewives* might attest, we love a good villain. Even though, as Toobin noted, the nation was not going to rush to support Newdow; we—and the news media—at least owed him the chance to take his best shot. Reporters must give us more credit for our ability to understand the important issues of the day; otherwise, we will go on conveniently ignoring the fact that the insertion into the Pledge of "under God" is only a half century old, and came about only because we wanted to reassert our faith in God in the face of yet another completely manufactured threat. I call on journalists to reevaluate these frames, and to do all that they can to stop helping the government deploy them.

References

Abrams, D. (Host). (2004, March 23). *The Abrams Report* [Television broadcast]. New York: MSNBC.

Across the nation. (2002, August 6). *Seattle Times*, p. A4.

Adams, J. (2002, June 27). One nation divided. *Newsday*, p. A3.

Adler, C., & Colmes, A. (2002, July 2). Interview with Michael Newdow. *Hannity & Colmes* [Television broadcast]. New York: Fox News Network.

Allen, C. (2003, October 5). Pledge of Allegiance: "Under God": An "injury" with almost no victims. *Los Angeles Times*, p. M3.

All things considered (2002, June 26). [Radio broadcast]. Washington, DC: National Public Radio.

Andersen, R. (1995). *Consumer culture and TV programming*. Boulder, CO: Westview.

Anderson, B. (2004). *News flash: Journalism, infotainment, and the bottom-line business of broadcast news*. San Francisco: Jossey-Bass.

Appeals court rules Pledge of Allegiance unconstitutional. (2002, June 27). *Startribune.com*. Retrieved July 5, 2002, from http://www.startribune.com/viewers.

Ask Ike to back new flag Pledge. (1954, April 30). *New York Journal-American*.

Barnicle, M. (Host). (2002, June 26). Federal appeals court declares Pledge of Allegiance unconstitutional. *Hardball with Chris Matthews* [Television broadcast]. New York: CNBC.

Bazinet, K. (2002, June 28). Pledge ruling on hold. *New York Daily News*, p. 6.

Begala, P., & Novak, R. (Hosts). (2002, July 3). *Crossfire* [Television broadcast]. Atlanta: Cable News Network.

Berdayes, L. C., & Berdayes, V. (1998). The information highway in contemporary magazine narrative. *Journal of Communication, 48,* 109–124.

Berkowitz, B. (2005, May 11). The Parents Television Council. *Media Transparency*. Retrieved July 7, 2005, from http://www.mediatransparency.org/story.php?storyID=62.

Binswanger, J. (Host). (2002, June 27). Michael Newdow discusses why he pushed to get Pledge of Allegiance out of schools. *The Early Show* [Television broadcast]. New York: Columbia Broadcasting System.

Biskupic, J. (2004, June 15). "Under God" stays in Pledge. *USA Today*, p. 1A.

Blackstone, J. (2002, June 30). *Sunday Morning* [Television broadcast]. New York: Columbia Broadcasting System.

Blitzer, W. (Host). (2002, June 26). Pledge of Allegiance ruled unconstitutional; WorldCom accounting scandal rocks Wall Street; new study says sparing rod is good for child. *Wolf Blitzer Reports* [Television broadcast]. Atlanta: Cable News Network.

Blitzer, W. (Host). (2004a, March 24). *Wolf Blitzer Reports* [Television broadcast]. Atlanta: Cable News Network.

Blitzer, W. (2004b, June 14). *News from CNN* [Television broadcast]. Atlanta: Cable News Network.

Bloom, D., & O'Brien, S. (2003, March 1). *Saturday Today* [Television broadcast]. New York: National Broadcasting Company.

Blumner, R. (2004, February 29). Readin', writin', 'rithmetic, loyalty oath. *St. Petersburg Times*, p. 7P.

Bordo, S. (1990). Reading the slender body. In M. Jacobus, S. Shuttlesworth, & E. F. Keller (Eds.), *Body/politics* (pp. 83–132). New York: Routledge.

Brassfield, M. (2002, June 27). No Pledge of Allegiance in school, Calif. Court says. *St. Petersburg Times*, p. 1A.

Broadway, L. (2002, July 14). Sermon inspired "under God." *Detroit News*. Retrieved April 28, 2005, from http://www.detnews.com/2002/religion/0207/29/a06-536445.htm.

Brokaw, T. (Host). (2002a, June 26). Pledge of Allegiance declared unconstitutional by federal appeals court. *NBC Nightly News* [Television broadcast]. New York: National Broadcasting Company.

Brokaw, T. (Host). (2002b, June 27). New outrage, action tonight in response to California federal court ruling on Pledge of Allegiance. *NBC Nightly News* [Television broadcast]. New York: National Broadcasting Company.

Brokaw, T. (Host). (2003, February 28). *NBC Nightly News* [Television broadcast]. New York: National Broadcasting Company.

Brokaw, T. (Host). (2004a, March 24). *NBC Nightly News* [Television broadcast]. New York: National Broadcasting Company.

Brokaw, T. (Host). (2004b, June 14). *NBC Nightly News* [Television broadcast]. New York: National Broadcasting Company.

Campbell, R. (1991). *60 Minutes and the news: A mythology for middle America*. Urbana: University of Illinois Press.

Canfield, O. (2002, July 1). Time to admire the laurel and salute the flag. *Hartford Courant*, p. B3.

Carlson, G. (Host). (2002, July 13). *The Saturday Early Show* [Television broadcast]. New York: Columbia Broadcasting System.

Caruso, D. (2004, August 24). Whistleblowers used to target fraud. *Associated Press*. Retrieved May 5, 2005, from http://www.yourlawyer.com/practice/news.htm.

Chadwick, A. (Host). (2004, March 24). *Day to Day* [Radio broadcast]. Washington, DC: National Public Radio.

Chapman, S. (2004, June 18). Justices do the right thing by punting on the Pledge. *Baltimore Sun*, p. 17A.

Chase, R. (2002, June 26). Lawmakers blast federal court ruling declaring pledge unconstitutional. *Associated Press*. Retrieved August 25, 2002, from http://www.lexis-nexis.com.

Chavez, E. (2002, December 9). Is there a God? *Sacramento Bee*, p. B1.

Chemerinsky, E. (2004). The myth of the liberal Ninth Circuit. *Loyola of Los Angeles Law Review, 37*, 1–21.

Chen, J. (Host). (2002, June 27). California court's ruling on the Pledge of Allegiance has lawmakers up in arms. *CBS Morning News* [Television broadcast]. New York: Columbia Broadcasting System.

Chen, J. (Host). (2004, March 24). *The Early Show* [Television broadcast]. New York: Columbia Broadcasting System.

Chung, C. (Host). (2002, June 26). Pledge of Allegiance ruled unconstitutional in court; Martha Stewart to face possible obstruction charges. *Connie Chung Tonight* [Television broadcast]. Atlanta: Cable News Network.

Christian Family Coalition (2005). Retrieved April 28, 2005, from http://www.mdccc.org.

Church-state issue will have to wait. (2004, June 16). *Seattle Post-Intelligencer*. Retrieved June 16, 2004, from www.seattlepi.nwsource.com.

Clark, R. (2001, October 10). The invisible uniform. Poynter Institute. Retrieved April 30, 2005, from www.poynter.org.

Clayson, J. (Host). (2002, June 27). Court rules Pledge of Allegiance unconstitutional when recited in schools. *The Early Show* [Television broadcast]. New York: Columbia Broadcasting System.

Coile, Z. (2004, March 25). Justices hear dead protest pledge. *San Francisco Chronicle*, p. A1.

Connor, T. (2004, March 25). God and the supremes. *New York Daily News*, p. 2.

Cooper, A. (Host). (2002, June 26). Is the Pledge of Allegiance unconstitutional? WorldCom caught in accounting scandal. *CNN Newsnight* [Television broadcast]. Atlanta: Cable News Network.

Cooper, A. (Host). (2004, March 24). *Anderson Cooper 360* [Television broadcast]. Atlanta: Cable News Network.

Cooper, C. (2002, September 28). Pledge foe insists his daughter backs him. *Sacramento Bee*, p. A6.

Cosby, R. (Host). (2002, July 14). *Fox Wire* [Television broadcast]. New York: Fox News Channel.

Costello, C. (Host). (2002a, June 27). Federal appeals court says Pledge of Allegiance can't be recited in public schools. *Daybreak* [Television broadcast]. Atlanta: Cable News Network.

Costello, C. (Host). (2002b, June 28). Judge puts hold on Pledge ruling. *Daybreak* [Television broadcast]. Atlanta: Cable News Network.

Coulter, A. (2005, April 7). Coulter: Fly Ashley Smith to Saudi Arabia to save Muslims' souls. Retrieved May 5, 2005, from http://mediamatters.org/items/200504070004.

Couric, K. (Host). (2002, June 27). Michael Newdow files lawsuit declaring Pledge of Allegiance unconstitutional. *Today* [Television broadcast]. New York: National Broadcasting Company.

Court reaffirms ban on Pledge of Allegiance. (2003, March 1). *Seattle Times*, p. A2.

Court rules that "God" in Pledge violates Constitution. (2002, June 27). *St. Louis Post-Dispatch*, p. A1.

Crawford, K. (2004, December 16). Breasts, butts . . . oh my! *Money*. Retrieved July 7, 2005, from http://www.cnnmoney.com.

Dale, K. (1954, February 7). Put God in the flag Pledge, pastor urges. *Washington Post*, p. 12.

D'Angelo, P. (2002). News framing as a multiparadigmatic research: A response to Entman. *Journal of Communication, 52,* 870–888.

Daniels, R. (1981). *Concentration camps: North America*. Malabar, FL: Krieger.

Daniels, R. (1993). *Prisoners without trial: Japanese-Americans in World War II*. New York: Hill and Wang.

Dean: I have all kinds of warts. (2004, January 23). CNN.com. Retrieved May 6, 2005, from http://www.cnn.com/2004/ALLPOLITICS/01/23/dean.interview.

DelFattore, J. (2003). *The fourth R: Conflicts over religion in America's public schools*. New Haven, CT: Yale University Press.

Denniston, L. (2002, June 27). Pledge of Allegiance is ruled unconstitutional; words "under God" back religion, say 2 on appeals panel. *Boston Globe*, p. A2.

Denniston, L. (2003, March 1). U.S. appeals court eases pledge ruling; holds position on unconstitutionality of phrase "under God." *Boston Globe*, p. A3.

Denniston, L. (2004, March 22). Father arguing case says law on his side. *Boston Globe*, p. A8.

Didion, J. (1990). *White album*. New York: Farrar, Straus, & Giroux.

Dobbs, L. (2003). *Lou Dobbs Tonight* [Television broadcast]. Atlanta: Cable News Network.

Docherty, G. (1954, February 7). Transcript of sermon delivered at New York Avenue Presbyterian Church. *Pittsburgh Post-Gazette*. Retrieved October 15, 2004, from http://www.post-gazette.com.

Dolan, M. (2002, June 27). Pledge of Allegiance violates Constitution, Court declares. *Los Angeles Times*, p. A1.

Dolan, M. (2004, March 23). They pray for judicial restraint. *Los Angeles Times*, p. A1.

Dolan, M., & Gerstanzang, J. (2002, tone 28). Ninth Circuit puts its ruling against Pledge on hold. *Los Angeles Times*, p. A-1.

Dole, K. (1955, March 12). Dr. Docherty originated "under God" in flag Pledge. *Washington Post*, p. 10.

Donahue, P. (Host). (2002, August 6). *Donahue* [Television broadcast]. New York: MSNBC.

Donahue, G., Tichenor, P., & Olien, C. (1995). A guard dog perspective on the role of media. *Journal of Communication, 45*, 115–132.

Duin, J. (2004, March 25). Atheist spars with skeptical justices over Pledge. *Washington Times*. Retrieved June 16, 2004, from www.washingtontimes.com.

Eaton, T. (2002, June 27). "Under God" in Pledge ruled unconstitutional. *Corpus Christi Caller-Times*, p. A1.

Edwards, B. (Host). (2004, March 24). *Morning Edition* [Radio broadcast]. Washington, DC: National Public Radio.

Egelko, B. (2002a, June 27). Pledge of Allegiance ruled unconstitutional. *San Francisco Chronicle*, p. A1.

Egelko, B. (2002b, July 13). Girl in Pledge case not an atheist, mom to tell court. *San Francisco Chronicle*, p. A15.

Egelko, B. (2002c, August 6). Mom wants girl out of dad's pledge lawsuit. *San Francisco Chronicle*, p. A3.

Egelko, B. (2002d, August 10). Bush administration seeks rehearing in court ruling on pledge. *San Francisco Chronicle*, p. A3.

Egelko, B. (2002e, September 28). "Pledge" dad lashes back in court. *San Francisco Chronicle*, p. A15.

Egelko, B. (2002f, December 5). Court blocks attempt to kill pledge lawsuit. *San Francisco Chronicle*, p. A9.

Egelko, B. (2003, March 1). Federal court stands pat on Pledge of Allegiance ruling. *San Francisco Chronicle*, p. A3.

Egelko, B. (2004a, June 14). Supreme Court sidesteps pledge issue, ruling father has no right to sue. *San Francisco Chronicle*. Retrieved June 16, 2004, from www.sfgate.com.

Egelko, B. (2004b, June 15). Pledge challenge tossed on technicality. *San Francisco Chronicle*, p. A1.

Elk Grove Unified School District and Gordon v. Newdow, 02-1624. Transcript of oral arguments before U.S. Supreme Court, March 24, 2004.

Entman, R. M. (1993). Framing: Toward clarification of a fractured paradigm. *Journal of Communication, 43*, 51–58.

Epstein, E. (2002, November 1). "Godless" forces to rally in the capital. *Washington Post*, p. A2.

Epstein, E., May, M., & Kim, R. (2002, June 27). Decision called everything from ridiculous to sublime. *San Francisco Chronicle*, p. A12.

Fenton, T. (2005). *Bad news: The decline of reporting, the business of news, and the danger to us all.* New York: Regan Books.

The firecracker that fizzled. (2004, June 15). *The Oregonian*, p. B8.

Fisher, M. (2002, June 27). A pledge that doesn't need fixing. *Washington Post*, p. B-1.

Fisher, W. (1987). *Human communication as narration: Toward a philosophy or reason, value, and action.* Columbia: University of South Carolina Press.

Fitzgerald. J. (2004a, March 24). God willing, atheist's appeal will fail. *Boston Herald*, p. 14.

Fitzgerald, J. (2004b, June 16). Justices hand God a win—but on a technicality. *Boston Herald*, p. 16.

Flap over Pledge. (2004, March 25). *Newsday New York*, p. A28.

Flythe, W. (1954a, April 28). Urge U.S. oath tell faith in God. *New York Journal-American*, p. 14.

Flythe, W. (1954b, May 10). Congress units okay "faith in God" Pledge. *New York Journal-American*, p. 10.

Flythe, W. (1954c, June 9). "God" Pledge goes to White House. *New York Journal-American*, p. 4.

Foskett, K. (2002, June 28). Bush, Congress blast ruling against Pledge. *Atlanta Journal-Constitution*, p. 1A.

Foss, S. (1996). *Rhetorical criticism: Exploration & practice*. Prospect Heights, IL: Waveland.

Franken, A. (2005). *The truth—with jokes*. New York: Dutton.

Franzen, E. (2004, March 24). Court shouldn't dodge issue. *Milwaukee Journal-Sentinel*, p. 16A.

Frith, S. (2002, June 27). Atheist who sued wanted to draw line between church, state. *Startribune.com*. Retrieved July 5, 2002, from http://www.startribune.com/viewers.

Gamson, W. A., & Mogdiliani, A. (1987). The changing culture of affirmative action. In R. D. Braungart (Ed.), *Research in political sociology* (Vol. 3, pp. 137–177). Greenwich, CT: JAL.

Gandy, O. (2001). Epilogue. In S. Reese, O. H. Gandy Jr., and A. Grant (Eds.), *Framing public life* (p. 365). Mahwah, NJ: Erlbaum.

Gearan, A. (2004, March 24). Court debates whether Pledge of Allegiance should keep phrase "under God." *Associated Press Online*. Retrieved June 22, 2004, from www.lexis-nexis.com.

Getlin, J. (2002, June 28). In New York, it's outrage, followed by "consider the source." *Los Angeles Times*, pp. A1, A20.

Gibb, T. (2002a, June 28). How the Pledge got God. *Pittsburgh Post-Gazette*. Retrieved April 28, 2005, from http://www.post-gazette.com.

Gibb, T. (2002b, August 19). Minister reprises "under God" sermon. *Pittsburgh Post-Gazette*. Retrieved April 28, 2005, from http://www.post-gazette.com.

Gibson, C. (Host). (2004, March 24). *World News Tonight with Peter Jennings* [Television broadcast]. New York: American Broadcasting Company.

Gibson, J. (2004, June 14). *The Big Story with John Gibson* [Television broadcast]. New York: Fox News Channel.

Gill, J. (2002, June 30). Lawmakers scramble to look pious. *New Orleans Times-Picayune*, p. 7.

Girl in Pledge case no atheist, mother says. (2002, July 12). *Washington Post*, p. A22.

Gitlin, T. (1980). *The whole world is watching*. Berkeley: University of California Press.

God and country. (2002, June 28). *Albany Times-Union*, p. A14.

God and the Pledge. (2002, June 30). *Cleveland Plain Dealer*, p. H2.

A Godforsaken ruling. (2002, June 27). *Los Angeles Times*, p. 14.

God save this court. (2002, June 28). *St. Petersburg Times*, p. 18A.

Goffman, E. (1974). *Frame analysis*. Boston: Northeastern University Press.

Gold, S., (2002, June 28). Keep God in the Pledge, an angry chorus cries. *Los Angeles Times*, p. A1.

Gold, S. & Bailey, E. (2002, June 27). The Pledge of Allegiance: 1 plaintiff, against the grain. *Los Angeles Times*, p. A1.

Goodman, E. (2004, March 29). Pledge plaintiff may be a pain, but he has a point. *Baltimore Sun*, p. 13A.

Greenhouse, L. (2004a, March 25). Atheist presents case for taking God from Pledge. *New York Times*, p. A-1.

Greenhouse, L. (2004b, June 15). 8 justices block effort to pull phrase in Pledge. *New York Times*. Retrieved June 16, 2004, from www.nytimes.com.

Gutierrez, H. (2002, June 27). Schoolchildren in metro area are not required to say Pledge. *Rocky Mountain News*, p. 46A.

Hallin, D. (1986). *The uncensored war.* New York: Oxford University Press.

Hannity, S., & Colmes, A. (Hosts). (2002a, June 26). Interview with Michael Newdow. *Hannity & Colmes* [Television broadcast]. New York: Fox News Network.

Hannity, S., & Colmes, A. (2002b, September 4). *Hannity & Colmes* [Television broadcast]. New York: Fox News Network.

Hansen, N. (Host). (2002a, June 27). Controversy over a California federal court's ruling that the Pledge of Allegiance is unconstitutional. *Early Today* [Television broadcast]. New York: CNBC.

Hansen, N. (Host). (2002b, June 28). Controversial decision on the Pledge of Allegiance on hold. *Early Today* [Television broadcast]. New York: CNBC.

Harrell, D., & Horner, M. (2002, June 27). Court rejects the Pledge in public schools. *Seattle Post-Intelligencer*, p. A1.

Harrington, C. (1954, June 15). Ike hails Pledge revision. *Washington Post*, p. 45.

Haswell, J. (1954, May 18). Public wants "under God" put in Pledge. *Washington Post*, p. 10.

Hayward E. (2002, June 27). Fed court rules Pledge unconstitutional in school. *Boston Herald*, p. 6.

Hedges, M. (2004, March 25). Atheist engages high court in debate of "under God" in Pledge. *Houston Chronicle*, p. A1.

Helderman, R. & Samuels, C. (2002, June 28). Va. schools forge ahead with national motto. *Washington Post*, p. B1.

Hemmer, B. (Host). (2002, June 28). Man whose case ruled out Pledge of Allegiance speaks. *American Morning* [Television broadcast]. Atlanta: Cable News Network.

Hemmer, B., O'Brien, S., Cafferty, J., King, J., & Stone, A. (2004, March 24). *American Morning* [Television broadcast]. Atlanta: Cable News Network.

Henderson, S. (2004, June 15). Justices duck fight over "under God." *St. Louis Post-Dispatch*. Retrieved June 22, 2004, from www.lexis-nexis.com.

A higher authority. (2002, July 3). *Pittsburgh Post-Gazette*, p. N4.

Holland, G. (2004, March 24). Supreme Court takes on Pledge of Allegiance case; new poll shows support for salute. *Associated Press Online*. Retrieved June 22, 2004, from www.lexis-nexis.com.

Holland, J. (2002, June 27). Congress, White House condemn decision. *Startribune.com*. Retrieved July 5, 2002, from http://www.startribune.com/viewers.

Holt, L. (Host). (2003, March 3). *Countdown: Iraq* [Television broadcast]. New York: National Broadcasting Company.

Hoppin, J. (2002, July 1). Goodwin isn't fazed by storm over the Pledge. *Cal Law*. Retrieved April 25, 2005, from http://www.law.com/regionals/ca/stories/020701a.shtml.

Hulse, C. (2002, June 27). Lawmakers vow to fight judges' ruling on the Pledge. *New York Times*. Retrieved August 31, 2002, from http://www.nytimes.com/2002/06/27/politics/CONG.html.

Hume, B. (Host). (2004, March 24). *Fox Special Report With Brit Hume* [Television broadcast]. New York: Fox News Network.

Insult to all. (2002, June 27). *San Diego Union-Tribune*, p. B-12.

Jacoby, J. (2002, July 4). The founders and God. *Boston Globe*, p. A11.

Jacoby, S. (2002, June 28). Much ado about propagandist Pledge. *Newsday*, p. A41.

Jacoby, S. (2004) *Freethinkers: A history of American secularism*. New York: Metropolitan Books.

Jackson, D. (2002, June 28). Rethinking the Pledge. *Boston Globe*, p. A23.

Jamieson, K., & Waldman, P. (2003). *The press effect: Politicians, journalists, and the stories that shaped the political world*. New York: Oxford University Press.

Japanese-Americans pledge loyalty to United States. (1941, December 8). *Los Angeles Times*, p. 6.

Jennings, P. (Host). (2002, June 26). Judge rules Pledge of Allegiance unconstitutional. *World News Tonight* [Television broadcast]. New York: American Broadcasting Company.

Kagan, D. (Host). (2004, March 24). *CNN Live Today* [Television broadcast]. Atlanta: Cable News Network.

Kasindorf, M. (2002, June 27). Court ruling on the Pledge ignites furor. *USA Today*, p. 1A.

Kasindorf, M. (2003, February 7). The court conservatives hate. *USA Today*, p. 3A.

Kasindorf, M., & Biskupic, J. (2003, March 3). Pledge appeal may go to Supreme Court. *USA Today*, p. 3A.

Keefe, B. (2004, March 22). Atheist takes Pledge to court. *Atlanta Journal-Constitution*, p. 1A.

Kinsley, M. (2005, June 12). The left gets a memo. *Los Angeles Times*. Retrieved July 7, 2005, from http://www.latimes.com/news/opinion/sunday/commentary/la-oe-kinsley12jun12,0,7389890.column?coll=la-sunday-commentary.

Kravets, D. (2004, March 22). Court to decide Pledge of Allegiance case. *Associated Press Online*. Retrieved June 22, 2004, from www.lexis-nexis.com.

Kurtz accepted another misleading claim from Luntz. (2004, October 11). *Media Matters for America*. Retrieved May 27, 2005, from http://mediamatters.org/items/200410110008.

Lane, C. (2002, June 27). U.S. court votes to bar Pledge of Allegiance. *Washington Post*, p. A1.

Lane, C. (2003, March 1). Pledge of Allegiance ruling is upheld; "under God" phrase splits appeals court. *Washington Post*, p. A1.

Lauer, M., & Couric, K. (Hosts). (2002, July 17). *Today* [Television broadcast]. New York: National Broadcasting Company.

Leave the kid alone. (2002, October 20). *Sacramento Bee*, p. E4.

Legion head supports change in allegiance Pledge. (1954, April 29). *New York Journal-American,* p. 10.

Lehrer, J. (Host). (2004, March 24). *The NewsHour with Jim Lehrer* [Television broadcast]. New York: Public Broadcasting System.

Limbaugh, R. (2005, April 27). *The Rush Limbaugh Show*. Retrieved May 5, 2005, from http://www.mediamatters.org/items/200504280002.

Lin, Carol (Host). (2002, August 10). *CNN Saturday Night* [Television broadcast]. Atlanta: Cable News Network.

Liptak, A. (2002, June 28). 2 officials seek review of decision on Pledge. *New York Times*, p. A14.

Liptak, A. (2003, March 1). Full Appeals Court lets stand the ban on "God" in Pledge. *New York Times*, p. A1.

Litigant explains why he brought Pledge suit. (2002, June 26). *CNN.com*. Retrieved December 8, 2003, from http://www/cnn.law.com/2002/LAW/06/26/Newdow.cnna.

Lopez, S. (2002, June 28). Our hands on our hearts and our heads in the sand. *Los Angeles Times*, sec. 2, p. 1.

Louey, S. (2003, March 4). School officials: Let Pledge stand for now. *Sacarmento Bee*, p. B1.

Lucas, G. (2004, March 2). Judge rules girl cannot attend Supreme Court hearing. *San Francisco Chronicle*, p. A-13.

Lule, J. (2001). *Daily news, eternal stories.* New York: Guilford.

Malkin, M. (2001, October 3). American journalism's true colors. *Townhall.com.* Retieved April 30, 2005, from www.townhall.com.

Mann, J. (Host). (2002, June 27). U.S. Court rules Pledge of Allegiance unconstitutional. *Insight* [Television broadcast]. Atlanta: Cable News Network International.

Mayor backs flag oath to include "under God." (1954, May 2). *New York Journal-American.*

McGinnis, S. (Host). (2004, March 24). *CBS Morning News* [Television broadcast]. New York: Columbia Broadcasting System.

Mintz, H. (2003, March 1). Ban on Pledge may go to high court. *Milwaukee Journal Sentinel*, p. 1A.

Mooney, J. (2002, June 28). Colorado will join in appeal of ruling. *Denver Post*, p. A2.

Morris, D. (1998). *Illness and culture in the postmodern age.* Berkeley: University of California Press.

Murphy, C. (2002, November 3). March of the Godless takes to the Mall. *Washington Post*, p. C3.

Nation in brief. (2002, December 5). *Washington Post*, p. A10.

Naylor, B. (Host). (2004, March 24). *Talk of the Nation* [Radio broadcast]. Washington, DC: National Public Radio.

Neary, L., & Siegel, R. (Hosts). (2002, June 26). Federal appeals court rules that the Pledge of Allegiance in public schools is unconstitutional. *All Things Considered* [Radio broadcast]. Washington, DC: National Public Radio.

New questions about old news. (2005, July 1). Media Matters for America. Retrieved July 7, 2005, from http://mediamatters.org/items/200507010007.

Newdow v. U.S. Congress et al., Civ. S-00-0495 MLS PAN PS (E.D. Ca. 2000).

Newdow v. The Congress of the United States of America et al. (2002) 9th Circuit U.S. Court of Appeals, No. 00-16423.

Newdow v. The Congress of the United States et al., 9th Circuit U.S. Court of Appeals, No. 00-16423. Plaintiff/Appellant's Response to Sandra Banning's Motion for Leave to Intervene.

Newdow v. U.S. Congress, Order and Amended Opinion and Amended Concurrence/Dissent, 9th Circuit, No. 00-16423. Issued February 28, 2003.

Nieves, E. (2002a, June 27). Judges ban Pledge of Allegiance from schools, citing "under God." *New York Times*, pp. A1, A20.

Nieves, E. (2002b, July 1). "Under God" iconoclast looks to next targets. *New York Times*, p. A8.

No Pledge allowed. (2003, March 5). *San Diego Union-Tribune*, p. B8.

Norris, M. (2004, June 14). *All Things Considered* [Radio broadcast]. Washington, DC: National Public Radio.

Norris, P. (1995). The restless search: Network news framing of the post–Cold War world. *Political Communication, 12*, 357–370.

Olvera, J., & Leedy, M. (2002, June 28). Students express support for Pledge. *Fresno Bee*, p. A1.

One nation, indivisible. (2003, March 9). *Seattle Times*, p. C2.

One nation under God. (2002, June 27). *New York Times*, p. A28.

One nation, under God. (2004, March 24). *San Diego Union-Tribune*, p. B-8.

O'Reilly, B. (Host). (2002, December 19). *The O'Reilly Factor* [Television broadcast]. New York: Fox News Channel.

O'Reilly, B. (Host). (2003, March 10). *The O'Reilly Factor* [Television broadcast]. New York: Fox News Network.

O'Reilly, B. (2004a, June 14). *The O'Reilly Factor* [Television broadcast]. New York: Fox News Channel.

O'Reilly, B. (2004b, June 15). *The O'Reilly Factor* [Television broadcast]. New York: Fox News Channel.

Osgood, C. (Host). (2002, June 30). Seven days; court's ruling on Pledge of Allegiance draws national outrage. *Sunday Morning* [Television broadcast]. New York: Columbia Broadcasting System.

Phillips, K. (Host). (2002, June 26). Federal appeals court rules Pledge of Allegiance unconstitutional. *CNN Breaking News* [Television broadcast]. Atlanta: Cable News Network.

Pledge challenger reports threats. (2002, June 28). *Milwaukee Journal-Sentinel*, p. 10A.

The pledge is safe for now, thank God. (2004, June 15). *New York Daily News*, p. 40.

Pledge "issue" a non-starter. (2004, June 15). *Milwaukee Journal-Sentinel*, p. 12A.

Pledge revision asked. (1953, April 22). *New York Times*, p. 38.

Pledge stands. (2004, June 15). *San Diego Union-Tribune*, p. B6.

Police apologize, drop charge vs. Sheehan. (2006, February 2). *Associated Press*. Retrieved February 2, 2006, from www.comcast.net.

President hails revised Pledge. (1954, June 15). *New York Times*, p. 31.

Press, B., Buchanan, P., Jansen, C., & Aspell, T. (2002, July 17). Wisdom of War against Iraq is questioned. *Buchanan & Press* [Television broadcast]. New York: MSNBC.

Public schools can't require flag Pledge with "under God" in it, federal court rules. (2002, June 26). *Americans United for the Separation of Church and State*. Retrieved May 5, 2005, from http://www.au.org.

Rather, D. (Host). (2003, February 28). *CBS Evening News* [Television broadcast]. New York: Columbia Broadcasting System.

Reaves, J. (2002, June). Person of the week: Michael Newdow. *Time.com*. Retrieved December 8, 2003, from http://www.time.com.

Reinert, P. (2004, June 15). "Under God" can stay in Pledge, court says. *Houston Chronicle*, p. A1.

Reinolds, C. (2002, July 18). One city "under God." *Atlanta Journal-Constitution*, p. 1JQ.

Revised Pledge gains. (1954, May 26). *New York Times*, p. 33.

Richey, W. (2004, June 15). Court keeps "under God" in Pledge. *Christian Science Monitor*, p. 1.

Riddell, L. (2002, June 28). Pledge ruling put on hold. Chattanooga Times, p. A-1.

The right Pledge ruling. (2004, June 16). *St. Petersburg Times*, p. 14A.

Roberts, J. (Host). (2002a, June 26). Controversial ruling in San Francisco regarding "under God" in the Pledge of Allegiance. *CBS Evening News* [Television broadcast]. New York: Columbia Broadcasting System.

Roberts, J. (Host). (2002b, June 27). Federal judge puts an indefinite hold on enforcing yesterday's ruling against reciting the Pledge of Allegiance. *CBS Evening News* [Television broadcast]. New York: Columbia Broadcasting System.

Roberts, J. (Host). (2004, March 24). *CBS Evening News* [Television broadcast]. New York: Columbia Broadcasting System.

Roberts, R. (Host). (2002, June 27). Ninth Circuit Court rules Pledge of Allegiance unconstitutional; Man who brought lawsuit to have Pledge of Allegiance banned talks about why the pledge is unconstitutional. *Good Morning America* [Television broadcast]. New York: American Broadcasting Company.

Rowe, P. (2002, July 2). Having it their way, or no way. *San Diego Union-Tribune*, p. E1.

Ruling gives Americans break from loaded issue. (2004, June 16). *San Antonio Express-News*, p. 6B.

Ruth, D. (2002, July 1). One nation under God also is really ticked off. *Tampa Tribune*, p. 2.

Safire, W. (2004, March 24). Of God and the flag. *New York Times*, p. A-21.

Salladay, R., & Coile, Z. (2002, June 28). Judge in Pledge case puts brakes on ruling. *San Francisco Chronicle*, p. A1.

Sanchez, R. (2002, June 28). For a single father, a long, lonely quest. *Washington Post*, p. A6.

Saunders, D. (2002, July 18). Doctor of the universe. *San Francisco Chronicle*, p. A25.

Savage, C. (2004, June 15). "Under God" to stay in Pledge of Allegiance. *Boston Globe*. Retrieved June 16, 2004, from www.boston.com.

Savage, D. (2004a, March 25). Justices debate "God" in Pledge. *Los Angeles Times*, p. A12.

Savage. D. (2004b, June 15). Justices keep "God" in Pledge of Allegiance. *Los Angeles Times*, p. A1.

Scarborough, J. (Host). (2004, March 24). *Scarborough Country* [Television broadcast]. New York: MSNBC.

Schudson, M. (1978). *Discovering the news: A social history of American newspapers*. New York: Basic Books.

The scoop that got spiked. (2006, January 11). *FAIR Action Alert*. Retrieved January 11, 2006, from www.fair.org.

Seigenthaler, J. (Host). (2004, March 24). *The News on CNBC* [Television broadcast]. New York: CNBC.

Sheehan, C. (2006, February 1). What really happened. *Truthout*. Retrieved February 1, 2006, from www.truthout.org.

Siegel, R., & Norris, M. (Hosts). (2004, March 24). *All Things Considered* [Radio broadcast]. Washington, DC: National Public Radio.

Sifton, E. (2004, April 13). The battle over the pledge. *The Nation*, pp. 11–14, 16.

Smiley, T. (Host). (2003, March 3). *The Tavis Smiley Show* [Radio broadcast]. Washington, DC: National Public Radio.

Smith, H., Storm, H., & Chen, J. (Hosts). (2004, March 24). *The Early Show* [Television broadcast]. New York: Columbia Broadcasting System.

Snow, K. (Host). (2002, June 29). Bush undergoes colonoscopy; Corporate America takes heat from politicians, public; Pledge of Allegiance ruled unconstitutional. *Saturday Edition* [Television broadcast]. Atlanta: Cable News Network.

Somebody bless America. (2002, June 27). *New York Daily News*, p. 42.

Spinner, W. (2002, December 5). Christianity debate to air nationwide. *New Orleans Times-Picayune*, p. 8.

State appeals ruling banning the pledge. (2002, July 26). *San Francisco Chronicle*, p. A22.

Taking the Pledge. (2002, June 28). *Washington Post*, p. C12.

Taking the Pledge. (2003, March 9). *Pittsburgh Post-Gazette*, p. E6.

Teichert, N. (2002, August 6). Mom asks court to remove daughter from Pledge case. *Sacramento Bee*, p. B2.

Torry, J. (2004a, March 25). Pledge of Allegiance case; justices put "under God" under scrutiny. *Columbus Dispatch*, p. 1A.

Torry, J. (2004b, June 15). "Under God" kept in Pledge in limited ruling. *Columbus Dispatch*, p. 1A.

Totenberg, N. (2004, June 14). *All Things Considered* (Radio broadcast). Washington, DC: National Public Radio.

Under God. (1954a, April 18). *New York Journal-American.*

Under God. (1954b, May 13). *New York Journal-American.*

"Under God" fight averted. (2004, June 16). *Boston Herald*, p. 36.

Under God, for now. (2004, June 17). *Cleveland Plain Dealer*, p. B8.

"Under God" preserved—on a technicality. (2004, June 15). *Denver Post*, p. B6.

Vanden Brook, T. (2002, June 27). Critics say court was "California dreaming." *USA Today*, p. 4A.

Van Susteren, G. (Host). (2002, June 27). Interview with Michael Newdow. *On the Record with Greta Van Susteren* [Television broadcast]. New York: Fox News Network.

Van Susteren, G. (Host). (2004a, March 24). *Fox on the Record with Greta Van Susteren* [Television broadcast]. New York: Fox News Network.

Van Susteren, G. (2004b, June 14). *On the Record with Greta Van Susteren* [Television broadcast]. New York: Fox News Channel.

Vargas, E. (2004, March 24). *Good Morning America* [Television broadcast]. New York: American Broadcasting Company.

Von Drehle, D. (2002, June 28). Judge blocks Pledge decision during appeals. *Washington Post*, p. A6.

Werkman, D. (2002, August 8). Elk Grove trustees file for rehearing in Pledge case. *Sacramento Bee*, p. N1.

Whitfield, F. (Host). (2002, June 27). Pledge plaintiff gets threatening phone calls. *CNN Live Today* [Television broadcast]. Atlanta: Cable News Network.

Whitfield, F. (Host). (2004, March 24). *Paula Zahn Now* [Television broadcast]. Atlanta: Cable News Network.

Williams, C., & Lengel, A. (2006, February 1). Sheehan arrested before speech. *Washington Post.* Retrieved February 1, 2006, from www.truthout.org.

Woodruff, J. (Host). (2002, June 26). Politicians turn attention to WorldCom scandal; Pledge of Allegiance ruled unconstitutional. *CNN Inside Politics* [Television broadcast]. Atlanta: Cable News Network.

Index